Music
Money
Maestros &
Management

The Hallé
A British Orchestra in the 20th Century

Robert Beale

Forsyth

Published by the Publishing Division of Forsyth Brothers Limited
126 Deansgate, Manchester, M3 2GR, United Kingdom

© Robert Beale 2000

British Library Cataloguing in Publication Data.
Data available.

ISBN 0 – 9514795 – 1 – 2

Acknowledgments

I am extremely grateful to successive Chief Executives of the Hallé Concerts Society – Clive Smart, David Richardson, Alan Dean and Leslie Robinson, in particular – for continuing to allow me access to the archives in times of great change and uncertainty for the Society. I must also thank the Hallé librarian, Patrick Williams, for letting me invade his space, the former Deputy Chief Executive, Stuart Robinson, for energetic help in getting to grips with the archive store, and Jane Lee and Wendy Pashley for constant helpfulness. Almost every other member of the Hallé staff has assisted my quest at some stage. Nonetheless, this is not an "authorised" account of the Hallé Concerts Society's history: the selection of material and the opinions expressed are entirely my own. Visits to the Royal Liverpool Philharmonic and City of Birmingham Symphony orchestras were possible with help from their respective archivists, Vin Tyndall and Beresford King-Smith; and I have had the benefit of enthusiasm and interest beyond the call of duty from the Henry Watson Music Librarian of Manchester Libraries, Martin Thacker. The whole research project has been conducted under supervision from the Department of Arts Policy of City University, London, where Freda James (née Steele) and others have assisted me, and above all I am indebted to Professor Patrick Boylan, for unfailing encouragement and wise counsel throughout a long and happy association. Finally, I must record my gratitude to Forsyth Brothers Ltd and the Manchester Musical Heritage Trust for making the publication of this book possible, and Pam Smith for producing the index.

Contents

Chapter 1

The day an orchestra nearly died

The new film, "Titanic", was in town on February 5th, 1998. But at the Bridgewater Hall in Manchester there were fears that another mighty vessel might be going down with all hands – the Hallé Orchestra.

It was a Thursday, and on Monday that week news had broken that the Hallé was in financial crisis and might have only three days' existence left. As the audience gathered in the hall, the atmosphere backstage was tense. Board members and others gathered in little knots in the corporate bar, and there were few entirely cool heads. It looked as if the orchestra that night might literally be playing for its life. The Hallé Board had met and approved an "action plan" to stabilise its situation, and there was to be an immediate re-structuring of the organisation. But there were voices which suggested the Hallé should simply close down. The *Manchester Evening News* was asking its readers to vote yes or no to the question: "Should taxpayers bail them out?"

The vote recorded was an 80 per cent yes, in fact – but the real answer to the question of how Manchester people felt about their orchestra came at the close of the concert that night. There was a tumultuous standing ovation, of a kind that I have never witnessed before or since. It seemed as if it would go on for ever. The players stood blinking in the stage lights, many clearly close to tears. It was, as the Leader of Manchester City Council said at the time, "unthinkable" that there should not be the Hallé Orchestra in Manchester.

But what had brought things to this pass? Why was an organisation formed in 1899, the Hallé Concerts Society, which had weathered so many storms before, on the verge of bankruptcy as the 20th century approached its end? More astonishingly still, why was an orchestra which had begun the decade by proclaiming its "New Beginnings" and confidence in the future, and had moved less than two years earlier into the first place ever to be designated a "home" for it – the wonderful, new £42 million Bridgewater Hall – fighting for survival?

It is the contention of this book that, whatever the immediate triggers of the crisis of February, 1998 in the Hallé Concerts Society, it is only much more long-term processes which really explain what brought it to that point. Had it been financially robust enough, it could probably have sustained a mammoth loss in a single year, as it had on some occasions in the past. Its debts were not particularly disastrous, in the context of those being run up by other British symphony orchestras at the time. But by the end of the 1990s the Hallé had been chronically short of money for so long, and successive hopes of "bailing out" from one source or another had proved illusory so many times, that a few big problems in a single year were enough to tip it into freefall.

The situation may seem uncannily familiar to anyone who has read Jilly Cooper's novel, *Appassionata*. Her imaginary Rutminster Symphony Orchestra faces a combination of falling audiences, decreasing Arts Council funding, reduced levels of local authority support and sponsorship income, combined with overspending, lack of success from recording – and even its own management planning a merger with another orchestra behind the players' backs: in fact it is at the point where it cannot survive another month without a cash injection from somewhere.[1] Another popular tome from the time, *When The Music Stops* by Norman Lebrecht, predicted a collapse of traditional musical institutions in the face of soaring costs and dwindling official support (and, in some cases, dwindling attendances).[2]

Other British orchestras have revealed worse problems since the Hallé's crisis, and the sums involved in the Arts Council's "stabilisation" programme indicate the extent to which they, too, were in trouble.[3] But the Hallé, which traces its history back to 1858 and is thus the longest-established professional symphony orchestra in the British Isles, had always seemed the most secure. It was proud of its tradition, its succession of conductors – including Charles Hallé himself, Hans Richter, Sir Thomas Beecham, Sir Hamilton Harty, Sir Malcolm Sargent, Sir John Barbirolli, James Loughran, Stanislaw Skrowaczewski and Kent Nagano – its audiences' loyalty, and its apparent financial solidity.

So what went wrong? And if an orchestra of this one's pedigree could go lame, what did that say about the way we support independent orchestras in Britain today? This book is an attempt to answer that question, and to do so from a long-term perspective. It examines the whole first century of the Hallé Concerts

---

[1]Cooper, 1996: 315, 879. In fact the Hallé is one of the few orchestras to which Jilly Cooper does not directly refer in describing her research for *Appassionata*. And in her story, salvation comes from a somewhat unlikely quarter: a lottery ticket bought in the name of the orchestra office cat (named John Drummond) wins the jackpot.
[2]Lebrecht, 1996: 505, 523.

[3]The Royal Liverpool Philharmonic Society received £5.4 million under the scheme in 2000, of which £3.25 million was to cancel accrued debt – Fresh start for RLPO, *Classical Music*, August 12, 2000.

Society's existence, from its formation in 1899 to its centenary. Financial crisis, in reality, has never been far away in those 100 years, and solutions have been many and various. Some of the problems, indeed, seem to have a habit of reappearing from one generation unto another. They have not always been tackled in similar ways, however.

Michael Kennedy, in his first book on the Hallé, made the point that high artistic achievement and financial instability seem to go hand-in-hand at various times in the story. It's an intriguing question as to which might be said to be the cause of the other: is it simply a question of aspiration outstripping resources? Or does the "backs-to-the-wall" situation produce better playing and inspired leadership? There is evidence for both propositions – and for some other observations on the relationship between financial and artistic ups and downs, too.

This is not, however, a complete history of the Hallé Orchestra or even of its activity in the 20th century. Some may be surprised to find no discussion at all of the work of Charles Hallé, the orchestra's founder (and there is no adequate treatment of the story of the Hallé Choir, either) – but this is about the Hallé Concerts Society, the body created to take Hallé's vision into the future: it is the story of what happened in the first 100 years *after* Hallé. Two comprehensive histories of the orchestra exist already, taking the story from its beginnings in 1858 to its 125th anniversary in 1983.[4] I have been careful not simply to duplicate the contents of those. My intention is rather to supplement them, and its justification is that I have been allowed to look at the Hallé's documentary archives, which include annual financial accounts from the whole 20th century (with one small gap in the sequence), Committee and Board minutes from 1922 to the present, and other papers whose preservation varies from period to period. I have not consulted Board minutes from later than mid-1995, not through lack of interest, but because documents which are closest to the present retain more delicate information than those from further into the past – as it is, I believe the Hallé Concerts Society is to be praised for making so much of its archive available for study, and I understand from those closely involved that the account of events from 1995 to 1999, which I have constructed from published sources only, is a fair summary of what went on.[5]

I have gone into some detail in respect of the performance record from 1985 to 1995 – but the main focus of my approach to the performed repertoire is an analysis of selected 10-year periods from the Hallé's Manchester concerts, spread through the 20th century. This is explained further in chapter 11 and in the forward to the Tables. This book is based on a research thesis for City University, London, and anyone wanting to read the original text is welcome to ask the author.

[4]Kennedy, 1960, and Kennedy, 1982.
[5]In almost every case, where a fact is cited without a reference, the source is a document in the Hallé archives.

But let us return to the Bridgewater Hall on the concert night of February 5th, 1998. That could have been the swan song of the Hallé: in fact it was something of a new beginning. Although the Titanic was an image in many minds at the time, the symphony they played that night was Mahler's first – "the Titan". I shall never forget the hope and determination embodied in that music, and the ringing fanfares which re-echoed at its close. It symbolised the fact that the Hallé has now begun a new era. It has looked extinction in the face and vowed to live.

The Hallé has entered the 21st century – the second century of the Hallé Concerts Society – with a new management structure, new ideas and high hopes. This is the story of the past, but the exciting prospect is the future.

Chapter 2

Nothing but the best – the reign of Richter

Charles Hallé died on October 25th, 1895, after holding 37 years of "Hallé Concerts" in the Free Trade Hall, Manchester. Three Manchester benefactors – textile merchant Gustav Behrens,[6] Hallé's business manager James Forsyth[7] and the industrialist Henry Simon[8] – were assigned the goodwill of the concerts by Hallé's executors (deed dated November 21st, 1895) and continued them for 1895-6 and the following three seasons. After this, if they so wished, the concerts would be their property. This became the position by the spring of 1899, but the three wished to see the concerts established on a more permanent basis and the ownership of them more widely shared. Consequently the Hallé Concerts Society was formed, incorporated on June 28th, 1899, and on December 6th the two surviving original guarantors (Simon had died in July) assigned the ownership of the concerts to it. Fifty members (soon afterwards increased to 200) guaranteed up to £100 each, which could be called on from time to time to make good any deficit on the activities of the Society. From summer, 1899, the concerts and orchestra were organised by a Committee of the Society, with Dr Hans Richter under contract as "permanent conductor" from October, 1900.

That is an outline of the birth of the Hallé, but it is worth remembering that the world into which it came was a very different one from ours, 100 years later. Manchester was a city of merchants and mill-owners, with a prosperous elite dwelling in towns such as Didsbury and Altrincham, and the middle classes in the leafy suburbs such as Moss Side and Whalley Range, whose well-to-do would parade their carriages in Alexandra Park of a Sunday afternoon. In the inner parts of the city, however, thousands lived in poverty and crowded housing. It is clear

[6]Gustav Behrens (1846-1936) was a Manchester businessman and philanthropist, and a close friend of Hallé during the latter's lifetime.
[7]James Forsyth (d. 1907), was Hallé's business manager and one of the Forsyth Brothers whose music store trades to this day in Deansgate, Manchester: it continued until after the Second World War as the box office for Hallé Concerts.
[8]Henry Simon was a Manchester industrialist and benefactor.

that the Hallé Society, in the beginning, belonged to the former category of citizens rather than the latter.

Behrens' first outline of his plans for the Society, drawn up prior to a meeting in the Lord Mayor's Parlour, Manchester Town Hall, on June 25th, 1898, declared that it would be non-profit-making, and that any surpluses would be accumulated in a reserve fund in order to give "greater freedom and scope to the management and make the engagement of artists and production of interesting musical works possible . . ." [9] The reserve fund, writes Michael Kennedy, began with a balance of £15,400, which presumably was a semi-private arrangement to provide working capital and avoid reliance on overdraft facilities when losses were sustained and before calls on the guarantors made up the shortfall. The surviving accounts do not mention the fund, rather surprisingly considering the extent of the losses which later ensued. Since the original three guarantors of 1895 had undertaken to pay the first £500 per season of any surplus to the executors of Hallé's will (i.e. for the benefit of Hallé's family) and in fact paid them £1809 over four seasons, it seems that at the outset there were no other surpluses to be retained. Whatever the position in regard to the reality of reserves, it is also clear that Behrens and his colleagues on the Committee assumed that their artistic horizons were limited by the potential trading income at any given time, although the fact that they had engaged Richter at a fixed fee of 50 guineas per concert – and with a guarantee of at least 40 concerts in total per season – was a high ambition in itself.

Richter (1843-1916), was a colleague, amanuensis and conductor of Richard Wagner, and conductor of, among other historic premieres, the first performances of Brahms' *Symphonies no. 2* and *3* and *Double Concerto*, Bruckner's *Symphonies no. 4* and *8*, Tchaikovsky's *Violin Concerto*, and the first complete *Ring* at Bayreuth. Prior to his engagement by the Hallé, he was chief conductor of the Vienna Court Opera, Vienna Philharmonic Society and Gesellschaft der Musikfreunde – his release from which was granted by Gustav Mahler – and known as a conductor throughout Europe.

Richter's first appearance with the Hallé in Manchester, which was also the first performance whose programme booklet bore the superscription "Hallé Concerts Society", rather than merely "Hallé Concerts", was on October 19th, 1899. It was the outcome of protracted negotiations which ended with Richter effectively in artistic control from the 1899-1900 season onwards,[10] although he was not able to conduct for the whole season because of his commitments in Vienna.

Richter was certainly the most eminent conductor in the world at the time he

[9]Quoted from Kennedy, 1960: 113.
[10]A detailed account of the negotiations leading to Richter's Manchester appointment – which began on the day of Hallé's death – is given in Kennedy, 1960: 100-107, 115-126. See also Fifield, 1993.

was engaged, and also among the most expensive. Christopher Fifield, in his biography of Richter, notes that Gustav Mahler (director of the Vienna Court Opera from 1897) had doubled Richter's salary as its conductor to try to keep his services, and that Richter was accused at the time of deserting Vienna for financial reward.[11] He was originally offered a minimum salary of £1500 for 42 concerts within a six-month period (including 12 in Liverpool and six elsewhere, and with the Liverpool Philharmonic Society undertaking to find £700 of the total).[12] At one point he asked for £3,000, saying he had been offered similar terms by both Boston in the U.S.A. and by Glasgow. This appears to have been the case,[13] and even higher fees were being demanded at the time by Felix Mottl, from both the Hallé and Liverpool.[14] The Hallé was unable to stretch to that level of remuneration, but, in the event, Richter's contract with the Hallé entitled him to a minimum of £2,100 for 40 concerts, and by this time Liverpool had dropped out of the process altogether, preferring to retain the services of Sir Frederick Cowen, who had conducted both the Hallé and Liverpool concerts from 1896. The result was that the Hallé Society was responsible alone for finding a very high salary for Richter. If the supposition is correct that a factor of nearly 200 represents the change in the buying power of money from 1899 to 1999 (see Chapter 12: beer in a public bar was 2d a pint before the First World War and is close to £2 a pint now), then Richter was being promised the equivalent of £10,000 a concert, with a guaranteed minimum of almost £4 million for six months' work.

The Hallé season before the First World War

No minutes of the Society's meetings survive from before the First World War, but some financial records do, and printed programmes, from which it is possible to infer certain aspects of the policies followed.[15]

The Manchester Hallé season consisted of a regular pattern of 20 concerts, mainly at weekly intervals, from October to March (plus an "Orchestra Pension Fund" concert which concluded each series), but the number of "country concerts" (engagements performed for other promoters both in and outside Manchester) varied from year to year. Between 1903 and 1913 these totalled between 16 and 30 per annum, and included four "Gentlemen's Concerts" every season, held in the Midland Hotel concert hall. There were also one, two or three engagements per season for the orchestra in the concerts of the private promoter Brand Lane[16] in Manchester.[17]

[11]Fifield, 1993: 275, 278.
[12]Kennedy, 1960: 100.
[13]Hart, 1973, says that Richter had agreed to become Nikisch's successor in Chicago, in 1893, but never went there because of his other duties.
[14]Kennedy, 1960: 102, 105-7.
[15]The history of the early years of the Society is given in detail in Kennedy, 1960: 97-186.
[16]Brand Lane was an impresario whose popular concerts in Manchester began before 1899 and were continued until the 1950s.
[17]For Brand Lane's concerts, see Kennedy, 1960: 109; 174-5.

A sketch of the Gentlemen's Concert Society's activity in the early 1900s may help to indicate their significance. The Society, begun near the end of the 18th century and described by itself as "the oldest musical society in the kingdom",[18] had its own concert hall in Manchester until 1898. The invitation which first brought Charles Hallé to Manchester in 1848 had been to the conductorship of the Gentlemen's Concerts, which usually included four orchestral concerts each season, as well as a small number of recitals. After encountering financial difficulty in the mid-1890s, the society sold its hall and the site was subsequently acquired by the Midland Railway Company (whose Central Station was adjacent) for the building of the Midland Hotel. However, the society secured a stipulation that the hotel should include a new concert hall with itself as priority user, and the Gentlemen's Concerts were held there from the opening of the hotel in 1903 until the demise of the society in 1920. In the years between 1898 and 1903, the society held concerts in the great hall of Manchester Town Hall.[19] During the period under discussion, the directors of the Gentlemen's Concerts Society included Gustav Behrens and E J Broadfield, also directors of the Hallé Concerts Society, and (until his death in 1907) Louis Grommé, whose son, E W Grommé, was to be a later Hallé chairman. Richter conducted most of the Gentlemen's Society's orchestral concerts each year from 1900 until 1907. Franz Beidler took the two concerts in early 1908 (as he did the Hallé engagements) while Richter was conducting the Covent Garden *Ring* cycle, and Henry J Wood was engaged for the following three seasons (while the Hallé renewed its commitment to Richter). Michael Balling conducted in 1912-13 and 1913-14, after which a roster of conductors was introduced, including Hamilton Harty. Subscriptions fell during the war, and by 1920 the society's overdraft exceeded the value of its investments. It had no guarantee fund and was wound up.

Money and music

If the Gentlemen's Concerts did not prosper in Edwardian times, neither did the Hallé's, particularly, either. After a peak of £16,018 in 1903-4, the Hallé's total annual income from concerts shows a fairly steady decline to £9,523 in 1911-12 and £9,674 in 1912-13 – because Manchester concert income fell over the years, as attendances dropped (see Table 2.2), and the number of other engagements, though varying from year to year, was also in decline in the long term. Overall expenditure followed a similar decreasing pattern – although in both respects the "Jubilee Season" of 1907-8 (celebrating 50 years of Hallé Concerts) was exceptional, and earned a useful surplus. Income of an orchestra in those days was a direct correlate of concert attendances, and though the "piecework" nature of the musicians' pay meant that costs lessened with fewer performances, the Manchester Hallé series was always of 20 concerts per season.

---

[18]Gentlemen's Concerts Society minutes May 11th, 1910, Henry Watson Music Library, Manchester.
[19]Fifield, 1993, is therefore not correct in his statements that Richter conducted Gentlemen's Concerts in the Free Trade Hall: the Gentlemen's Society minutes refer to their own hall as "the concert hall" and some use of this phrase may have misled Fifield.

The percentage of total income derived from the Manchester concerts varied in the years from 1903 to 1913 between 52% and 72%. Hallé accounts from 1902-3 to 1908-9 also show the main Manchester series producing a regular surplus, but losses on the "country" concerts in every season. In 1909-10, 1910-11 and 1911-12 both headings show deficits, but that on the "country" concerts greatly exceeds that on the Manchester ones in 1909-10 and 1911-12, with only 1910-11 reversing the position. From 1913 to 1923, by contrast, this pattern is the other way, with "country" concerts either earning more, or losing less, than Manchester ones. It would be unwise to draw firm conclusions from this comparison, however, without information on how overheads were calculated and included in expenditure for "Manchester" and "country" concerts respectively. The basic contracts made both with conductor and players were for the Manchester series, and "country" concerts were extra to that. However, Hallé players, like those of the Scottish Orchestra, were hired on six-month contracts and paid a weekly wage from 1913 onwards.[20]

But even in an age of freelance employment for most musicians, there were clearly advantages to be gained from the Hallé's accepting engagements outside the main Manchester series, apart from the simple question of whether the fee earned exceeded the expenses charged to each one. Continuity of work was a factor that would increase the value of association with the Hallé, from an individual musician's point of view. Performances rehearsed for one venue could be repeated in another. Soloists could be offered more attractive fees for groups of concerts than single occasions would permit. "Country" concert venues included Bradford, Dundee, Newcastle, Sheffield, Liverpool, Leeds, Belfast and Huddersfield in 1912-13, and Bradford, Dundee, Kendal, Edinburgh, London, Londonderry, Sheffield, Leeds, Hull, Huddersfield, Wigan, Belfast, Blackpool, Southport and Preston in 1913-14. The Hallé Orchestra had a national reputation (built on Charles Hallé's own indefatigable touring in earlier years), and provided its members with a great deal more employment than 21 concerts in Manchester.

Orchestra members' payments were certainly sufficient to attract players from the Continent, at least to take up principal positions. Richter told Otto Schieder in 1903, offering him the position of principal bassoon, that he would be guaranteed £200 for the Hallé Manchester series (i.e. £10 per concert) and that income from other Hallé engagements would enhance this by at least £60 per season.[21] That was one fifth of Richter's own payment per concert. But Hallé accounts show that payments to all orchestra members for the Manchester series usually totalled about £130 per concert, which implies an average payment of around £2 each, so rank-and-file remuneration must have been considerably less

[20]Kennedy, 1960: 178, 180. This must have applied only selectively, however (perhaps only for principals). Sidney Partington, who joined the orchestra in 1932 and was for many years principal second violin, told me (personal communication, October, 2000) that before the Second World War many players were paid only per concert.
[21]Fifield, 1993: 394.

than that for principals. Charles Reid states[22] that before the First World War, Hallé players could enhance their earnings by "up to" £5 a week from "country" engagements.

After a surplus of £96 for 1903-4, and a small declared loss (£13) for 1904-5, which was later made up by collection of late payments, the next two seasons produced deficits for the Hallé of £109 and £354. The "Jubilee Season" (1907-8) and the following one were, however, very successful, wiping out the accumulated loss and leading to an accumulated surplus of nearly £600 by 1909. Results then turned sharply down, with a deficit of £600 on 1909-10, and of £1,066 on 1910-11 (Richter's final season), resulting in the first call on guarantors since 1902 (when a call of £5 each had realised £890). The call of June 16th, 1911, was for £7 each and raised about £1,000.[23] The 1911-12 season lost £387, and 1912-13 lost £737. A further call was made in June 1914, after a very large deficit in 1913-14 – leaving the accumulated deficit at over £1500.

The maestro

Richter's last two seasons (1909-10 and 1910-11) both showed deficits on the main Manchester concert series for the first time in the Society's history, and the programme for his farewell concert on March 23rd, 1911 (the Pension Fund concert) stated that he was retiring on medical advice, one year earlier than his contract required. He gave his last British concerts the following month, and his last Bayreuth performances of *Die Meistersinger* (at wide intervals) that summer. His sight was failing badly, and he was 68 years old.[24] It must have been with some relief, however, that the Hallé Society turned to conductors (including Michael Balling, Richter's successor from October, 1912) who did not require fees as high as Richter's 50 guineas a concert. Balling (1866-1925) was a German-born opera conductor, had a long previous association with the Bayreuth Festival and was highly regarded by Richter. Balling's fee of 25 guineas meant that on a full season of 40 concerts he would be more than £1,000 cheaper than Richter, which on a turnover in the region of £10,000 was a significant saving (and the equivalent of the maximum loss the Society had so far made in any one season). Whatever one makes of the conversion factor to present-day values from those of the early 1900s, it is plain that Richter's salary represented over 20% of the Hallé's total turnover – a major commitment by any standard.

Relations between the Hallé Committee and Richter, however, remained excellent throughout his regime, despite the latter's insistence on a purge of the orchestra's players when he signed his first five-year contract in 1900,[25] and though there were vocal factions who complained about his narrow repertoire there is no

[22]Reid, 1971.
[23]Kennedy, 1960: 143.
[24]Fifield, 1993.
[25]Fifield, 1993: 337.

evidence that the Committee members wished him to resign any earlier than he did, or that the reason given for his departure was not genuine.[26]

Kennedy records controversy[27] in Manchester and criticism in the contemporary press about Richter's neglect of English and French composers, other than Elgar, from about 1906 onwards. It is interesting that Ernest Newman's[28] Hallé programme notes of the time laud Elgar's music for its "European" qualities: both his analysis of *The Dream Of Gerontius* and that of the first symphony, on their first performances, make that point, and it would seem that by "European" he meant, in effect, "Germanic". Richter's repertoire was limited in some ways but remarkably far-sighted in others (see Chapter 11 and Tables 2.1 and 2.2). Richter was not solely devoted to the Hallé, either. He continued his summer activities in London and elsewhere after accepting the Hallé contract. His London seasons continued until 1902, and from 1903 to 1910 he conducted opera at Covent Garden every year. At the outset of his Hallé commitment he wrote in his diary: "My London players really are my favourites."[29]

Richter did incur disapproval for his absences in the 1907-8 and 1908-9 Hallé seasons (so that he could conduct the first complete *Ring* cycle in English at Covent Garden). He consequently missed the orchestra's 50th anniversary concert in January, 1908, and was responsible for the engagement of Franz Beidler, Wagner's son-in-law, for this instead – a decision which was attacked as an attempt to "insinuate" Beidler into the Hallé conductorship. Richter, however, then severed his connection with Covent Garden and renewed his Hallé contract for three years.

When Richter was absent, guest conductors were paid considerably less than his fee: Henry Wood, for instance, received 25 guineas in 1909. For the interregnum season of 1911-12, only two conductors received the Richter rate (Sir Edward Elgar and Franz Schalk), while others were paid from 25 to 35 guineas. Expenditure on artists was at first rarely at the level of Richter's concert rate, but this changed. The only artist to be paid equal fees to his in the early years of the decade was Lady Hallé,[30] Sir Charles' widow (whose fee never subsequently exceeded Richter's). Fritz Kreisler, who received 45 guineas in 1903, was a frequent visitor, receiving 50 guineas in 1905 and 60 guineas from 1908 on. Mischa Elman was paid 60 guineas in 1906 (75 guineas the following year), and Pablo Sarasate £60. Pianists Ferruccio Busoni and Leopold Godowsky, however, received 40

[26]Kennedy, 1960: 142-3, 169-70.
[27]Kennedy, 1960: 136-144.
[28]Ernest Newman (1868-1959) – real name William Roberts – was a Liverpool-born and Liverpool University educated bank clerk, without formal musical training, who became a music critic on the *Manchester Guardian, Birmingham Daily Post, The Observer* and finally, from 1920 to 1958, *The Sunday Times*.
[29]Fifield, 1993.
[30]Lady Hallé (b. 1839) was Wilma Norman-Neruda, described by Kennedy, 1960: 82 as "the greatest woman violinist of her day".

guineas each, both at the beginning of this period and its end. It appears to have been a purely market-driven payments pattern: relative unknowns, such as Bela Bartok in 1903, would appear as soloists for 10 guineas (the same amount was paid to an orchestra member playing a concerto – though Bartok did receive 20 guineas on his return in 1905). Percy Grainger, in 1905, was paid 15 guineas.

However, celebrity recitalists – introduced in the Hallé series for the first time in the 1911-12 season – were able to earn large fees (eg. a combined £254 for singers Clara Butt and Kennerly Rumford, and £147 for the virtuoso violinist Eugene Ysaye, accompanied by Raoul Pugno).

The Hallé project in context

When Charles Hallé founded his orchestra in 1858, it was an entrepreneurial venture in a city where a concert society already existed. He was not unique – other examples of conductors who were their own orchestral impresarios in the late 19th and early 20th centuries are Leopold Damrosch and Theodore Thomas in New York, and Henry Wood and Thomas Beecham in London. Opportunities for such individual enterprise were available in metropolitan centres, with their substantial communities of resident musicians.

But in most major cities in both Britain and the United States, concert-giving societies as the bases for orchestras, whether initiated by musicians or by well-to-do music-lovers, were more the norm.[31] Liverpool had its Philharmonic Society, founded in 1840. It appointed a conductor from time to time (Hallé held the job from 1883 until his death, succeeding the composer, Max Bruch) and employed an orchestra which, from Hallé's time, at any rate, was substantially the same as the Hallé Orchestra in membership.[32] And in Manchester there was the Gentlemen's Concerts Society. The City of Birmingham Orchestra was different – it came into existence in 1919, after a number of other short-lived attempts at orchestra-founding, with the support of Birmingham Corporation.[33] The Bournemouth Municipal Orchestra was a similar enterprise, which traces its history back to 1893.[34]

The Hallé Concerts Society was unusual in that it came into being to continue the personally-named concert series which Hallé had promoted at the Free Trade Hall in Manchester: few other orchestras in the world today are named after their founder. But the fact that from the outset the Hallé Concerts Society struggled financially was not unique. The City of Birmingham Orchestra was subsidised heavily by its Corporation from the start; the Boston Symphony Orchestra in the

[31]Businessmen and financiers enabled the foundation of the Boston Symphony Orchestra, in 1881, the Chicago Orchestral Association 10 years later, and the Philadelphia Orchestra in 1900 (Hart, 1973, Arian, 1971).
[32]Lewis, 1998.
[33]King-Smith, 1995.
[34]Street & Carpenter, 1993.

USA was set up anticipating losses of $50,000 per annum, and the New York Philharmonic had to raise $50,000 to remain viable between 1903 and 1906, later setting up its own group of "guarantors" in 1909, who raised $118,000 to cover the then deficit and establish a fund for the future.[35] The Hallé guarantors may have felt they were hard done by, but they were not exceptional.

Richter was the first conductor actively wooed to Manchester by the fledgling society, and his engagement indicates a bold policy of creating, by building on the legacy of Charles Hallé, a world-class orchestral institution in Manchester. It was, if you like, an artistically-led policy. Richter's time at the Hallé is described by Kennedy, 1960, as a "part of a golden age",[36] despite the limitations of his choice of repertoire. But the Hallé Society, by 1913, had sustained trading deficits on more years since 1900 than it had achieved surpluses,[37] and was having to issue substantial calls on its guarantors to remain solvent.

The use of "calls" on the guarantors could be compared with income from private donation or even commercial sponsorship in today's conditions (though the proceeds were always entered in balance sheets, not trading figures), as most donors were people with private fortunes derived from business. The accounts indicate other non-performance income of £48 in 1909, £226 in 1911, and £98 in 1913. However, in the period as a whole, proceeds of calls were equivalent to only 1% of performance income, and other income to 0.3% of performance income. The role of the guarantors was to make good any losses which seemed irrecoverable from trading alone: they were not seen, however, as a regular source of income with which to carry out plans calculated to result in a loss from the outset. The orchestra was paid only when it performed, and thus expenditure and income rose and fell together in relation to the number of engagements obtained. If there is a case for supposing that artistic goals can lead towards particular financial outcomes, the evidence of this early part of the Hallé's story is that any such cause-and-effect is rather between high aspiration and *poor* financial performance.

There is a theory – first formulated by the American arts economists Baumol & Bowen – that the gap between performance earnings and costs in organisations such as symphony orchestras grew inevitably in the 20th century because of the impossibility of labour-saving deals in artistic performances. This has become part of the common coin of American discussion of orchestras' problems, where "the earnings gap" needs no further definition. But it does not show that large symphony orchestras' earned incomes and total expenditure were ever in balance in the past – and the early need for donations in Chicago and New York proves that in those two cases they were not. The same was true of the Hallé. If there was ever a "golden age" artistically, there was no golden age financially.

---

[35]Shanet, 1975.
[36]Kennedy, 1960: 143. The same phrase is used by him to describe Barbirolli's era (279).
[37]See Kennedy, 1960: 143.

The idea that symphonic music once "paid its way" seems to be a fiction indulged in by British writers with little evidence to support it. Norman Lebrecht wheels it out more than once in his book, *When The Music Stops*.[38] John Pick and Malcolm Anderton argue in *Building Jerusalem*[39] that many arts activities in Britain flourished with little financial patronage (other than by ticket sales and subscriptions) before the 1940s, and it seems that their reference to Hallé's founding of his orchestra in 1858 and its subsequent operation is designed to support this argument. Hallé, after all, wrote in his memoirs that in some seasons his concerts made profits of up to £2,000 a year, as Pick and Anderton observe. But we must not overlook the fact that Hallé was his own manager, conductor and even soloist much of the time, and he was almost certainly referring to surpluses achieved without allocation of fees to himself at all. It is clear that, as soon as the Hallé Concerts Society committed itself to the fees required by Richter and the soloists engaged alongside him, it was extremely difficult to make ends meet, despite ticket prices which were much higher than Hallé's and (as I shall argue in chapter 12) the Hallé's highest, in real terms, of the entire 20th century. The audience, for whom evening dress was as much *de rigueur* as it was for the orchestra, was, with few exceptions, socially exclusive.[40]   Thus, from the beginning, the Hallé Concerts Society could not survive without its safety net of private guarantors – and the Gentlemen's Concerts Society failed, after the First World War, because it had no guarantee scheme.[41]

Whatever one's view of the size of fees paid in recent years to conductors and soloists by the Hallé (in common with other orchestras) – and the effect of ever-higher admission prices for classical music concerts – it is salutary to remember that both were higher, once one allows for inflation, in the Edwardian "golden age". The Hallé then was a rich people's club – and so, no doubt, was music-making generally.

Richter was, of course, the source of a huge part of the Hallé's costs after 1899. But he established a place for the Hallé not merely as the left-over of one man's achievement, but as a permanent institution of international repute, and it is doubtful whether a less famous name could have accomplished such a feat. It is true that his reign was a period during which audiences declined – whether because of his conservative programming (which was the subject of criticism at the

---

[38]Lebrecht, 1996: 28, 211, 504.
[39]Pick & Anderton, 1999 – Particularly in the final chapter: 253-274.
[40]See Kennedy, 1960: 132. Prices under Hallé himself were from 1s to 2s 6d from 1858 onwards, so any conception that Hallé sought particularly to bring music to "mill workers and other simple folk" (Kennedy, 1960: 86) must be balanced by an awareness that his admission charges, in modern terms, would have been the equivalent of about £15 (for standing room) to £50 per performance.
[41]Jack Westrup wisely writes: "The economic position of orchestras has never been completely stable", adding that independent orchestras in England and the USA relied until the Second World War on high admission prices and the generosity of private patrons (article "Orchestra" in The New Grove, 1980, ed. Stanley Sadie).

time)[42] or because of worsening economic circumstances generally, is difficult to judge at this distance – though I incline to the latter view, in the light of the whole subsequent pattern of events in the Hallé's story. But in Richter the Hallé bought an enhanced reputation, rather than breadth of repertoire or audience-building. Whether the investment would prove justified, only the future would tell.

[42]Kennedy, 1960: 141-3.

Chapter 3

War and peace – Beecham and Harty

Everything changed with the First World War. Michael Balling was in Germany in the summer of 1914, and did not return. The Hallé Committee feared that wartime conditions would affect its attendances, but resolved to carry on. It found particular help in the form of the entrepreneur-conductor Sir Thomas Beecham, who offered to conduct any number of its concerts for no fee.

Beecham (1879-1961) was the heir to the fortune of the St Helen's-based family business, Beecham's Pills, begun by his grandfather and continued by his father, Sir Joseph. Educated at Oxford (although he did not complete his degree) he began conducting opera in London in his early twenties, and formed his own New Symphony Orchestra in 1905, followed by the Beecham Symphony Orchestra in 1908. His father's wealth and connections enabled him to conduct opera at Covent Garden and Drury Lane from 1910, and in 1913 he took over the bankrupt Denhof Opera Company in mid-tour when it was stranded in Manchester, and turned it into the Beecham Opera Company, which thereafter performed in London and toured the provinces. He was knighted in his own right in 1916, and succeeded to his father's baronetcy shortly afterwards.

Beecham provided funds which kept the Royal Philharmonic Society orchestra members on full pay in 1914, and also helped the London Symphony Orchestra's 1915-16 series. He rescued the Royal Philharmonic Society's 1916-17 season and undertook to conduct all its concerts for five years and to raise a £10,000 guarantee fund, providing he had absolute control of its musical affairs – a characteristic Beecham "takeover" of the kind he would attempt later with the London Symphony Orchestra, also.[43] He was said to have paid the full fees of all conductors who took his place in the Hallé Manchester series from 1914, but at least one admitted later that he received "a small expenses fee only".[44]

[43]See Lebrecht, 1996: 101-2.
[44]Reid, 1962.

But after a season of Beecham's "novelties" in 1915-16, receipts for Hallé Manchester concerts were at an all-time low. Additional "Proms" seasons were presented in 1916 and 1917, and lost £722 3s 8d in total. Gustav Behrens and E W Grommé (Behrens' successor as chairman of the Hallé) personally settled that debt, paying half each, in 1922.[45] After a visit in spring, 1917, with his opera company, Beecham bought out a "Saturday Proms" series presented by The Manchester Orchestra Ltd (a players' co-operative, mainly of Hallé Orchestra members) and organised a 1917-18 Hallé season of 32 weeks, consisting of Thursday and Saturday concerts and ending with seven weeks of performances by the Beecham Opera Company, with the Hallé Orchestra in the pit, at the Queen's Theatre (subsequently renamed the Manchester Opera House, the name it retains to this day). His 1918-19 season consisted of four weeks of Proms, eight weeks of opera, orchestral concerts from February to April, and a spring opera season. It lost £725. (In fact, from 1909 to 1921 only one Hallé season – 1914-15 – recorded a surplus, and that was a relatively small one, due more to a reduction in "country" concerts, which came with the onset of war, than anything else).[46]

This first Beecham era ended for the Hallé, as it did for numerous other musical organisations, with the proceedings for bankruptcy against him which began in 1919 – a severe embarrassment, which kept him out of musical affairs from 1919 to 1923. The proceedings arose from his father's death in 1916, in the middle of a purchase of the huge £2,250,000 Covent Garden estate in London. The sale of Sir Joseph Beecham's art collection enabled Thomas Beecham to continue his operatic and musical ventures temporarily, but by the end of the war he was over £100,000 in debt, and Sir Joseph's trustees would allow him only a limited income pending the completion of administration. One of Thomas Beecham's creditors petitioned for a Receiving Order against him in May, 1919, and he was unable to satisfy the Official Receiver until March, 1923.[47] A claim that he owed the Hallé Society £732 19s 6d was finally settled in 1923, and the Hallé accepted £200.[48]

For 1919-20, "Proms" were abandoned, and the young Irish organist, pianist and conductor Hamilton Harty accepted the permanent conductorship of the Hallé Orchestra[49] on the basis of the traditional winter programme of 20 concerts a season plus *Messiah* and the annual Pension Fund concert. In that season there was a loss of £1,528, and players' salaries were reduced. The orchestra's strength

[45]Receipt from Forsyth Bros. and correspondence, in Hallé archives.
[46]Kennedy, 1960: 219.
[47]Reid, 1962.
[48]This no doubt explains a couple of letters from Harty to Behrens in 1923 in which he suggests the Hallé should be hosts to Beecham in a forthcoming visit to Manchester, and then comments that he is "very sorry about the Beecham affair ... that is too bad", but hopes he will not be handicapped in his own musical ambitions for the Hallé by "a debt incurred before I had any connections with the Society" – Documents in Hallé archives.
[49]Being appointed "on Beecham's recommendation", according to Procter-Gregg, 1976: 14, and also that of Albert Coates (Hammond, 1978).

stood at 73.[50]

Harty (1879-1941) was the son of an organist and choirmaster in Hillsborough, County Down, 12 miles south of Belfast. At 14, the gifted Hamilton gained his first musical appointment, as organist of a nearby church, and within a year moved to Belfast (to another organ bench) and joined an orchestra as a violist. One year later he moved to Dublin, took lessons at the Royal Irish Academy of Music and began to gain a reputation as a piano accompanist of rare gifts and extraordinary reading ability. He married the soprano Agnes Nicholls in 1904, who was a personal friend of Hans Richter. In 1911 Richter invited Harty to conduct his tone poem, *With The Wild Geese*, in London, and he was engaged for the following London Symphony Orchestra season. He conducted in Dublin and at Covent Garden in 1913, and first appeared with the Hallé Orchestra at the Westmoreland Festival in 1914, also conducting on occasion during the First World War (including a concert in January, 1915), and taking Beecham's place at the Hallé *Messiah* in 1918 and Bach's *Mass in B Minor* in 1919.[51] He had also become known to Manchester concert-goers as a conductor of the Gentlemen's Concerts during the war.[52]

Harty caused a furore in 1920 by dismissing the women players who had joined the orchestra in the war years, but, with the restoration of regular concerts to Thursday nights, and, in addition, four operatic evenings on Saturdays, a better financial pattern was apparent, and the 1921-22 season ended with £30 profit.[53] The Manchester Hallé season of 1922-23 consisted of 22 midweek concerts and four on Saturdays – the latter were operatic evenings, with the "Beecham Operatic Chorus", as in the previous season. Harty had conducted a festival week of opera with the Hallé and Beecham Chorus in Manchester in 1921, and did so again in 1925, though in 1922 he and the orchestra took part in the Carl Rosa Opera season instead.[54] . "Country concert fees to be paid as formerly" one of the earliest surviving Hallé Committee minutes says in 1922 (there appear to have been up to 28 planned at the time, though 14 of these were "pending") but the amount of Harty's fees for them is unclear.

With the survival of Committee minutes from June, 1922, onwards, it is possible to gain an impression of the some of the processes involved in the formation of Hallé policy. The minutes show that Harty was present at most Committee meetings (which were held, normally, once per month from September to June), and although his position as permanent conductor gave him a leading

[50]Kennedy, 1960: 219.
[51]Kennedy, 1960; Greer, 1978; Hammond, 1978.
[52]Gentlemen's Concerts Society minutes, Henry Watson Music Library, Manchester.
[53]Kennedy, 1960: 196-219.
[54]Kennedy, 1960: 219.

role in decision-making,[55] the other Committee members made their views on repertoire known from time to time and, apparently, saw their proposals acted on. Harty personally was also the chief link between the Hallé and both the BBC and the Columbia Gramophone Company, with which he had an individual contract separate from the Hallé's (Harty recorded with the London Symphony Orchestra, also).

Programmes were announced in an annual prospectus, but Harty often changed them as the series proceeded.[56] Just as during Richter's incumbency, when (in March, 1909), Elgar's *Symphony no. 1* had been repeated "by request" after its premiere the previous December, a decision could be taken to repeat a work within a single season: for instance, Elgar's *Symphony no. 2* in 1926 and Lambert's *Rio Grande,* repeated at the Pension Fund concert in March, 1930, after its premiere the previous December. And programmes could be changed at short notice: the Beethoven *Missa Solemnis* on February 4th, 1926, was changed by the Committee meeting the previous December to one of the Bach *Mass In B Minor –* "in view of many pressing requests". The Committee also made – or at least endorsed – decisions about who should lead the orchestra for particular concerts.

From the 1925-6 season onwards, Harty's fee was fixed at £50 per concert (Richter's had been 50 guineas, at a time when money was worth twice as much, according to the Prices and Incomes Index, and two-and-a-half times as much if we go by the "beer standard")[57] – after rising from £31 in 1921-2 to 40 guineas in 1922-3, and 45 guineas in 1923-4. An exception was the Bantock *Omar Khayyam* performance of December 1st, 1921, for which Harty received 50 guineas: presumably on account of his exceptional efforts in playing the entire accompaniment on the piano, from the full score, when the orchestral parts failed to arrive.[58]

For most of the 1920s and 1930s,[59] the 20 midweek concerts in Manchester (and the Pension Fund concert at the close of the season) were once again the major feature of the Hallé's activity. "Country" concerts varied in number from 37 to 17 per season (in the surviving records). Over the seven seasons from 1928-29 to 1934-35, for which annual accounts survive, the proportion of income derived from Manchester main series concerts appears to vary between 37% (in 1929-30 – an exceptional year, because 24 Manchester "Promenade" concerts were also

[55]See Kennedy, 1960: 213. His personal secretary (and "intimate friend" – Kennedy, 1960 – or "mistress" – Kennedy, 1982), Olive Baguley, was also secretary to the Hallé Concerts Society until his departure in 1933.
[56]See Kennedy, 1960: 219.
[57]See chapter 12.
[58]Kennedy, 1960: 248, and Hirsch, 1978: 69.
[59]Records are not complete, as annual accounts do not appear to have survived from 1923-4 through to 1927-8, although summaries of Manchester concert income and expenditure are available for these years, as in fact they are for the whole of 1921-2 to 1942-3.

given,[60] as well as 37 "country" concerts), and 72% (in 1934-5), and average income per concert appears to have varied between £361 (in 1932-3) and £409 (in 1934-5) for Manchester, while "country" concerts show average income between £142 (1933-4) and £227 (1935-6). But as in the equivalent figures for 1903-13, records do not show any allocation of overheads.

Support from the city

The Hallé had been requesting aid from Manchester City Council, without success, since the beginning of the First World War,[61] and in 1922 embarked on negotiations with the council's Town Hall Committee on a proposal for eight "popular concerts" on consecutive Sunday afternoons in December, 1922, and January, 1923, to be given in the Free Trade Hall under Harty.[62] The hall (normally rented by the council to the Hallé) was to be made available free of charge, standing room would be available free of charge, and tickets were to be priced at 1s and 2s. The Hallé were to bear all costs (estimated at £224 per concert, ie £1,792 in total), but the Corporation would guarantee against loss up to £1,000. Two Corporation representatives were to assist in the management of these concerts. A letter was sent to the *Manchester Guardian* explaining that the plan would not entail any change in the management of the Hallé Concerts Society, or risk of loss to its guarantors, as "misleading" reports of it had emerged. The subject was sensitive politically and the plan, having been passed by the Town Hall Committee, was withdrawn by the committee's chairman shortly afterwards.[63]

That proposal having failed to gain approval, Dr Walter Carroll, Manchester City Council Education Committee's musical advisor, approached Harty, asking whether "selected schoolchildren" from primary schools might be admitted to orchestral rehearsals. After this idea, also, foundered, because the Education Committee would not contribute an appropriate fee, Harty himself put forward the idea of a children's concert in the afternoon before the second December performance of *Messiah*: "as . . . the band can be utilised (as a rehearsal) without extra cost, and the hall too is available free of special charge".

The idea of Municipal Concerts was then raised again: a plan was produced by the City Council for concerts with cheap seats (from 8d to 3s 6d), with 500 seats reserved for children at 6d each – this time with the council bearing the costs. The Hallé decided it could quote a rate of £200 a concert for these, and five dates were agreed between October and December, 1924. The first incurred a loss to the Corporation of £169 10s 11d, but, with 2,346 tickets sold, "the result was

[60]A BBC promotion from which the Hallé derived neither profit nor loss, according to E W Grommé, the Hallé chairman (quoted in Kennedy, 1960: 232).
[61]Kennedy, 1960: 200f.
[62]Both Birmingham and Glasgow by this time were supporting municipal orchestras (Hammond, 1978).
[63]Kennedy, 1960, tells the tale, involving opposition from the *Manchester Evening News* and *Manchester City News*.

considered to be in every way satisfactory." Similar losses were incurred at the next two Municipal Concerts, with similar attendances (the third sold out at 2,402) and the Hallé Committee was told "the Town Hall Committee considered the results to be most gratifying."

Harty seized the moment by suggesting that the Corporation be invited to take over the Hallé's Good Friday concert (which had made a loss for several years) for 1925, and the orchestra and choir should perform *Messiah* on that date. The Corporation declined, but *Messiah* was given anyway, at "popular prices", and the BBC agreed to broadcast it for a special fee of £100 – as it had *The Dream Of Gerontius* earlier in the year. Thus, because of the example provided by the Municipal Concerts, the Hallé promoted its own first concert deliberately given at reduced prices with a subsidy to meet its cost – in this case from broadcasting.

The Hallé Committee asked that another series of Municipal Concerts should be arranged for 1925-6. This was finalised as a series of 10: nine at a rate of £210 each (£10 of this being for "artists" – i.e. soloists), and a free children's concert was given on the afternoon of Friday, December 18th, "in lieu of rehearsal" – using Harty's plan of performing in the rehearsal time of the second *Messiah* performance. A problem arose because five of these concerts were to be on days when the Liverpool Philharmonic's rehearsals were held: a solution was reached (at Liverpool's suggestion) by holding the Hallé's rehearsals at 2.30pm, instead of 1.30pm, allowing players who were members of both orchestras to attend a 10am rehearsal in Liverpool on the same day on each occasion (clearly a product of a time when trains were fast and reliable). The Municipal Concerts continued on the same pattern until 1929-30. Later[64] they were reduced to seven, in 1933 to four, and after five in 1939-40 they were discontinued.[65]

From 1926 Carroll organised an annual concert by a schoolchildren's orchestra and choir – the choir, trained by Gertrude Riall, performed in a Hallé Municipal Concert on March 4th, 1929, and the famous Columbia recording of *Nymphs And Shepherds* and *Brother Come And Dance With Me* followed (made on June 4th, 1929). The record, COL 9909, became one of the biggest selling items in Columbia's catalogue, and even in the 1950s was one of the most requested items on BBC Radio's "Children's Favourites". The Manchester Schoolchildren's Choir appeared in the final Municipal Concerts of 1930 and 1931 also.

The instigation of the Municipal Concerts represents the first recognition by the Hallé and Manchester Council that they had a common interest in making concerts available for the benefit of the less well-off, and that in order for music of the quality provided by the Hallé to be accessible in this way, drastically reduced admission prices were necessary. Educational need was part of the justification for

---

[64]Kennedy, 1960, says in 1930-31, but the programme books indicate there were still ten in that season.
[65]Kennedy, 1960: 218.

the plan from the beginning, but only part, as the concerts were not limited to a schools' audience.

Money and music

The 22 Thursday concerts of 1922-3 showed a surplus of £640, following one of £584 the previous season. However, the Saturday concerts now showed a total loss of £567 3s 1d, and were abandoned. The orchestra's size was increased to 86 for the 1923-24 season.[66] The first 12 concerts (including two performances of *Messiah*) showed a loss of £33 16s 4d, at a point when the previous two years had shown a surplus. It was clearly to be a difficult year.

An invitation to give concerts at the British Empire Exhibition at Wembley, London, in 1924 was refused on the grounds that the society could only constitutionally accept engagements of that kind "if no financial loss can accrue to our Society from such engagement". But, at the same time, Harty agreed to give three concerts at the Queen's Hall, London, in the autumn of 1924, under the auspices of the Columbia Gramophone Company Ltd., with a guarantee which, he said, was to be of "up to £800 for any loss". In the event, the concerts lost over £1296, and the Columbia company contributed only half that sum, not the full £800. The Hallé minutes record a "misunderstanding", as Columbia had actually agreed to meet half any loss, up to a total loss of £1600. If the Hallé Committee was dismayed by its conductor's incurring such a deficit, it was not registered in its minutes. But after 21 concerts of the Manchester season, the main series results showed a £95 loss, whereas in previous years at the equivalent point there had been surpluses of £540 and £694 – an indication of an incipient problem of major proportions. It was at this point (March, 1924) that agreement was made with the BBC for parts of Hallé concerts to be broadcast.

A month later the Society's bank balances showed a deficiency of £1011, which was not finally cleared until November the same year. The orchestra's contract with the Columbia Gramophone Company was renewed for a five-year period, on payment of £100 to the Hallé "as well as a fee for each performance" (this was revised in January, 1926, as a £100 payment for "sole rights" and a guarantee of at least 20 recording sessions during the five years – session fees were now not specified).

The final loss for the 1923-4 season was £258 12s 10d – a setback which was to prove difficult to overcome. The first half of the 1924-5 season showed an £85 loss, and the full series of 20 concerts lost £27. But the Hallé's balances were still £665 6s 5d in deficit: a continuing reflection, it would seem, of the loss on the Queen's Hall concerts and the "misunderstanding" with Columbia.

The 1925-6 season seems to have been a finely balanced one, financially. By

[66]Kennedy, 1960: 221.

December, the first seven concerts had lost £514 16s 10d (the figure was £401 18s 11d the previous year). But by March, 1926, the Hallé's bank balances were £236 5s 6d in credit, and by June £203 19s 7d in credit, with the annual accounts showing a surplus of £57 1s 6d. For 1928-29 the Hallé recorded a surplus of £146 on a turnover of £16,458 (which included £1,921 income from seven recording sessions). For 1929-30 the surplus was £91 on a turnover of £22,148, a peak in concert income not to be emulated until 1941-2 because of the "Prom" concerts in Manchester and £1,827 from five recording sessions. The results for 1930-31, however, show a deficit of £310 on a turnover of £18,416, representing a similar number of concerts to the previous season, except for the lack of a "Proms" series, but with Manchester concert income down by 14%.

The Hallé's results showed a sharp down-turn from 1931-32 onwards. Calls were made on the Society's guarantors every year from 1932 to 1935. The trading loss for 1931-2 was £1583, and more annual deficits followed (£737 in 1932-33, £611 in 1933-34, £383 in 1934-35), though the figure was reduced to £153 by 1935-6. The Depression must have been the single most important factor in this pattern. Overall income, which had exceeded £16,000 in 1928-29 and 1930-31 (in addition to the huge figure for 1929-30, the year of the 24 Promenade concerts), dropped dramatically in the following two seasons – to £13,155 and £13,210, respectively – and reached its lowest (£11,139) in 1933-4, growing only gradually thereafter.

The 1930-31 season saw a reduction in attendances at Manchester concerts, but the dramatic losses in 1931-2 and the next two seasons were mainly because of the reduction in the number of "country" concerts.[67] Manchester income recovered in 1934-5 and 1935-6. Income figures for Manchester concerts include broadcast fees, and it seems clear that these played a significantly greater part in Hallé finances when times were hard.

The formation of endowment funds to provide a base of financial security is a frequently-observed phenomenon in the history of the major American symphony orchestras in the years between the two World Wars.[68] The idea of an Endowment Fund to help the Hallé through difficult periods came, first, in April, 1926, from Gustav Behrens, one of the original personal guarantors and now Treasurer, with an offer to contribute £1000 to such a fund if nine other people would do the same. Almost a year later, Harty was recorded as "again" strongly urging that the society's finances should be stabilised and proposing that the fund should now be formed by asking each guarantor to pay £5 per annum, even if there were no loss on the society's activities, but his suggestion does not seem to have found support

---

[67]But also in part due to Harty's own attitudes, according to Kennedy, 1960: 239.
[68]The Philadelphia Orchestra accumulated its endowment fund between 1916 and 1923; the New York Philharmonic's was first established in 1911 (after enormous losses incurred under Gustav Mahler's conductorship) by Joseph Pulitzer, and increased by fund-raising thereafter (see Hart, 1973, and Shanet, 1975).

(a similar idea, of "subscribing" membership, finally became part of the Hallé's finances in the "democratization" of 1946). Behrens renewed his offer in 1929, and the Hallé Endowment Fund was finally established. But it was clearly not sufficiently long-established to sustain the Hallé through the hard times that were just around the corner.

The maestro

The assessment in Michael Kennedy's first book on the Hallé[69] is that, in programming, Harty was "hardly the man to pioneer". Harty's "public relations" may have been calculated to avoid acquiring the reputation of a modernist, but the reality was not so simple. And analysis of Harty's programmes[70] points to another conclusion entirely in regard to Harty's Hallé repertoire. Kennedy's assessment in 1960, though made in comparison with Henry Wood's Promenade Concerts of the time, seems a little one-sided. To describe the concerts themselves as "makeshift" and "a half-hearted compromise between the glories of the past and the ventures of the future" is perhaps harsh. The critic Samuel Langford may have "sensed . . . that Harty, for all his brilliance, was not of the highest calibre", but the Hallé, under Harty, were heard in London in 1928, shortly after a visit by Furtwangler and the Berlin Philharmonic, and critical comparisons were in the Hallé's favour (as also noted by Kennedy – his second history of the Hallé[71] contains a considerable revision of his opinion of Harty's work).

Philip Hammond, in the major work on Harty's life and work,[72] quotes Harty's own views on "modern" music. In 1920, before taking up the Hallé baton, he professed not to have any liking for "the terrible cleverness of the moderns". But he added that he admired Stravinsky and Ravel greatly: they were "all that is witty" – adding "I hope to have something new at each concert, and also at each a solid proportion of music that can be enjoyed without the learning of a new language every week." His dislikes apparently included Franck, Scriabin and some Brahms. Nine years later Harty was pursuing the same theme. "Strauss and Elgar are still with us and as far as one can see are the end of that particular line [i.e. Bach-Mozart-Beethoven-Brahms-Wagner] . . . bright young people of today . . . profess to find pleasure . . . in certain latter-day developments . . . (but) music has wandered aside into barren and unfruitful wastes . . ."[73] But Leonard Hirsch, a member of the Hallé Orchestra from 1922 and leader of the second violins for much of his career, writing in the same work[74], stated: ". . . he made the Hallé one of the best disciplined, most artistic and most adventurous orchestras in the world". John Barbirolli is quoted as saying of Harty: "During his period the Hallé reached

[69]Kennedy, 1960: 214-216, 220, 228, 229.
[70]See chapter 11.
[71]Kennedy, 1982: 13-18.
[72]Hammond, 1978.
[73]Interview April 20th, 1920, with the *Musical Times*, and lecture, "Some Problems Of Modern Music", 1929, both quoted in Hammond, 1978.
[74]Greer, 1978: 73.

heights that have certainly never been surpassed."[75] And others have given Harty great credit for his achievement: Denis McCaldin, for instance, who states that his appointment "revitalized the orchestra and its repertoire . . ."[76] It will be observed in chapter 11 that Harty's main Hallé series programmes show a greater degree of novelty, and a higher proportion of the work of living composers, than those of any other Hallé conductor in the periods analyzed.

From 1926 onwards at least 34 items were issued on record by Columbia featuring Harty and the Hallé, including Beethoven's *Piano Concerto no. 3* and *Symphony no. 4*, Berlioz's overture *Le Carnaval Romain*, the Hungarian March and Dance of the Sylphs from *Faust,* the Queen Mab Scherzo from *Romeo Et Juliette*, and the Royal Hunt and Storm from *Les Troyens*, Brahms' *Hungarian Dances No. 5 and 6*, and the *Violin Concerto*, Dvorak's *Carnival Overture,* Elgar's *Cello Concerto* and *Enigma Variations*, Haydn's *Symphony no. 101*, Liszt's *Hungarian Rhapsody no. 12*, Mendelssohn's *Symphony no. 4*, Mussorgsky's *Prelude to Khovanschina*, Mozart's *Symphony no. 35*, Rimsky-Korsakov's *Capriccio Espagnol* , Schubert's overture, *Alfonso And Estrella*, *Rosamunde* music and *Symphony no. 9*, and Tchaikovsky's *Piano Concerto no. 1*.[77]

One thing is clear from Harty's time with the Hallé, however. The kind of changes in repertoire he made, after the Depression hit attendances, did not lead to any appreciable change in box-office fortunes (see Table 3.2 and chapter 11). These were still influenced far more by national economic circumstances. It is clear that the Hallé Committee felt that Harty should reduce the amount of "modern music" in the programmes to gain larger audiences – but Harty in fact reduced the level of variety (both in overall number of composers represented and in historical concentration), rather than the proportion of contemporary music. After he left, the proportion of music by living composers did fall, however. Neither change can be said to have affected attendance levels particularly: these simply recovered gradually as the economic situation improved.

When it became apparent in mid-1932 that Harty was no longer to give the Hallé his attention throughout the season (he was appointed artistic advisor and conductor-in-chief of the London Symphony Orchestra, and applied for leave of absence to visit America the following January), the Musical Committee was strengthened by the addition of R J Forbes, Principal of the Royal Manchester College of Music, and Leonard Behrens, son of the founder guarantor, former chairman and still treasurer of the Hallé, Gustav Behrens; and a sub-committee of the latter two, plus the Hallé chairman, E W Gromme, was formed "to act for the executive in case of urgent happenings". Sir Thomas Beecham and Sir Edward Elgar were approached regarding vacant dates in the next season, and Beecham, who had been requested to include *Ein Heldenleben* in his programme for February

---

[75]Atkins & Cotes, 1983: 92.
[76]McCaldin, 1987: 384.
[77]Information from Greer, 1978.

2nd, 1933, secured extra rehearsal time on the ground that the extra expense would be "justified in the circumstances". Harty announced his resignation from the Hallé conductorship three days later, and his last concert as permanent conductor was the Pension Fund performance of March 23rd, 1933. By May, Beecham was assuming a leading role. He asked for, and obtained, extra sectional rehearsals before the beginning of the next season – which were to be given free "and will be quite a few".

Harty's time with the Hallé included one of the most difficult financial periods in the orchestra's history – attributable almost entirely to the Depression of the early 1930s – and represent the point at which the Hallé became aware that it represented a tradition of artistic achievement which could prove difficult to sustain in adverse economic circumstances. Its problem, however, was not so much rising costs as falling attendances, and it was slow to accept that price reductions could be an incentive to audiences. The Hallé Committee tried most other courses of action available to cut costs and find new income – reducing the orchestra's pay, accepting local authority help with whatever strings were attached, seeking recording openings, beginning an Endowment Fund, reform of the guarantor system, and forming a Ladies' Committee (with the intention, one assumes, of fund-raising). Indeed, the Hallé was now substantially dependent on privately donated income, as were most American orchestras of the time. None of this was to have as significant an effect, however, as co-operation with the BBC – and that part of the story is described in chapter 4.

Auntie to the rescue – the alliance with the BBC, and the onset of war

The fact that the Hallé was rarely able to balance costs and expenditure from performance income alone, from its foundation as a society, and that this was not unusual for symphony orchestras in cities in both Britain and the U.S.A., has been already mentioned.[78] In Britain, however, the position was affected to a major extent by the formation and activity of the BBC. The Liverpool Philharmonic Society's orchestra functioned as a kind of off-shoot of the Hallé (joint membership of the two orchestras ended only in 1939), but from 1934 the BBC was able to provide year-round employment for musicians in both Manchester/Liverpool and Birmingham, through its Northern Orchestra and Midland Orchestra. The City of Birmingham Orchestra, like the Hallé, struggled financially in the 1930s, and a link with the BBC was a lifeline in both cases.[79]

Relationships with the newly-emergent BBC took up a large proportion of the Hallé Committee's discussions in the 1920s and 1930s. The uneasy progress in co-operation between the two organisations was finally to lead to an alliance, which at the time ensured the Hallé's survival, in 1934, and which lasted until 1943. The BBC contract from 1934 was year-round but not full-time, and many BBC players were Hallé and Liverpool Philharmonic Orchestra members, too.

The newly-created BBC, in the 1920s, was a publicly-funded body with enormous musical aspirations, in the north west of England as elsewhere. A first approach to the Hallé came early in 1923 (from what was then the Westinghouse Company and the Broadcasting Committee) for permission to "relay" concerts. Harty was initially against the idea, but by January 1924 he had had further discussions with the British Broadcasting Company and undertook to enter into an agreement for broadcasting orchestral performances "at the choice of the Hallé Concerts Society Executive".

[78]Chapter 2.
[79]King-Smith, 1995.

Two months later this was defined as follows: "The BBC to have the right to take not more than one hour out of any programme, the selection and the length of items of the orchestral performances to be left to Mr Hamilton Harty." The limitation on length arose, it would seem, from a fear that broadcasting of full concerts would affect attendances. In October, 1924, the BBC asked to change the arrangement to one where it could choose to broadcast either selected portions of all the 20 Hallé concerts, or 10 complete programmes of alternate ones. The Committee did not accede.

The financial terms were for £21 per concert to be paid for the Manchester station, plus 10 guineas each for the option to use four other main stations, with a minimum of three (in total £52 10s 0d) guaranteed. The BBC asked for further options to broadcast from eight relay stations at £2 10s 0d each, and was told that the guaranteed minimum should be for £63 if such "greater facilities" were to be granted. The technology was advancing rapidly, nonetheless, and by January, 1925, the BBC was able to offer £100 in return for a broadcast of a complete performance of *The Dream Of Gerontius*, from the "Higher Power Station" (in addition to the usual £21 for an excerpt of less than an hour from the Manchester station). The same fee was paid for a broadcast of *Messiah* that spring (see chapter 3).

The orchestral players looked for their share of the fruits of broadcasting, and in December, 1924, the Hallé Committee met the orchestra committee (of players' representatives), to hear that extra remuneration was "only a fair proposition" as the orchestra provided "some portion of the entertainment". It was also argued that broadcasting of Hallé concerts had to a great extent replaced concerts formerly given from the BBC studios by an orchestra of 40 to 50 specially recruited, and that if extended "it would probably lead to a certain amount of unemployment amongst musicians". This argument, however, was supposed to support the idea of the Hallé players, rather than anyone else, receiving extra payment! No decisions were taken.

It seems a fair conclusion that Harty's acceptance of broadcast concerts was at least in part a defensive measure against the formation of a competitor orchestra by the BBC. It is also a reasonable assumption that Hallé players made up a good number of the former BBC orchestra's membership, and thus missed the extra income it had provided.

By May, 1925, the BBC was in dispute with the Musicians Union over broadcasting fees, as the union was negotiating for a nationally agreed rate for "relays", and approached Harty, asking for his full co-operation "to secure the best possible concerts for broadcasting". The BBC offer was that 10 out of the 20 Hallé concerts in the next season should be broadcast in full, for an inclusive fee of £1,000, and this appears to have been accepted.

For 1926-7, Percy Pitt[80] of the BBC told Harty that the BBC Central Board would renew the arrangement, with a guaranteed £1,000, but wanted the right to transmit the whole Hallé series in part or in full. The Hallé executive decided it would rather renew on the old terms – but the question was overtaken by the industrial relations situation arising from the players' desire to receive extra fees from broadcasting. The BBC refused any extra payments, and the Hallé decided there should be no broadcast concerts, "in order to avoid a possible serious loss to the Society", announcing that because the lack of broadcast fees would make a deficit on the season likely, the orchestra would have to be reduced in numbers. New contracts were issued to 70 players, and almost all signed, despite Musicians Union instructions to the contrary. A further 10 contracts were then issued by Harty, effectively undermining the effort to achieve economy by reducing the orchestra's size (although it had been larger still beforehand).

So 1926/7 was a season without broadcasts – but now they were sorely missed. By December, 1926, the Hallé Committee, wishing to re-establish its relations with the BBC, suggested to the orchestra that "certain fees" might be paid into their pension fund, in lieu of extra payment, if broadcasting were resumed, but this was not accepted. The Hallé Society, it was then decided, would itself undertake to meet any demands made by the orchestra, and Harty was to approach the BBC "at once". He reported a BBC proposal which "would involve the reconstitution of the Society" – presumably some kind of plan for joint operation – but when this failed to find acceptance he had a resumption of broadcast concert fees as before to offer, with 10 concerts paid for at £100 each – the only other obligation on the BBC being to pay any broadcast fees demanded by soloists or delete their items from the broadcast. The orchestra members do not, however, seem to have demanded any new extra payment. In 1929 the arrangement for broadcast Hallé concerts was renewed at a rate of £125 each for eight concerts.

The BBC had not given up its desire to have its own orchestra in Manchester, and Harty, at least, seems now to have seen the value of coming to agreement on an arrangement which would improve his players' earning power considerably. Early in 1928 Harty presented a scheme to the Hallé Committee, which was quickly accepted, under which the Manchester radio station would engage a "permanent" orchestra of 27 players, who would also be members of the Hallé Orchestra: they would be left free for Hallé rehearsals and performances in Manchester (assuming rehearsals were always on the same day as performances), including Municipal Concerts as well as the main series. Those who were principals in both orchestras were to be free for up to 20 other concerts undertaken by the Hallé, and for all other dates the BBC would have "first call" on the players.

This may have been satisfactory to Harty, but the BBC was not without further

---

[80]Percy Pitt was a conductor who had worked with Richter and a former close associate of Sir Thomas Beecham in his London operatic ventures (Greer, 1978: 73).

ambitions. A major disagreement came in 1930, when the BBC again formed its own, exclusive Northern Orchestra. Harty complained to the Committee that "serious harm had been done to the Hallé Orchestra" by the BBC making large offers, some of which had been accepted, to some of the leading Hallé players. The BBC were not justified, he believed, in using public money to compete against private organisations, and should "subsidise" the Hallé to some extent to help repair the damage done.

The Hallé Committee took the matter very seriously, seeking a meeting with the BBC Governors, which was held on August 6th at Savoy Hill, the BBC's London headquarters. Harty's speech to the Incorporated Society of Organists at Torquay, on August 30th, on "Music And The Wireless", was his opportunity to make the issue public, and his remarks about "the amiable bandits of Savoy Hill" had a major impact.[81]

The issue became one of principle for the independent orchestras, and the BBC backed down, saying in September, 1930, that it would "loan" the members of its orchestra to the Hallé, prior to disbandment, and discuss "extended co-operation" in the future. Soon afterwards a conference organised by the London Symphony Orchestra resolved that the activities of the BBC should be "limited to the studio" – and the Hallé Committee agreed in principle. With a BBC decision in March, 1931, to retain a Nonette for studio work, whose members would be released only for Hallé concerts in Manchester, a stalemate appears to have been reached. Harty declared that if his orchestra was not kept intact for all its concerts, he could not continue as conductor – but it is clear that from this point on, if not before, his commitment to the Hallé as his prime musical interest waned. The Hallé Committee, on the other hand, did not discuss matters further beyond negotiating the broadcast of Hallé concerts in the 1931-2 and 1932-3 seasons: 10 concerts for £1,250 was the final deal in each case.

Income from recordings had helped the Hallé to a degree in the five years from January, 1926, under the contract with Columbia. This was superseded in 1928 by a new five-year exclusive contract to run alongside Harty's personal one of similar date, but it does not seem to have included a guaranteed number of sessions, as did its predecessor, and its value would therefore have been less, financially. Recording income does not appear as such in the accounts after a figure of £200 for two sessions in 1931-32.

Concern about the future became acute after the "disastrous" results – the Committee minutes' word – of the first part of 1931-2, and radical measures seemed to be needed. Harty proposed a scheme for the Hallé players to "take over" the work of the Scottish Orchestra in their forthcoming Edinburgh and Glasgow

---

[81]See Kennedy, 1960: 232, and Hammond, 1978, who says that Harty was particularly angered by the way in which the BBC had not advertised positions in its new orchestra but approached players (including some of his own) directly.

series, in order to offer Hallé musicians an attractive contract, even if it meant Manchester Hallé concerts becoming a fortnightly series. A meeting with Glasgow representatives was arranged, but nothing further seems to have come of the scheme. It could have led to something close to a full-time contract for Hallé players – an idea from Harty which seems to have been ahead of its time (although the BBC Symphony Orchestra had been formed, on a full-time basis, in 1930).[82]

In April, 1932, the Committee heard that the Hallé's partners in the Bradford Subscription Concerts Society (an important source of "country" engagements for the Hallé Orchestra) were in a "precarious" position and could only carry on if the cost of the Hallé Orchestra and its conductor were to be reduced by 10 per cent. This was accepted, and the players were asked to take a 10 per cent wage cut, which they eventually accepted. The "Hallé Light Orchestra" was also formed – arising from a suggestion by Harty – with the intention of competing for work beyond the scope of the full orchestra. Harty agreed to "carry on next season", taking any cut in pay applied to the orchestra, and without a formal contract – but he asked for "a certain amount of freedom in case of important engagements abroad". This was, as it now appears, the beginning of the end of his relationship with the Hallé.

Terms for the players were modified. In May, 1933, they agreed to perform in some towns on a "sharing" basis, with only half their fees and travel expenses guaranteed by the Society, and the following month the 10 per cent pay reduction was restored for Manchester concerts only. Another idea, with parallels in the contemporary American symphony orchestra pattern, tried in 1932 was the formation of a Ladies' Committee, with the intention of helping in fund-raising. There seems to be little evidence of its activity, however.[83]

Something had to be done to increase funds in the immediate future. In July, 1932, a new guarantee scheme was instituted, intended to appeal to those who could not guarantee up to £100: guarantors could join the scheme by commitment to any multiple of £10, with no more than a fifth of the total so guaranteed being subject to "call" in any one season. A circular stated that "the concerts are a public institution, and the responsibility for continuing them should be shared more widely" (September, 1932). The new scheme no doubt explains why the Hallé was

[82]For Michael Kennedy's view of this episode, see Kennedy, 1960: 239. Harty's proposal would also incidentally have deprived John Barbirolli of one of the first major achievements of his career. Barbirolli's tenure at the Scottish Orchestra (1933-6) was compared to the "revival of a corpse" – see Reid, 1971.
[83]The only evidence I know of is that a Mrs Quas-Cohen, JP, of Hale, who is also mentioned in the Hallé minutes as a leading light on the Hallé Ladies Committee, wrote to John Barbirolli while he was in the United States, in February, 1942, to put him in the picture regarding the state of the Hallé (which she did not then regard very highly). This is of interest for two reasons – first, it shows that the Ladies Committee was still sufficiently active for a member to be seen by Barbirolli as a source of information on the Hallé, and, second, it shows that the orchestra was not completely foreign to his thoughts prior to 1943.

able, from this point, to make annual calls on its guarantors until 1935.

The call of 1932, for £10 from each of the original guarantors (more than the cost of a top-price season ticket for the entire season of 20 concerts), yielded approximately £1,450. In 1933, "original" guarantors paid £2 10s, and new guarantors 15s per £10 pledged (yielding approximately £640). In 1934 "original" guarantors paid £2, and new guarantors 12s 6d per £10 pledged (yielding approximately £550). In 1935, "original" guarantors paid £1 10s, and new guarantors 8s per £10 pledged (yielding approximately £445).

Considered as a proportion of performance income, the proceeds of calls over the five-year period from 1930-31 to 1934-5 amount to 5% (2.5% if considered over the entire 10 years 1925-6 to 1934-5) – an indication of the extent to which the Hallé was now dependent on voluntary contributions from private sources, in addition to its local authority income (in respect of the Municipal Concerts) and its close relationship with the publicly-funded BBC. Indeed, its calls on guarantors from 1932 to 1935 may be seen as a similar phenomenon to the periodic "appeal" which was a familiar part of American symphony orchestra finances between the wars.[84]

After Harty's departure, R J Forbes, principal of the Royal Manchester College of Music, took an increasingly significant part in Hallé affairs, being appointed Orchestral Advisor "until the appointment of a permanent conductor" in April 1934. He had taken part in protracted negotiations over the end of the BBC Nonette and the reinstatement of all but one of its members to the Hallé Orchestra, in the summer of 1933. The Nonette members' contract finally terminated in October 1934, and Forbes brought forward the proposal in April, 1934, that the BBC should in future engage 30 players twice a week, and 50 once a week, for its own orchestra, with the Hallé regarded as the "northern pool" from which such players would come.

It may have appeared that this restored the Hallé's place as "the greatest force in music in the North" (a phrase used by the Hallé chairman, E W Gromme, on November 10th, 1930), but the BBC's detailed proposals, revealed in June, 1934, showed that it would in future be making the running. The Hallé (and others employing the players concerned – the Liverpool Philharmonic Society in particular) were required to employ the musicians for a minimum number of concerts per season and "would have a say in the appointment of players to fill vacancies". The Hallé accepted this, and proposed a two-year contract for a minimum of 20 concerts each season.

It seems clear that the falling number of "country" engagements at the time and the acute financial crisis it faced must have made the Hallé seek the security of a co-operative existence with the ever-growing BBC, and the arrangement

[84]Rosenbaum, 1967; Hart, 1973.

continued until the middle of the Second World War. The BBC today reckons the continuous story of its own Manchester orchestra (now the BBC Philharmonic) to date from 1934.[85] A parallel pattern of events took place in Birmingham, where the CBO, facing heavy losses, helped the BBC to establish its Midland Orchestra in 1934, with Leslie Heward as its conductor in addition to his CBO position, and the players were salaried by the BBC on 12-month contracts and hired by the CBO when available.[86]

The BBC was the first major national institution in Britain with a mission to provide orchestral music for the masses.[87] That it did this at first entirely through broadcast performances did not affect the fact that it was able to provide year-round employment to musicians in place of the winter-season contracts which had previously meant that members of even such renowned orchestras as the Hallé disappeared to seaside piers and promenades to earn their living every summer.[88]

Money and music

The Hallé itself was becoming the vehicle for Manchester appearances by eminent soloists, who were by this time receiving much higher fees than conductors. Ferruccio Busoni, Alfred Cortot and Josef Hofman were each paid 100 guineas for an appearance in the early 1920s, and Pablo Casals' fee was 130 guineas by 1924, though it reduced to 110 guineas in 1925. It was a sign of impending hard times that fees generally dropped from 1926-7 on: Hofman accepted 75 guineas in 1926, Cortot £85 in 1927. Leopold Godowsky performed for 75 guineas in 1928, and Wilhelmina Suggia, Wilhelm Backhaus and Benno Moiseiwitch each accepted 70 guineas at various times from 1925 to 1932. Cortot and Artur Schnabel took 80 guineas (Cortot in 1930, Schnabel in 1930, 1931, 1933, 1934) and in 1931 Backhaus was paid the same fee, though accepting 70 guineas again in 1933. From 1934 Schnabel was able to charge 100 guineas, and Sergei Rachmaninov 150 guineas. Soloists' fees then continued to rise, as did inflation generally, until the outbreak of war: Rachmaninov's rose to 200 guineas in 1938, Fritz Kreisler charged 325 guineas the same year, and Casals was paid 175 guineas.

The Hallé, however, was able to make some economies after Harty's departure by engaging conductors who were less expensive. In 1933 Beecham was paid 60 guineas, Elgar 55 guineas, and Pierre Monteux 50 guineas – but a young man such as John Barbirolli commanded only 25 guineas. The following season (1933-4) Beecham received £70 per concert for five engagements, and Monteux, Adrian Boult, Albert Coates and Nikolai Malko 50 guineas each: Barbirolli received 30 guineas. Beecham again obtained £70 per concert for his six engagements in 1934-5 and seven in 1935-6, and Malcolm Sargent, who took a major role in the Hallé

---

[85]See Wyatt, 1994.
[86]See King-Smith, 1995.
[87]See Minihan, 1977: 203-9.
[88]Kennedy, 1960.

season from 1936-7 onwards, was paid 40 guineas a concert, as was Sir Henry Wood in 1939-40 and 1940-41.

Payments to the orchestra members, however, were much the same in monetary terms as they had been 25 years before, despite a fall in money's value to about half what it had been. In 1907, the average cost of all the players together was £131 per concert in Manchester: in 1932-3 it was £132.[89] Charles Reid[90] states that, after the 1930s slump, Hallé players earned only £3 3s 0d from the Society, for two concerts per week (one Manchester and one "country").

In the acute decline of the Depression years, audiences fell as low as 40% – an average 51% in 1931-2. Star pianists such as Schnabel and Rachmaninov seem to have been the only "draws" to beat the trend. There was an 86% house in February, 1934, and 92% in October, for Schnabel – the former performance conducted, auspiciously, by the 34-year-old John Barbirolli – and 95% for Rachmaninov in March, 1935.

The Hallé hesitated at first to win audiences back with lower admission prices. However, the top ticket price was reduced to 10s in 1932, and the lowest price to 2s 6d in 1934. When exemption from Entertainment Tax came in the 1935-6 season, the Hallé priced its tickets at 2s to 8s 6d, and standing room at 1s – though premium rates were charged for the appearances of Bronislaw Huberman, Vladimir Horowitz and Rachmaninov – inspired, no doubt, by high attendances at the Schnabel and Rachmaninov appearances the previous season.

After Harty's departure it was perhaps inevitable that programming should be less adventurous, as a succession of guest conductors appeared (Beecham more often than others). Nicolai Malko and Rachmaninov gave the English premiere of the latter's *Variations On A Theme Of Paganini* in 1935, however, and George Szell, with Eileen Joyce as soloist, brought Dohnanyi's *Variations On A Nursery Theme* to Manchester for the first time the same year (13 years after its publication).

Interregnum – and Sargent

The search for a new Permanent Conductor was to overshadow all other artistic matters in the Hallé Committee's discussions for several years to come. In February, 1934, it was decided to approach several conductors and offer each a small number of consecutive concerts in the next season, "with a view to their becoming candidates for the position of Permanent Conductor". The following month Beecham was invited to become, not conductor, but President of the Hallé

---

[89]Calculated from records in Hallé archives.
[90]Reid, 1971.

Concerts Society (in succession to Elgar, who had recently died),[91] while R J Forbes, as Orchestral Advisor, had authority to make changes in orchestra personnel. The Hallé chairman, E W Grommé, told the annual meeting in 1934 that the Committee was in no hurry to appoint a permanent conductor "as long as we can rely on Sir Thomas Beecham".[92] It was decided that none of the invited conductors for the next season should be described as "guest conductors" in programme books, but that the Committee would consult further with Beecham. Wilhelm Furtwangler, Bruno Walter, George Szell and Nikolai Malko were all apparently under consideration in early 1935, but by the middle of the year none had shown interest, and plans were being made for the next season relying on Beecham, with Malcolm Sargent and Malko each appearing twice (other conductors included Ernest Ansermet, Landon Ronald, and Forbes).

The indecision nearly produced a fatal split in the Hallé Committee in December, 1935, when Forbes offered his resignation, and was dissuaded only by the adjournment of the meeting until January and adoption of a resolution dissociating everyone from "any suggestion or idea that Mr Forbes has ever been tempted to use his position for any interest other than the wholehearted support of the Society." Forbes did later resign as Musical Advisor to the Hallé (in May, 1936). In suggesting, at that juncture, the appointment of Philip Godlee to the Committee, however, he introduced one of the Hallé's greatest chairmen of later years. Before long Forbes' role in relation to orchestra personnel seems to have reasserted itself. From 1936, Beecham was busy running Covent Garden Opera, taking his London Philharmonic Orchestra on an exchange visit to Germany, and guest conducting in both Manchester and Liverpool (he left Britain for the United States in 1940 and did not return until the war was over). Malcolm Sargent was seen as the candidate for the Hallé conductor's post when the decision should be made. He conducted more concerts in the Hallé series of 1937-38 than any other.

By then, however, the financial corner had been turned. In the second half of the 1930s, Manchester concert income grew steadily, and "country" concert income improved, too. Prices were now lower than for many years, and attendances were booming – and since inflation generally in the 1930s was quite severe, the real price of tickets was falling rapidly. After a loss of £153 for 1935-36 (the lowest since 1930-31), and a call on the guarantors in July, 1935, reducing the accumulated deficit to under £100, the Hallé recorded surpluses of £707, £723 and £1,161 in the next three seasons. The Endowment Fund was now sufficient to provide extra funds for the balance sheet, and by the summer of 1939 the Hallé had an accumulated surplus of £2,582.

---

[91]The office of "president", originally accepted in 1915 by Earl Balfour, Manchester East MP from 1885-1906, Prime Minister from 1902-05 and subsequently First Lord of the Admiralty, Foreign Secretary, and twice Lord President of the Council, had been offered to Elgar on Balfour's death in 1930. The fact that it was not provided for in the Hallé's Articles of Association was to provide a useful exit from a tight corner for Philip Godlee in the Barbirolli era – see chapter 5.
[92]See Kennedy, 1960: 268.

In April, 1939, Sargent was appointed as Conductor-in-Chief and Musical Adviser until 1940-41, an arrangement that was renewed for 1941-2 also. For 1942-43, the Hallé proposed to offer most of the series to Leslie Heward ("with a view to the appointment of Mr Heward as permanent resident conductor for 1943-44"), but he was not well, and in the end Sargent took 14 dates.

But the Second World War was bringing a remarkable change in the entire situation of the Hallé Concerts Society. Although the 1939-40 season was hit by the requisition of the Free Trade Hall for war purposes (it was then almost completely destroyed in the Manchester Blitz of December,1940), it soon became apparent that there was a growing demand for concerts, and that people would attend them in cinemas, theatres and churches, now that they were provided at popular prices. Also, new outside funds were becoming available.

Chapter 5

Death or glory – the re-making of the Hallé

Orchestral life in Britain took on a pattern of its own, distinct from that in the United States, in the Second World War and after. American orchestras remained private enterprises with little public funding, while in Britain the wartime popularity of orchestral music and the provision of grants (first from charitable trusts, later from the CEMA – Council for the Encouragement of Music and the Arts – and its successor, the Arts Council) and local authority support enabled the establishment of full-time, salaried orchestras in Liverpool, Manchester, Birmingham and Bournemouth[93]. The London Philharmonic Orchestra also followed this pattern until it lost its London County Council grant in 1951. In Leeds, the Corporation established the Yorkshire Symphony Orchestra at the end of the war, but, with no Arts Council support, it was unable to continue after 1955.

By 1942-3, the Hallé's performance income (£33,166 – from 122 concerts and 22 recording sessions) was already more than twice that of any season from 1931-2 to 1939-40, and the Carnegie United Kingdom Trust[94] was in its third year of supporting its concerts outside Manchester, resulting in a large increase in the number of such "tour" engagements. It was also now clear that the newly-established CEMA would offer support if the Society took the plunge of offering full-time contracts to its musicians.

[93]In Bournemouth's case, the musicians were employed directly by the local authority, as the Bournemouth Municipal Orchestra, until 1954: Street & Carpenter, 1993.
[94]The Carnegie United Kingdom Trust and the Pilgrim Trust, from which the CEMA at first derived much of the aid it distributed, were American-based foundations (in the case of the latter, indirectly, as it had been established with money from the U.S. Harkness Foundation in 1930; its chairman by the outbreak of war was Lord Macmillan, who became Minister of Information before becoming the first chairman of CEMA). The Carnegie Trust had made some donations to support the arts before the war. The role of the trusts and their relationship to CEMA is described in Minihan, 1977: 216 and Hewison, 1995: 30-37.

The Hallé's hand was forced, effectively, by the BBC's decision to form its Northern Orchestra as a full-time body. The Hallé announced that it would do the same, but the majority of Hallé/BBC players accepted BBC contracts, and it became clear that by the spring of 1943 the Hallé would have few musicians left from its old membership. It was, as Philip Godlee observed in a later reference,[95] a case of "death or glory", and it was at this stage that the offer was made to John Barbirolli to return to Britain from the United States to accept the permanent conductorship of the orchestra, with (as the telegram from R J Forbes rather disingenuously put it) "important developments pending".[96] Lesley Heward had already been offered the post and, according to Beresford King-Smith,[97] had accepted it, sending his resignation to the Birmingham committee on December 26th, 1942, but was by then very ill: he died on March 15th, 1943. Sir Henry Wood was also approached, before a formal invitation went to Barbirolli, because of a misunderstanding about Barbirolli's availability.[98]

John Barbirolli (1899-1970) was a London-born cellist and conductor who achieved brilliant early success with the Scottish and Leeds Symphony Orchestras and in opera at Covent Garden, and in 1936 was appointed to the New York Philharmonic in succession to Toscanini. Initially much admired, he was eventually "squeezed out" as the New York society celebrated its centenary with two seasons (1941-42 and 1942-43), employing a large roster of guest conductors. Barbirolli also conducted extensively in other parts of the USA, particularly Los Angeles, where he entertained hopes, at one stage, of a permanent appointment. Ever a patriot, however, he had resisted pressure to take American citizenship, and had revisited England in the summer of 1942 to conduct without fee, as his contribution to the war effort.[99]

The resourceful Barbirolli, whatever his initial feelings about being launched into a situation where the first bookings were about a month away and he had fewer than half the minimum players needed,[100] created what was in effect a new orchestra in four weeks, and it gave its first performance (in a cinema in Bradford, not in Manchester) on July 5th, 1943. He signed his first contract with the Hallé in October, 1943, for one year, accepting £3,750 for a minimum of 150 concerts, with concerts over that number to be paid at £42 each. In September, 1944, a new contract raised his gross fees to £4,000 for the same workload.

---

[95]Speech to the Hallé AGM, December 8th, 1950.
[96]Quoted and illustrated in Kennedy, 1960.
[97]King-Smith, 1995: 75-6.
[98]Kennedy, 1960: 288, 300.
[99]See Reid, 1971, Kennedy, 1971, and "Barbirolli In America 1936-1943", in *Glorious John*, ed. Paul Brooks (The Barbirolli Society, Oxford, 1999).
[100]He had been through a curiously similar experience in California only the previous autumn, as it happened, and there are indications that he had not completely made up his mind to stay in England when he left the USA in 1943, although he remembered that his immediate response to the Hallé telegram was: "This is it!" – see Reid, 1971: 235, and "Barbirolli in California 1940-43: A little-known chapter", *The Barbirolli Society Newsletter*, December 1994.

The season just ended had seen a record number of engagements by the "old" Hallé Orchestra – 144. In contrast, the new one gave 194 concerts in its first nine months (1943-4), 258 in 1944-5, and 236 in 1945-6 (the accounts show 296 concerts in a 16-month period). In 1944 it received £1,500 from Manchester City Council. The orchestra's strength stood at 70.[101]

T E Bean was appointed General Manager and Company Secretary of the Hallé in 1944, in succession to Richard Hesselgrave, who had administered its affairs from 1933, working from Forsyth's music shop in Deansgate, Manchester.[102]

Money and music

At the outset at least, by far the largest segment of Hallé Concert Society income (more than 75% in 1944-5) was from concerts outside Manchester – a huge increase in the relative contribution of "country" concerts to the Hallé's economy. The "main series" Manchester concerts, held in the Albert Hall Methodist Mission in Peter Street from 1945 to 1951, produced about 18% of income in 1944-5, and other sources were school concerts and recording income. By 1946 the Committee was remarking on "enormous audiences"[103] at its Sunday concerts at the Belle Vue amusement park in Gorton, about a mile from the city centre (where they had been held since August, 1943), which must have tilted the balance in favour of Manchester concerts to some extent, but the proportion of Manchester concerts to outside ones appears to have been about one to four in 1946-7, one to 3.5 in 1947-8, 1948-9 and 1949-50, and one to three in 1950-51. In the exceptional year of the Free Trade Hall's re-opening (1951-2), the numbers of Manchester and "outside" concerts were almost equal, and thereafter the ratio is about one to two.

Grant income from the newly formed Arts Council was £4,000 in 1945-6, with £1,552 coming from Manchester Corporation, after which the Hallé was able to record a surplus of £6,021 in the balance sheet and £12,500 in General Reserve, a remarkable result after about three years of trading which began with a positive balance of only £2,500. Arts Council grants continued on a yearly basis and increased in 1948-9 to £9,433, the next year to £10,000, and by 1953-4 to £12,000. However, the Hallé's path over these years was to be far from smooth financially.

---

[101]Reid, 1971.
[102]Hesselgrave was appointed Secretary of the Society in 1933, to take the place of Olive Baguley, who had departed along with Sir Hamilton Harty. Hesselgrave had previously been the Hallé booking office manager, on the staff of Forsyth Bros., and from 1933 gave the Hallé first call on his services while continuing in Forsyth's employment. The Hallé Committee specifically decided he would not be known as Manager. His role became full-time with the Hallé in October, 1942.
[103]Hallé annual reports 1945 and 1946.

In the immediate post-war years, there was universal agreement that the Hallé players' heavy work rate could not continue indefinitely. Philip Godlee, the Hallé's chairman, reported in 1945 that performing five times a week was "excessive . . . and bound eventually to jeopardise . . . musical standards". In 1945 and the following year he called for a reduction in the average number of concerts to three per week ("normal for the great orchestras in other countries") as well as an increase in the orchestra's strength to the pre-war number of 95. Negotiations were in progress with the City Council for aid on a long-term basis, as financial support was seen as vital for fulfilling these aims. In 1947 Godlee reported that there had been a "satisfactory outcome", and the Hallé was able to claim indemnity against its losses from the City of Manchester, up to a total of £9,000 per year, for the next three years.

These guarantees were called upon in each succeeding year (the full amount in 1948-9 and 1949-50), so it came as a severe shock when the Hallé was told that the City Council had not agreed any grant or guarantee for 1950-51, against a claim for £7,664. For the last time in the Hallé's history, a formal "call" on the private guarantors was made, but this was little more than an accounting exercise. The balance sheet already showed around £5,000 as "amounts received from guarantors in advance of calls", and only £880 was transferred from those amounts or raised during the year. The old method of dealing with unsustainable losses was no longer applicable. Few of the old-style guarantors still existed: a new category of membership had been introduced in 1946 under which people paid their "guarantee" in small annual instalments and could not be called on to donate more[104].

The Hallé was thus brought to a major crisis in 1951-2. The loss of the expected City Council payment, the lack of sufficient funds from guarantors, and the increased expense of paying the musicians rates which "now compare favourably with those paid elsewhere",[105] plus that of increasing the size of the orchestra in time for the re-opening of the Free Trade Hall in September, 1951 (along with mistakes in estimating the demand and scale of income from ticket sales in the new hall) were the principal causes.

The General Reserve now stood in the region of £10,000, and as trading losses of over £9,000 per year were recorded in 1949 and 1950, which had to be carried in each case until Manchester paid its guarantee, the threatened loss or reduction of that guarantee made the position indeed precarious, and the bank overdraft needed to finance everyday operations was increasing rapidly.

---

[104]An Extraordinary General Meeting of February 9th, 1945, established this, at the same time bringing to an end an unfortunate episode of disagreement with Sir Thomas Beecham over his relinquishing the "presidency" of the Society, the post Beecham had been granted in 1934, in succession to Balfour and Elgar, but for which the Hallé's Articles of Association did not in fact provide – see Kennedy, 1960: 312-321.
[105]Annual report 1950.

That this was dealt with so quickly and effectively is evidence of the abilities of Kenneth Crickmore, appointed General Manager in succession to T E Bean in September, 1951. Despite the initial refusal by the City Council of the Hallé's claim for 1950-51, he ultimately obtained £6,485, and was then able to record (with the help of a new three-year outright grant of £9,000 per annum) first a reduced loss for 1951-2, and two years of increasing surpluses – £5,451 in 1952-3 and £15,067 in 1953-4. His introduction to Manchester of the Hallé Proms (a summer series of popular programmes) and "Industrial Concerts" (later renamed "Opus One" concerts: a series of popular content, for which employers made block bookings at low prices) brought the number of engagements per year rapidly up from 209 (in 1951-2) to 267 (in 1953-4). Godlee's dream of cutting the players' workload to three concerts a week was a long way off.

Though Manchester Corporation's grant was not renewed in 1954-5, a new "Joint Scheme" involving most of the local authorities of Lancashire and Cheshire, including Manchester, which was designed to provide equally for the Hallé and Liverpool Philharmonic Orchestras, partly took its place. The Hallé's reserves by then stood at around £40,000, and were to be added to over the following 12 years (and from 1958, the Hallé Orchestra's centenary year, Manchester resumed its own direct grants, in addition to contributing to the "Joint Scheme").

A Crisis of Finance

That is the story in summary, but it is fascinating to explore it in a little more detail – partly because of the key role played by Barbirolli in the battles with parsimonious councillors, and partly because there are distinct parallels between the pattern of events around the re-opening of the Free Trade Hall in 1951 and those which accompanied the opening of the Bridgewater Hall in 1996 and its aftermath.

Barbirolli used to tell how he asked, early in 1944, what were the resources "available in the form of guarantees" which Godlee's 1943 letter had assured him existed, and how long the Hallé could keep going if public support fell. The answer, apparently, was "a fortnight".[106] Matters had improved by 1946, as noted above. But the Hallé was still a precarious organisation, financially, when it attempted to enlarge its orchestra and change its programming pattern on its return to the Free Trade Hall in 1951. The ensuing crisis was the most serious faced by the Hallé in its history to date – as Michael Kennedy[107] observes.

Barbirolli met the Committee in January, 1946, with a request for the enlargement of the orchestra, pointing out that this, and the need to retain the services of the best musicians, would mean inevitable increases in costs. He was back in October with one of many requests for wage rises for his players, and

[106]Reid, 1971: 269.
[107]Kennedy, 1960.

suggested that "in presenting the case for a civic grant these increased commitments should be taken into account." The outcome was a memorandum prepared by Bean for submission to Manchester Council in March, 1947, presenting the case for a civic grant and an estimate of the probable sum required.

The Town Clerk of Manchester, Sir Philip Dingle, replied with a request for increased representation of the City Council on the Hallé Committee. This was readily conceded as the price of seeing the Council meet the financial requirements set out in the Hallé's submission. Agreement was reached in August, 1947, on a civic guarantee for £9,000 for 1947-8 (in addition to £6,000 paid for school concerts), and in return three councillors were co-opted to the Hallé Committee. This produced an immediate benefit in the Hallé's relations with the Arts Council, whose grant for 1948-9 was fixed at £9,000 also. Soon afterwards, Bean embarked on a series of meetings with civic representatives of towns outside Manchester regularly visited by the Hallé, and there are lists in the Hallé minutes, from this point onwards, of local authority grants from the out-of-Manchester venues visited by the orchestra.

A Hallé Management Committee of six was set up in January, 1948 (including Ald. Abraham Moss, one of the three co-opted Manchester City Council members, and with J L Hodgkinson in attendance for the Arts Council), and met fortnightly. The full Hallé Committee, now renamed the "Executive Committee", met bi-monthly from this point.

However, three decisions of December, 1948 – to enlarge the orchestra to around 100 members, to increase orchestra pay rates to a level comparable with the BBC Northern Orchestra, and to undertake an overseas tour every year – brought new financial headaches. Bean drew up a precisely costed statement of the implications, incorporating the assumption that engagements would not exceed 200 per annum in future (in fact, so low a figure was never achieved). It showed that the Hallé would need to find additional income of £19,000 in 1949-50, and (once the Free Trade Hall was re-opened and the orchestra enlarged) of £32,600 per annum.

Hodgkinson endorsed a suggestion by Moss that Manchester should call a meeting of representatives of all local authorities in the region to discuss support for the Hallé, and Moss broached the idea with Manchester's Town Hall Committee, assuring his Hallé colleagues that it would not be seen as "a way of limiting the call on the Manchester rate." This was the effective birth of what was to be known as the "Joint Scheme" of support for the Hallé and Liverpool orchestras.

The Hallé's Arts Council grant for 1949-50 was fixed shortly afterwards at £10,000 – an increase of £1,000, but, on its own, far from the amount that T E Bean had considered necessary to meet the costs of the new policy, which would have included about £7,000 more from local authority sources than was available in 1948-9.

But opinion in the City Council was changing. Alderman Moss said that Manchester might expect the Arts Council to take a greater share of meeting the Hallé's deficit in future. The Arts Council view, on the other hand – as stated in the annual report of 1950 – was that the permanent orchestras should "normally" be subsidised by itself and local authorities in equal shares. Against this background, Bean's booklet *The Future Of The Hallé Orchestra: A Problem Of Finance* was published, in February, 1950, and the Hallé distributed 10,000 copies of it.

It was very much aimed at the City Council. Philip Godlee's foreword said: "If Manchester wants the Hallé, with its fame today based on an achievement second to nothing in its long history, then she must be prepared to stand in with the National Exchequer and a score of Local Authorities and devote a fraction of a penny rate to the purpose."

When Moss's conference to discuss the needs of the Hallé and Liverpool orchestras was finally held, in July, it merely set up a committee to consider matters further. The Hallé had a rather better result in 1949-50 than expected (mainly by taking on more engagements than had been budgeted), and recorded a deficit of only £337 – assuming Manchester paid its £9,000 guarantee. But by the end of 1950 it was clear that the imbalance predicted by Bean would still rapidly come about. And there were signs that the Corporation was not likely to continue its support at the previous level, let alone increase it, in 1950-51.[108]

Moss was still pursuing the "Joint Scheme". Another conference of regional authorities was to be held, and in 1951 he persuaded the Hallé Committee to reverse its earlier decision and not request renewal of its City Council "grant", or make any public comment about its situation, until the results of this conference were known. The damage to cash-flow resulting from this seems to have triggered the severe crisis which came later in the year.

In March, 1951, the Hallé learned that a previously estimated surplus of £1,383 for the year had changed to an estimated deficit of £1,543, and that the £9,000 from Manchester Corporation was now expected to be only £5,000. By June, estimates showed a doubling of the deficit, even after all grants and guarantees. Moss pleaded again for a postponement of discussion until after the "regional conference" (it was finally held in November and proposed a "common pool", for the benefit of the Hallé and Liverpool Philharmonic orchestras, with an "emphasis on guarantees").

---

[108]Kennedy, 1960, details the continuing controversy within Manchester City Council, from 1949 onwards, over support for the Hallé.

In August, Bean offered his resignation: he was to become manager of the Royal Festival Hall in London. By September Kenneth Crickmore had been appointed General Manager. Crickmore had already progressed from being a cinema manager to Director of the Sheffield Philharmonic Society and personal manager to Sir John Barbirolli. The Sheffield society, from 1943 onwards, had provided a regular series of "rental" engagements for the Hallé Orchestra in the winter season – almost always consisting of programmes already rehearsed for Manchester concerts, and thus of great financial benefit to the Hallé. He was consulted by the Hallé over its programme planning, acting as Barbirolli's representative on the issue, for a number of years before his appointment to its staff.

One week before Crickmore's appointment, the Hallé Treasurer, Leonard Behrens, drafted an account for 1950-51 for the Committee showing a deficit of £6,484. He added: "Also I had as you know secreted a budgetary reserve to meet unforeseen contingencies, which is fortunately not required." It is impossible to discover what he meant by this: no other budgetary or income and expenditure figures for the period show such a contingency provision, and the Hallé's General Reserve, shown on its balance sheet year by year, now stood at slightly over £10,000.

One week after Crickmore's appointment, however, his figures for 1950-51 showed a deficit of £7,664, and it was decided to apply for £5,000 "already agreed" to the Corporation, plus an additional £1,485. The City Treasurer replied that the Corporation had not voted any guarantee for the period in question. Despite the looming crisis, the orchestra was increased in size to 88 players for the new season, as planned.[109] Crickmore reported that he was working on a budget for the 1951-2 season with an estimated deficit of £16,000 to £17,000, after all grants and guarantees except Manchester Corporation's.

He proposed an application to Manchester Council for an outright annual grant of £17,500 in 1951-2, less anything to be raised in a public appeal; and for £7,500 for each of the following two years. All possible cuts in expenditure on administration and sundries were to be made forthwith, and the "Hallé Appeal Fund" was launched.

But the Hallé Committee was told on January 10th, 1952, that its application to Manchester City Council for a three-year funding package was "unlikely to be successful". This probably represents the most gloomy outlook it faced in the whole 1951-2 crisis. A document dated January 15th, 1952, headed "Notes for Sub-Committee" refers to the prospects of a deficit of £12,500 for 1951-2, even with a Manchester Corporation grant of £5,000, and the need to save £20,000 in 1952-3. It suggested three alternative solutions: Scheme A would be to reduce the orchestra to its former size and give 25 extra concerts; Scheme B would be a 10 per

[109]Kennedy, 1960: 356.

cent salary and fees cut with 30 extra concerts; Scheme C would be reduction of the orchestra by five or six players, with a 5 per cent salaries cut and 30 extra concerts.

It continues: "(a) Reduction in salaries brings us into dispute with Union following a recent application from Union for increases in pay. (b) Reduction in size of Orchestra brings us into possible dispute with Sir John Barbirolli. (c) A possible compromise . . . Point applicable to all schemes. The only way of inserting 30 extra concerts without going back to the bad old days of long hours of travel for the Orchestra would be to give these extra concerts in Manchester. The only way in which 30 extra concerts in Manchester could be certain to be of financial benefit would be by giving programmes of an entirely different nature to our normal Thursday and Sunday concerts, to an entirely different type of audience."

Various programming ideas were floated. "Industrial concerts", with support from local firms, on similar lines to those given by the Liverpool Philharmonic Orchestra, appealed. Reintroducing popular concerts at Belle Vue was another suggestion. Taking part in the "Brand Lane concerts" (popular programmes played by an ad hoc orchestra recruited by a private promoter) was rejected. Barbirolli felt that the schedule could be increased by 20 to 30 concerts in the season, if there were a reversion to the previous system of duplicated fortnightly mid-week Manchester concerts on Wednesdays and Thursdays, the Committee was told (the first season in the Free Trade Hall had 20 weekly Thursday concerts, on the pre-war pattern). This was adopted.

Leonard Behrens resigned as Hallé Treasurer in 1951, and Sir James Lythgoe, a former Treasurer of Manchester City Council, took on the role. The Musicians Union requested an increase in basic rates in 1952: Crickmore was told to negotiate for a 10 per cent cut in all salaries above the basic, for 1952-3. The Hallé Committee had said it "could not see any way of carrying on in 1952-3" without such a cut. Effectively, Scheme B had been adopted.

The first Industrial Concert was to be given in the summer of 1952, conducted by Barbirolli, with others following in the 1952-3 season. An Associate Conductor was needed for these and other popular concerts, including summer Proms, which were also planned by Crickmore[110], and George Weldon was the first choice for this post.[111] It was clear from the start that these more popular concerts would be allowed less rehearsal time than the existing ones.

---

[110]In his time in Sheffield, the City of Birmingham Symphony Orchestra had brought its summer Proms to the city with success.
[111]King-Smith, 1995: 100, quotes the opinion of David C F Wright that Weldon, who had been relieved of his command as conductor of the CBSO, without warning, in December, 1951, was made Associate Conductor of the Hallé by Barbirolli because the latter was furious at his "despicable" treatment by the Birmingham committee.

The 1952 Proms were organised with the first "Industrial" in their framework. Weldon was appointed soon afterwards, to conduct a minimum of 60 concerts, at a fee of £25 each, from June 1952 to July 1953. (The average payment to guest conductors previously had been more than 60 guineas, so this was a clear saving).

The crisis had not yet gone away, however. In March, 1952, Barbirolli was said to be "cutting down rehearsal time whenever possible in the hope that one or two extra concerts over and above the budgeted number could be given." A press conference was held on the Society's financial position and future.

With the help of Barbirolli's letter of May, 1952 (see below), Crickmore was able to report, in July, that Manchester Corporation had voted an outright grant to the Hallé of £9,000 for each of the three years ending 1952, 1953 and 1954.

There was still an extremely tight rein on finances. Economies were made in the orchestra's subsistence allowances by holding morning rehearsals in Manchester before evening concerts in nearby towns: players who might have claimed for a double journey from home in these circumstances were to be told this was not acceptable. When Barbirolli wanted to increase his principal cello's salary by 10 per cent (£2 per week), he stated that he would make economies in extra players' fees to offset the expenditure, and when an industrial court awarded increased rates of pay to musicians in December, 1952, the Society decided to continue paying existing rates to all players who were already on or above the new rates, anyone refusing to accept to be given three months' notice.[112]

Crickmore's November budget for 1952-3 showed a predicted surplus – but he also reported that any serious drop in concert bookings in the second half of the season could still have a "disastrous" effect. He planned 225 concerts, to be given over 46 weeks (at one point he had proposed 234 over 48 weeks), plus a visit to Bulawayo in Rhodesia, with the orchestra's strength at 85. The surplus, after a Manchester Corporation grant of £9,000, with £10,000 from the Arts Council and £3,480 from other corporations, would be £582.

The orchestra had been saved – but Philip Godlee's dream of only 200 engagements a year had been completely abandoned. The "Industrial Concerts" scheme was an undoubted success, and the concept was discussed with approval in the Arts Council annual report of 1955. But as a result the Hallé's workload changed considerably after 1951. Arts Council annual reports show that in 1948-9, 1949-50 and 1950-51, it gave fewer concerts than the Liverpool (with one season's exception) or Birmingham orchestras, or than the London Philharmonic – but subsequently its workload outstripped the other three. "Industrial Concerts and Proms were new and successful features in Liverpool, Birmingham and Manchester,

---

[112]This decision was consistent with the line adopted by the Orchestral Employers Association, and backed by the Arts Council, at the time.

and the Hallé was the last of the three to adopt them.[113] It was phenomenally successful in audience numbers, too, using the enormous King's Hall auditorium at Belle Vue for its Sunday concerts in the early years, and duplicating its midweek concerts at the Free Trade Hall from 1952-3, with near-capacity attendances.

The maestro

Barbirolli's role in the Hallé story from 1943 onwards is clearly central. More than any other principal conductor (with the possible exception of Harty), he immersed himself in the orchestra's fortunes and played a key part in its battles for public financial support. His ambitions for the orchestra were undoubtedly great from the beginning – he told the *Star* newspaper in London, in June, 1943: "I hope eventually to make Manchester the Vienna of England, with a great symphony orchestra playing for opera as well as in the concert hall."[114] He rejected more than one offer of alternative posts to that of conductor of the Hallé. The London Symphony Orchestra offered him its conductorship in May, 1944,[115] and he could have been paid £6,000 per annum for it,[116] half as much again as his then Hallé salary.

In December, 1948, he was offered the conductorship of the BBC Symphony Orchestra. When Godlee outlined the situation to the Hallé Management Committee, he had already discussed it with Barbirolli and was able to say that the latter was "not anxious to leave the Hallé" but wanted assurances that in the next 10 years the Hallé would: 1. be enlarged to its pre-war strength of around 100; 2. increase its pay rates to be in line with the BBC's; 3. make an annual tour abroad; and 4. be assured of "adequate" rehearsal time. Godlee had also already talked to the Lord Mayor of Manchester and was looking forward to discussions with others in the City Council in order to gain "support for these reforms".

At a special meeting on December 21st, Kenneth Crickmore attended as Barbirolli's spokesman and "urged the committee to consider the matter solely from the angle of whether or not they wanted the Hallé Orchestra to become an orchestra of international standards or whether it was to be merely a 'provincial band'. If a decision were given in favour of making the orchestra equal to the best, he would give his assurance that he would stay with the Hallé Orchestra for as many years as he is wanted." The committee and Crickmore then agreed to a modified form of Barbirolli's requirements.

---

[113]The Liverpool Philharmonic began its Industrial series in 1946, performing in each case on three consecutive evenings, with all seats sold at one price and bookable in groups at places of work, and with a later start time than the subscription series. (Lewis, 1998: 124, 127-8, 332). The CBO/CBSO gave a Summer Proms series in Birmingham from 1945 and "Industrial" concerts from 1950, and exported its "Proms" performances to other cities, including Sheffield – King-Smith, 1995: 84, 95, 98.
[114]Reid, 1971: 242.
[115]Kennedy, 1960: 309 and 327.
[116]Reid, 1971.

Barbirolli's personal sacrifice was genuine. He refused an offer of conducting in Australia (for the third year running) "in view of the difficulties which the Society is likely to encounter as a result of the recent decision on policy", and shortly afterwards one visiting soloist at least (Ida Haendel) offered to reduce her fees "in appreciation of Mr Barbirolli's decision to remain with the Hallé Orchestra". He also plunged into the battle to secure more support from public funds, addressing the Manchester and Salford Trades Council, the Lancashire and Cheshire Federation of Trades Councils and the Arts and Amenities Group of the Labour Party at the House of Commons.

After Barbirolli's knighthood in June, 1949, he presided by moral authority more than by contract. But throughout, his role as artistic director as well as permanent conductor was recognised. His formal contract with the Hallé of October, 1950, actually reduced his conducting fees from £4,480 per annum to £4,250, for 120 concerts, but its overall value (including an increased travel allowance and increased secretarial allowance) was a little greater than before. Even so, his overall compensation amounted to slightly less than £50 per concert – a lower figure, even in nominal terms, than Richter had been paid before the First World War.

Barbirolli returned from a tour of Australia in early 1951 unwell (he eventually had an operation for appendicitis and was out of action for more than two months). But his indisposition was not until he had convened a special meeting of the Hallé Management Committee at his flat in Appleby Lodge, Rusholme, to discard Manchester Corporation's modest plans for a festival to inaugurate the rebuilt Free Trade Hall later in the year and substitute a scheme in which he would "start afresh". The original plan was to invite nearby orchestras such as the Liverpool Philharmonic and Yorkshire Symphony (Leeds) to share a week of music with the Hallé. Barbirolli, however, wanted only those orchestras he considered of equal international standing to the Hallé, and the festival took place with the Hamburg Radio Orchestra, BBC Symphony and Concertgebouw of Amsterdam as guests instead. In March the Hallé Committee was told that Manchester's Town Clerk (Sir Philip Dingle) had asked for the BBC Northern Orchestra and "the Sale Choir" to be included, but this request was ignored.

A letter from Barbirolli to members of the General Committee, prepared for a meeting on December 4th, 1951, refers to his loyalty and preparedness to make sacrifices "to maintain the great orchestra which we now possess". He continued by saying that he judged that the Committee could not give him or the players an answer to the question whether there would be jobs for them at all next season unless it approached Manchester Corporation and found out "once and for all [underlined] what they are prepared to do about the Hallé." He continued: "I do earnestly suggest to the Committee that any question of 'taking a gamble' is put aside and that a realistic, professional approach is made forthwith . . . Do not let us continue the procedure, of which I have never frankly approved, of talking airily of £25,000 or £50,000, etc. Let us state exactly what we require and what will happen if we don't get that sum." He added that he had in the past often complained about extravagance in administration, with "many memos" from him that were "never acted upon", and that the building of "palatial offices" in St Peter's Square, compared with the Hewitt Street rehearsal facilities, had had "a disastrous psychological effect" on the orchestra.

It is impossible to know now what the relationship between Barbirolli and Crickmore was like after the latter's appointment to the Hallé general managership, but it is well known that Barbirolli trusted him implicitly for many years. It is therefore open to conjecture whether Crickmore's report at the same meeting – that Sir John was still considering an invitation to become permanent conductor of the Covent Garden Opera and demanded to know what steps the Committee proposed to take to ensure the orchestra's continuance before replying (by January 1st) – was in fact "stage-managed" by Crickmore – Barbirolli had often been sounded out on the prospect of a move to Covent Garden in the early post-war years, but there was no firm offer then.[117]

Crickmore first informed the Hallé Committee of the Covent Garden offer in May, 1951, and Barbirolli's contract had already been renewed on the same terms as the previous year (except for an increase of £250 in expenses) in July. At all events, Barbirolli now said that if the Committee would make an immediate and realistic application to the Corporation regarding the society's financial future, he would reply that his commitments prevented his accepting Covent Garden's offer. (Nonetheless, Barbirolli began a period of frequent guest conducting at Covent Garden – in 1952-3 he conducted 50 of the Royal Opera House's 147 performances,[118] which evoked an outburst of praise from Sir Kenneth Clark in his Arts Council annual report).

But Barbirolli was still ready to ride into battle on the Hallé Orchestra's behalf. In May, 1952, he sent a further letter to Philip Godlee and the members of the Committee, which seems to have been aimed as much at the City Council as the Hallé. In short, it was a new threat to leave Manchester unless the Hallé received more help.

The letter states (*inter alia*): "My ambition is to be at the head of the Hallé when its centenary comes in 1958 . . . In considering your invitation to stay, at least till then, I have to make conditions . . . I will gladly take a 10 per cent cut in salary in the present financial emergency." The "conditions" were "those welcomed, not only by your Committee, but by the Manchester Corporation representatives themselves, namely, that Manchester shall have an Orchestra worthy of ranking with the world's best."

---

[117]Lady Barbirolli, personal communication.
[118]Reid, 1971.

He cited the "offers from all over the world" he was repeatedly refusing, including permanent conductorship at Covent Garden, an orchestra in the Dominions offering £60,000 a year (the Hallé's total annual expenditure on all conductors was about £10,000 per annum at the time) and various prolonged tours. If he were to select from those, he added, "I would not have . . . to watch every halfpenny as I do now on the question of extra players, hire of music, which do not beset any conductor of my standing in any other part of the world."

He suggested that Manchester give "a clear indication of our future for, say, the next three years . . ." This seems to have worked, in that the Corporation voted an outright grant to the Hallé of £9,000 for each of the three years ending 1952, 1953 and 1954, as the Hallé Committee heard in July, 1952. In August Crickmore told them that Barbirolli was ready to sign a three-year contract, under which he would conduct 10 per cent more concerts (132, compared with 120) for the same salary as before. In September this offer was accepted "with grateful thanks".

The picture that emerges from this sequence of negotiations, carried through against the background of the Hallé's most serious post-war financial crisis, is one of a conductor who used the offers he received from elsewhere as a lever, both against the Hallé Committee and the City Council – but, remarkably, not for self-betterment but for the improvement of the standing and conditions of the orchestra. Barbirolli finished with a worse contractual package, personally, than he began with.

One must bear in mind the part played by Crickmore in all this, as both General Manager of the Hallé and as Barbirolli's personal manager – a dual role in which he seems to have aspired to being a British Arthur Judson.[119] The fact that Barbirolli trusted Crickmore does not necessarily mean that Crickmore worked exclusively in Barbirolli's interests, rather than his own. Barbirolli's final refusal of Covent Garden's invitation was immediately after the death of Philip Godlee, the Hallé chairman (on September 27th, 1952), with whom he had had a particularly close relationship, and it may be that in the circumstances the emotional ties he felt with the Hallé overrode all other considerations.

His loyalty to the Hallé Orchestra was legendary. In November 1952 he refused to appear at the Edinburgh Festival with the Philharmonia Orchestra and stated that he would prefer a future engagement with the Hallé. Early in 1954 he decided to go back on the offensive for causes such as obtaining annual overseas tours for the orchestra and securing sufficient salaries to enable it to keep those he considered key members. It is likely that his "demands" to the Committee had been discussed with Crickmore before they were produced, and possibly influenced by Crickmore's own agendas, the latter knowing that the Committee wanted,

---

[119]Arthur Judson, at this time, was both manager of the New York Philharmonic and an international artists' agent, an arrangement which has been remarked on by Peterson, 1986: 163-4; and Lebrecht, 1991 and 1996.

above all else, to retain Barbirolli's services for as long as possible. It is notable that Barbirolli's first request at this point was for Crickmore to be "freed in order to attend to wider international policy issues" – which meant Crickmore going abroad to negotiate such arrangements personally, Barbirolli continued. After this came a reference to his own fees, which he pointed out were less than a third, per concert, of those he commanded elsewhere. Nonetheless, his statement concluded, he would be prepared for any increase to be put aside to help pay for foreign tours for the orchestra (a suggestion the Hallé Committee seized upon with alacrity – thus beginning the "Foreign Tours Reserve" which appears in later Hallé accounts, and which ultimately became the Hallé Trust Fund – now the Charles Hallé Foundation).

Part of the reason for the Hallé's growing international reputation was the sequence of tours in which Barbirolli led them from wartime onwards. These began with concerts for the troops in Belgium, France and Holland at Christmas and New Year, 1944-45 (at Eindhoven, Holland, the auditorium was barely 10 miles from the front line and after one concert the town was strafed by enemy aircraft); Austria (including Salzburg and Vienna) in 1948; Holland in 1949 (an exchange with The Hague Residentie orchestra); Belgium in 1949; Portugal in 1950; Bulawayo in Rhodesia (now Zimbabwe) in 1953; and Paris in 1955.

Barbirolli had considerable fame as a recording artist before he joined the Hallé, but the sequence of performances by them made in the early years of the LP era includes many now seen as classics. Between 1952 and 1955, for The Gramophone Company, these included Brahms' *Symphony no. 3*, Elgar's *Symphony no. 2*, Schubert's *Symphony no. 9*, Sibelius' *Symphony no. 2*, Vaughan Williams' *Sinfonia Antartica*, and a number of collections. From 1955 to 1962 he recorded for the Pye label.

The beginning of commercial television brought Barbirolli immediate offers: in particular one to conduct the London Symphony Orchestra in a televised series. He stood by his undertaking to support the Hallé's interests, however, and the matter was taken up by Crickmore in early 1955, securing an arrangement with Associated Rediffusion for 24 concerts a year for three years, to earn the Hallé £75 to £100 more per performance than its usual "rental" fee, and a further £25 per performance to the Hallé for the services of Crickmore as "joint producer".

Chapter 6

The golden age – Barbirolli supreme

The 10 years following 1955 were a period of remarkable stability for the Hallé Concerts Society, the apogee of a time aptly characterised by Michael Kennedy as the "golden age of Barbirolli".[120] Sir John celebrated the Hallé Orchestra's centenary in 1958 with a European tour and special programmes in Manchester, and was awarded the Freedom of the City.

Modest financial surpluses were recorded for 1954-5 and 1955-6, and financial reserves were built up steadily thereafter. Manchester Council began making a grant of its own in addition to its contribution to the "Joint Scheme" of Lancashire and Cheshire local authorities. This was not achieved without anguish, following an Arts Council decision to reduce the Hallé's grant in 1955-6. Barbirolli made a speech to members of the City Council on November 13th, 1956, in which he stated that the Hallé had been offered an American tour for its centenary year – 1958 – but had had to suffer "the humiliation of having to stay at home" because of its financial position; and that the Hallé Committee had been "forced to break undertakings given me when I refused the offer of the BBC", that committee having included representatives of the Corporation at the time. His appeal evidently worked: a special grant was made for the centenary year and the City Council made it clear that its offering aid to meet the Hallé's budgeted deficit was on the condition that similar sums would be forthcoming from the Arts Council – a turning around of the "pound for pound" concept, this time to elicit greater support from a now-reluctant Arts Council. The fact that Alderman Abraham Moss was chairman of the city's Town Hall Committee at the time was no doubt to the Hallé's advantage.

The Arts Council restored the value of its grant in 1957-8 and increased it substantially in 1959-60 and succeeding years, and the City Council grant grew rapidly, overtaking the total derived from the Joint Scheme in 1962-3 (it had

---

[120]Kennedy, 1960: 279.

begun with a value of less than half that of the Joint Scheme), and exceeding it by more than a third in 1963-4 and succeeding years (see Table 7.1). By 1965-6 the Hallé's reserves, at £82,622, were the highest hitherto recorded (and not to be exceeded, even in nominal terms, until 1974-5).

The contract with Associated Rediffusion for regular televised performances (see chapter 5), negotiated by Crickmore in 1955 and which was continued until 1964, brought resources to the Hallé which enabled it to give a large number of concerts in London and the South of England.[121] The television programmes themselves were the subject of criticism,[122] but it is probably the case – even if it was not entirely appreciated at the time – that the mere fact of such television exposure helped to build the Hallé's reputation with the non-specialist public, on a national and local scale, in a way that could never have been achieved without it. The Associated-Rediffusion contract undoubtedly helped the Hallé's financial situation considerably (as did a recording contract with Pye in 1956). It allowed the Hallé to perform regularly at the Royal Festival Hall, a fact that was noted with approval by the Arts Council in its annual reports of 1961 and 1963. The contract also supported the Hallé's "public orchestral rehearsal" series in Manchester in association with the Society for the Promotion of New Music, commended in Arts Council reports of 1961, 1962 and 1963.

The pattern of concerts invented by Crickmore after the crisis of 1952 (a winter season of 15 paired weekday programmes at fortnightly intervals, frequent Sunday concerts, and Industrial concerts once a month, each given twice, with a series of summer "Proms" given almost daily over a fortnight) became firmly established.

Artistic policy

The fundamental aims of the Hallé were considered in some depth early in 1955, and the conclusions reached then set the pattern for some years to come. It was noted that the duplicated midweek concerts had not made much progress towards the "original goal" of two large audiences on successive nights, but that there were more patrons than could be accommodated on a single night, so the pairs arrangement would continue. Barbirolli undertook to "slightly reduce the severity" of his mid-week programmes, without endangering their artistic level. Internationally famous soloists, it was noted, only filled a hall if they played popular repertoire, but it was felt that it was nonetheless justifiable to engage them, even at fee levels that ensured a loss on a full house for a particular concert, if it enhanced the appeal of the season as whole and thus benefitted season ticket sales, and if a soloist could be persuaded to undertake a short tour with the orchestra at a reduced fee per concert (almost all Hallé midweek and Sunday programmes were at this time duplicated as Friday and Saturday concerts in the

---

[121]Nearly 130 over a period of five years, with support worth £35,000 in total, writes Reid, 1971.
[122]Reid, 1971.

Sheffield Philharmonic Society series, and "rentals", as such fixed-fee engagements were called, were also undertaken in Bradford, Hanley, and other northern towns). Choral concerts were considered problematical, as many people were said to find them "anathema", and although Sunday was the obvious day for the Hallé Choir to perform, the Sunday series was for a popular audience and "few choral works can by any stretch of the imagination be labelled 'popular'". It was decided that choral concerts, unless of a popular nature, should not be included in the Sunday series.

Kenneth Crickmore, awarded an OBE in 1958, underwent major surgery the same year but returned to work. He was appointed Director of the Hallé in 1959 and Clive Smart joined him as Secretary, succeeding him as General Manager and Secretary in 1960. Stuart Robinson became Concert Manager in 1961 and soon after was congratulated for his part in the "rescue" of the orchestra and its officials when its contracted airline became insolvent during a Hallé tour to Greece, Turkey, Cyprus, Yugoslavia and Italy.

From 1960 Crickmore was contracted as a consultant and to provide services including the negotiation of "major contracts", and co-opted to the General Committee. However, relationships between him and the Hallé went badly wrong in 1963. First, his personal company, Society for the Enjoyment of Music Ltd., which handled the Hallé booking office as agent, was found to owe outstanding money, and solicitors became involved. Crickmore claimed money was due to him in respect of the Associated-Rediffusion contract. Crickmore was still also Barbirolli's personal manager, and Barbirolli attempted to mediate between the Hallé and Crickmore while the latter was in America representing him in relation to his new appointment as chief conductor of the Houston Symphony Orchestra. Crickmore's departure from the Hallé developed into a rancorous affair. Crickmore became ill in 1964 and died in California in April, 1965, and the dispute had to be settled with his estate and his companies. The chief loser, unfortunately, was Barbirolli personally, who was forced to sue in the American courts for the money due to him from his Houston contract. [123]

John Denison MBE, musical director of the Arts Council, became the Hallé's Arts Council assessor from 1955-6, and remained on the Hallé Committee in this capacity until 1963-4, although jointly with Eric Thompson from 1957-8. The Hallé crossed swords with the Arts Council from time to time after 1960, but the amounts available from both Arts Council and Manchester Corporation increased steadily.

[123]Kennedy, 1982: 87.

The maestro

The orchestra's fortunes had been intimately bound up with Barbirolli since 1943, and in 1955 he announced that he would be unable to continue as Permanent Conductor beyond the centenary season of 1957-58. This was later modified to an offer to remain as Musical Director until the end of 1959-60, and in 1957 withdrawn completely, with an undertaking that "as long as it was mutually advantageous he would remain with the society". He undertook to appear 60-70 times a year rather than his former 120 engagements. Although he retained the same secretarial allowance and expense payments as before, his fee was to be £41.60 per concert (virtually halving his already reduced salary, now £5000 per annum). [124] It could, of course, be that he hoped for vastly improved opportunities from the extra time he would have available, but nonetheless shows that Barbirolli by now felt he was never going to break his ties with the Hallé completely.

The Hallé Committee presented him with a policy statement which informed him that in future the General Manager would be responsible to the Committee for carrying out programme policy ("in line with the suggestion made by Sir John himself some years ago"); that mid-week concerts from 1958-9 onwards should "introduce rather more variety than hitherto": he would not conduct more than eight programmes out of the series of 15; and that in future foreign tours would be undertaken only when adequate fees could be obtained. In May, 1958, Barbirolli relinquished the title of "Musical Director" (no subsequent principal conductor was granted it until Kent Nagano in 1992) and became Conductor-in-Chief and Musical Adviser to the Society.

But the Hallé needed Barbirolli's artistic advice, perhaps more than it was willing to concede officially. In 1960 he presented the Committee with a memorandum emphasising his need to audition all existing orchestra members to keep standards high; reminding them that quantity of strings was "essential to quality in a symphony orchestra" and that "for many years we have been the largest permanent public symphony orchestra in Britain"; recommending the value of annual foreign tours; and stating that his programme policy was "to lead the concert-going public, without driving it beyond their own capability of enjoyment and artistic satisfaction" – while referring to the "barrenness" of many composers of the day.

He had begun negotiations to become the principal conductor at Houston, Texas, which was to be compatible with his existing concert commitment to the Hallé. The announcement was made publicly in December, 1960. He told the Hallé he would then continue as Conductor-in-Chief, but no longer Musical Adviser; that he would accept full public responsibility for the artistic policy of the society, but wanted a young conductor to be given a block of concerts each season,

[124]Some of the details of the preceding negotiation are recounted in Kennedy, 1982: 68-9.

with a free hand to arrange his own programmes arnd rehearsals; and that he would no longer be responsible for the engagement and dismissal of musicians. The Committee accepted these terms and announced them to the press as representing Sir John's "closer ties" to the Hallé for the future. Lawrence Leonard was the first recipient of the opportunities under the "young conductors scheme", as it was described.

The close association continued in practice. Barbirolli celebrated a 21st anniversary season in 1963-4, and decisions were taken (in 1962) to spend extra amounts on engaging two "top" guest conductors per season (priority was to be given to "first class conductors rather than soloists"). The search for a successor became officially part of the Hallé's long-term policy. But Barbirolli was engaged in 1964 for a further three years, with an annual salary of £10,000, in return for conducting 70 concerts a year, including half of both the entire midweek series and the Sunday series. Of this, £6,300 represented fees, the rest being made up of secretarial salary and allowance, rent of office, etc., and a car and travel allowance.

George Weldon, Associate Conductor since 1952, died in 1963, and Maurice Handford, formerly Hallé principal horn, was appointed to conduct the Industrial Concerts and some others. In January, 1964, he and Lawrence Leonard were made Assistant Conductors for two seasons, with an option of a third, and it was envisaged that other conductors might be offered similar appointments (in fact Handford became the sole Associate Conductor from 1966).

The perception that after 1958 Barbirolli's connections with the Hallé would be looser undoubtedly had some negative repercussions in business terms. The BBC told the Hallé the orchestra would not be required for the Henry Wood Proms in 1960 (there had been six Hallé/Barbirolli concerts in each series for several years previously). Crickmore reported that engagements such as these and the Swansea Festival were being lost because they were obtained in the past "on the name of Sir John".

Barbirolli and the Hallé's recordings for Pye between 1955 and 1962 included Dvorak's *Symphonies nos. 7, 8* and *9*, Tchaikovsky's *Symphonies nos. 4, 5* and *6*, Elgar's *Symphony no. 1*, Nielsen's *Symphony no. 4*, and Vaughan Williams' *Symphony no. 8*. He returned to The Gramophone Company (now EMI) in 1962, and although he was now free to record with a number of British and overseas orchestras he maintained a steady stream of issues made with the Hallé. These included Delius' *Appalachia* and *Brigg Fair*, and a selection of shorter works, Elgar's *The Dream Of Gerontius*, another *Symphony no. 2* and a *Falstaff*, another Schubert *Symphony no. 9*, a series of the Sibelius symphonies and a selection of Sibelius' shorter works, Vaughan Williams' *Symphony no. 2*, and a typical "Viennese programme". The Elgar *Symphony no. 2* and *Falstaff* recordings were mentioned with pride in the Arts Council annual report of 1965, and *The Dream Of Gerontius* in the following year.

Touring continued to be a regular part of the orchestra's life after 1955, with visits to the Ravello Festival in Italy in 1957; a centenary tour of Europe in 1958, including visits to Hagen (Charles Hallé's birthplace), Linz, Warsaw and Prague; Switzerland in 1961; Greece (with Isaac Stern), Turkey, Cyprus, Yugoslavia and Italy in 1961 (the tour affected by the insolvency of the Hallé's airline); Scandinavia in 1963; Switzerland and Italy in 1965; Germany in 1966; the Bordeaux Festrival in 1967; Mexico and South America (a 42-day tour) and Switzerland, Austria and Germany, all in 1968.

Money and music

Seat prices were increased by 6d per ticket in 1960, for the first time since 1951, and more substantially in 1963, which apparently resulted in a decrease in season ticket sales, especially for Sundays. The Proms of 1962 and 1963, however, exceeded budgeted income levels. This corresponds with concert attendance levels generally, which, according to the Arts Council, were "abundant" in 1956, in "decline" in 1959, and "for the most part satisfactory" in 1961. The Hallé's Manchester concerts were said to have a 90% average attendance, [125] though to be falling, at the mid-week concerts, in the following year.

The ten years from 1965 to 1975 represent a more comfortable climate for the economics of the regional symphony orchestras as a group than at any time since the war, marred only by the effect of uncontrolled inflation in the later years of the period. Of 1970-71 and the following year, Arts Council annual reports were able to record "increased attendances" at concerts, the former describing life in provincial cities and towns where ". . . the visits of the Royal Ballet, the next Hallé concert . . . [inter alia] . . . are real events: anticipated, talked about and criticised . . ."

But, ominously, the season of 1965-6 was the last for which the Hallé recorded a surplus on activities for eight years. The society's balance sheet position deteriorated each year until 1968-9, and especially in 1967-8, Barbirolli's "silver jubilee year", which included a four-week tour of South America (including an appearance at the Mexico Olympics) and contained no summer Prom series in Manchester. In fact, 1967-8 represents the largest one-year decline in the Hallé's balance sheet position, when considered as a percentage of the relevant year's operational costs, until 1996-7 and 1997-8.

The cost of the tour of South America – although it was supported by the British Council and the Hallé Trust Fund and at the time was reported to have had a "satisfactory financial result" – along with expensive artist bookings and a large number of "special" concerts given to mark the jubilee, must have been contributory to the poor result, but it is all readily explicable as an indulgence of Sir John for his 25 years' work with the Hallé. It was also the first season in which

---

[125]Arts Council annual reports 1956, 1959, 1961.

the mid-week concerts were given once only (on Thursdays), instead of in pairs on Wednesdays and Thursdays, and although the change had been brought about by poor attendances, especially on the Wednesdays, the initial effect was a substantial loss of revenue, as the aggregate audiences were considerably lower under the new arrangement.

When a Hallé Manchester concerts sub-committee reported in October, 1966, its main recommendation had been the abandonment of paired weekday concerts and, instead, a pattern of 14 to 16 Thursday concerts and 14 to 16 Sunday concerts in the season. This was essentially based on the simple evidence of falling attendances and falling demand for season tickets for the weekday series. But it is also of interest because of its statement of programming policy and the factors considered relevant to it at the time.

The "limited spending power" of the concert-goer was cited: if prices were increased because of a particular artist's fee, people would probably miss attending another concert to which they would otherwise have gone, it stated (the assumption is clear that most people planned their attendance over a whole series rather than concert-by-concert, even when they were not season ticket holders). But "the works presented, together with the standard of presentation, form a greater attraction than the artists", the report continued. This had meant that the point had been reached, in the opinion of many, where financial implications were overruling artistic policy, in that popular works were being included simply for box office reasons (this probably explains the exceptional nature of the programmes of 1966-7, shown in Tables 5.1 and 5.2). Giving up the Wednesday series in favour of Thursdays only also had the advantage, Clive Smart recalls, of allowing for more rehearsal time in the Free Trade Hall itself for no extra cost.

The sub-committee's proposal was for a separate artistic policy, within overall policy, for each of the Hallé's four main concert series, each catering "for a particular range of musical interest". Thursdays were to have "comprehensive repertoire", with an emphasis on major works and first class artists and conductors. Sundays were to be "predominantly based on the standard repertoire, being planned to provide "entertainment": contemporary music "must only be a subsidiary part" of this series, which should be able to attract new patrons. The Industrials should "present the standard repertoire at popular prices and thereby attract new patrons to Hallé concerts", and special concerts should be presented only with industrial sponsorship or in aid of charity. This was essentially the pattern followed in this period, as noted above. Notwithstanding the unusual arrangements for Barbirolli's 25th season (and one must bear in mind that its many "special" concerts may well have arisen from artist bookings made previously, on the assumption of paired weekday concerts), it is observable that these principles were adopted with considerable success in attaining the objectives contemplated. The full potential of the Industrial concerts was achieved only from 1971-2 onwards, however.

But Barbirolli's ability to introduce ambitious special projects extra to the normal series was limited, even at the height of his fame and after he had served the Hallé for 25 years. His suggestions for concerts to commemorate his 25th season were for "an outstanding performance of the Verdi *Requiem*, with international artists" and three concert performances of Verdi's *Otello* (the work in whose premiere his father and grandfather had played in 1887 at La Scala, Milan). It is notable that even at this point he had to ask the Hallé Committee's permission for these events. It is even more notable that the Committee gave its permission only for the second project, and then for only two performances.

The last years of 'JB'

By 1968, the Hallé had not appointed a new permanent conductor for 25 years: indeed, if one bears in mind the exceptional nature of Barbirolli's appointment in the middle of the Second World War, it had not done so in "normal" conditions since Harty in 1919. Seeking a successor to Barbirolli was officially part of Hallé policy from 1962, but it was only from 1968 onwards that the issue became an urgent one.

Barbirolli had retired as conductor-in-chief of the Houston Symphony Orchestra, though keeping the title of Conductor Emeritus, in 1966 (he was succeeded there by André Previn). But it was clear this would not mean his giving any greater time to the Hallé than during the past 10 years. Maurice Handford was made Hallé Associate Conductor shortly afterwards, but bluntly told that if Barbirolli were to relinquish his post as Conductor-in-Chief after the 1967-8 season, the Committee "would intend to appoint someone other than Mr Handford as Principal Conductor". Handford renewed his appointment with the Hallé until 1970, when he accepted the post of Staff Conductor of the CBSO, in addition to his commitments in Calgary in Canada, and in Romania.

In 1967, after the main plans for his silver jubilee season of 1967-8 had been ratified, Barbirolli discussed his future vis-a-vis the Hallé with the chairman, Sir Geoffrey Haworth, and asked the Hallé Committee for "some form of life association with the Society". The first proposal was that he should be named "Conductor Emeritus For Life", on the Houston analogy, but when Barbirolli's formal letter came, in March, 1968 (it was written while he was working in Houston) renouncing the position of Conductor-in-Chief but adding ". . . I have no wish ever to leave our great orchestra . . .", the Committee opted for the title "Conductor Laureate for Life".

Smart negotiated new contractual terms under which all the allowances previously paid to Barbirolli (which had been about a third of his gross emoluments) were discontinued, and he was to be paid £300 per concert for all hired engagements, but £250 per concert for Hallé Manchester concerts and one concert each in the Sheffield and Bradford "rental" series. He was also to undertake foreign tours with the orchestra "on the same basis as previously" – i.e.

for expenses only – and the Committee expressed its thanks to Barbirolli for his generosity, and to Lady Barbirolli for being willing to accompany him on tours and take care of his needs. Barbirolli's concern for "his" orchestra had not abated, and memoranda were still sent such as this (regarding the appointment of a new principal cornet, to replace Bram Gay): ". . . Must look for a young, brilliant player . . . Northern if poss. Enquire among the brass bands – that is where I found Bill Lang, and had to teach him the clefs and keys!"

A sub-committee reported soon afterwards on the matter of succession. It was "apparent", it stated, "that no obvious successor to Sir John would be readily available." It recommended an appointment at the earliest possible date, but without taking hasty action. A letter on the subject from John Cruft, the Arts Council music officer, was "noted" in January, 1969, and the subject disappeared from Committee discussion for some time. There were other matters claiming attention: financial difficulties in 1969 and the Peacock Enquiry[126] among them.

Financially, the Hallé's fortunes declined during the last five years of the Barbirolli era. Barbirolli himself, of course, was not available as he once had been – by the end he was making few appearances, and the great recordings of his later years were mainly with other orchestras than the Hallé. And it seems clear that although artistic standards were remarkably high (especially in terms of repertoire and the quality of guest artists – there is a question over the playing standards of the orchestra in the latter part of the 1960s), plans were always limited by financial realism. Nonetheless, audience sizes were healthy (see chapter 12), and the "tuning" of each Manchester concert series to its target audience had become a skilled procedure. It was accepted that price would determine attendance at concerts, and, to counter the accusation that its artistic policy was being overruled by financial considerations, the Hallé put a new focus on the differences in audiences catered for by its various series, balancing high aspirations for the midweek series with the need to attract new concert-goers through the others.

The number of concerts given per year was now lower than in the years immediately following Crickmore's 1952 changes, and amounted to slightly less than four per week on average. The relative proportions of earnings from concerts in Manchester and outside are not available in surviving documents from every year, but summaries from 1966-7 to 1970-71 indicate the following: concert income from Manchester averaged 35% of the total; concert income from hired engagements outside Manchester averaged 41% ; and concert income from other performances outside Manchester plus school concerts averaged 23% of the total. Manchester concerts tended to have much higher soloist and conductors' fees

[126]The Committee chaired by Professor Peacock, which produced the *Report on Orchestral Resources in Great Britain* (Arts Council of Great Britain, 1970). See further, chapter 7.

charged to them, so the proportions of *net* income (i.e. after deduction of promotional costs, artist payments, etc) from the above three categories are on average 17%, 57% and 30% respectively – an indication of the dependence on touring which was still at the heart of the Hallé's economics – or, to put the same point differently, the way in which available resources were used to sustain the high-prestige Manchester concerts at the expense of others.

Chapter 7

A national and international orchestra – James Loughran

James Loughran became Barbirolli's successor late in 1970, in what might appear (from the distance of 30 years) to have been a smooth transition. In fact there had been a virtual interregnum since Barbirolli's "silver jubilee" season of 1967-8, with the Conductor Laureate still a father figure, but Handford in a caretaker role.

The appointment of Barbirolli's successor is an episode whose details have not been fully understood before. In mid-to-late 1969, plans for tours and special concerts in both 1971 and 1972 were being discussed with Barbirolli, though his part in the Manchester season of 1969-70 was limited to six concerts altogether, and a similar number was planned for 1970-71. But during the season of 1969-70, in addition to the regular guest conductors, who included Daniel Barenboim and Moshe Atzmon of the Sydney Symphony Orchestra, the young American Lawrence Foster was asked to undertake a short residency with the Hallé, in what he later described as "an experience I'll never forget . . . after that I cancelled everything for a month".[127] The search was on in earnest.

The sub-committee charged with seeking a new principal conductor opened discussions with Barenboim, but in January, 1970, these proved abortive. Smart recalls that Barenboim had a plan for a transformation of the Hallé, with help from Granada Television, into an orchestra which would play in London and on television frequently, in a development similar to the Associated-Rediffusion relationship with Barbirolli. But this could not be brought to fruition.

In February, 1970, there was a unanimous recommendation for a three-year contract to be negotiated with Atzmon. An invitation was issued, and negotiations proceeded. Barbirolli died in July, 1970, and, strangely, it seems that around that

---

[127]Speech from the podium at the Bridgewater Hall, March 5th, 1998.

point the Atzmon appointment became no longer realisable. By November, the invitation was withdrawn – because Atzmon wanted changes in the orchestra personnel before he would accept.[128] It is clear that the whole process had been undertaken against a background of financial uncertainty and a search for economies. What part that played in the ultimate result cannot be precisely determined – nor how much the death of Barbirolli affected the process in what was until then still very much "his" orchestra.

But enquiries were in hand regarding another conductor, and in November, 1970, negotiations were sanctioned to conclude an agreement with James Loughran, the young conductor of the BBC Scottish Symphony Orchestra, and the announcement of his appointment as Principal Conductor and Musical Advisor, in December, met with an "outstanding press". Michael Kennedy[129] points out that popular opinion still favoured Barenboim for the post, and others were convinced that Foster should have taken it. But two respected journalists had suggested to Smart that Loughran was the right man to succeed, well before Barbirolli died: Neville Cardus, at the celebration dinner given in his honour by the Hallé, in April, 1966 (as Smart recalls), and Michael Kennedy, in January, 1969.

James Loughran, born in 1931 and educated in Glasgow, had been a repetiteur with opera houses in Germany, the Netherlands and Italy before winning the Philharmonia Orchestra conductors' competition in 1961. He was Associate Conductor of the Bournemouth Symphony Orchestra from 1962 to 1965, and conductor of the BBC Scottish Symphony Orchestra from 1965 to 1970. He recalls hearing the Hallé play, on tour, in the spring of 1970 – and "I fell in love with the Hallé Orchestra". He was asked to take a concert in October, 1970, with Gina Bachauer as soloist and Beethoven's *"Eroica"* symphony on the programme. This had a major impact, and the announcement of his appointment to the principal conductorship was made soon afterwards.[130]

On appointment, he discussed his plans with the Hallé Committee, and stated his intention to invite "the very best guest conductors" to Manchester. The Committee considered his programme drafts for 1971-2 and expressed their observations, which were "predominantly favourable" . After seeing a revised draft they resolved to tell Loughran "there seemed to be very little Haydn and Mozart and earlier works".[131] He was also told, a year later, that "as a matter of musical policy the Hallé Choir should be adequately represented in the Thursday series".

---

[128]I confirmed the reason for Atzmon's refusal with him on his visit in February, 2000, to conduct the orchestra.
[129]Kennedy, 1982: 110.
[130]Personal communication.
[131]Loughran comments that in fact there were two Haydn symphonies and 12 works by Mozart.

In 1972 an orchestra management committee was formed, comprising the General Manager, Loughran, the leader, Martin Milner,[132] the co-leader, Michael Davis,[133] and the orchestral manager. There was also an orchestra liaison committee, whose formation allowed members of the orchestra to be involved in official machinery for the first time. But the new conductor's position was secure: the Committee had ventured to express a hope for more Bach and Britten in the season of 1973-4, but when Loughran met them in January, 1974, he assured them he was "satisfied that he was well up to the targets which he had set himself when he accepted the appointment." With attendances so consistently high, few were likely to contradict him when he assured them that the orchestra was now in a very healthy state, receiving the response that his policies were "warmly welcomed".

Despite Barbirolli's enormous personal prestige, there had been references in the late 1960s to the falling level of playing standards in the orchestra. Charles Reid says that in Barbirolli's later years the "old magnificence" of his performances with the Hallé was only intermittent, and attributes this to the variety of guest conductors working with the orchestra by this time.[134] The *New York Times* critic Harold Taubman wrote in 1970 that standards at the Hallé had descended to an indifferent level.[135] And Gerald Larner of *The Guardian* was describing the CBSO, not the Hallé, when he wrote "there is no better British orchestra outside London" in autumn, 1970.[136] But there are frequent references in Hallé annual reports in the 1970s to the high artistic levels achieved in James Loughran's early years, and the success of foreign tours and recordings under his baton. Michael Kennedy notes the high approbation Loughran received from the critics for his performances at this time.[137]

One aspect of orchestral life should be noted, however, which may have more significance in relation to critical attitudes than appears at first sight. The Hallé performed much less frequently in London after the end of its links with Associated Rediffusion in 1964 (it had given 14 London performances in 1958-9, and 11 in 1963-4; after that there were never more than six, and in 1969-70 only three); while the CBSO, after the building of the motorways enabled it to get its players back to base before the "witching hour" of midnight (in terms of overtime

---

[132]Martin Milner (1928-2000) was the longest-serving leader in the Hallé's history. Born in Bolton, he studied at the Royal Manchester College of Music and joined Beecham's Royal Philharmonic Orchestra at the age of 18. He became the Hallé's leader in 1958, and was described by Barbirolli as "the best I ever had".

[133]Son of the Hallé's long-serving principal second violin, Eric Davis, and now leader of the BBC Symphony Orchestra: he served as co-leader with Martin Milner from 1972 to 1979, and returned to take Milner's place on the latter's retirement in 1987, serving until 1991.

[134]Reid, 1971: 407.

[135]Taubman, 1970: The Symphony Orchestra Abroad (American Symphony Orchestra League, Vienna, VA), quoted in McCaldin, 1987.

[136]See King-Smith, 1995: 160.

[137]Kennedy, 1982: 114, 116, 121, 122.

payments), was giving more, with 19 central London performances in 1969-70 – as pointed out by Beresford King-Smith.[138] The mere fact of one orchestra being given notices more frequently than another by the London critics of the national papers may, in time, have had its effect on perceptions.

Artistic policy

The year 1969 saw a national enquiry into orchestral provision, which became known as the Peacock Report.[139] The Hallé's evidence to it concluded a short history of the orchestra with these words: "It has been described as Britain's only truly National Orchestra in that it serves the country as a whole and is one of Britain's principal musical ambassadors abroad"; and its statement of policy included the following: ". . . presentation of concerts by the orchestra in all the major towns and cities throughout this country, including London . . . the maintenance of a broadly-based repertoire presented at the highest artistic level catering for both majority and minority audiences whether their tastes are for the established repertoire or not." The latter phrases presumably reflect a defence of the Hallé's different series in Manchester, aimed, as pointed out above, at different kinds of audience.

The submission also conceded that the artistic policy had been restricted "over the years" for economic reasons: by the need to increase the number of "product services" (this was a term coined to include concerts, recordings and other earning activities by the orchestra) to a level which would balance the budget. The Hallé, it said, had budgeted for several years on the basis of 200 product services a year, but that figure had always had to be exceeded. In fact, the number of engagements per year did fall to around 200 or below after 1969.

The submission mentioned that the "normal" rehearsal time for a main series weekday concert was 11 to 14 hours, whereas Sunday concerts were allocated three to six hours, Industrial concerts three hours per programme, and Proms concerts three hours each.[140] It also claimed that Manchester attendances suffered if programmes contained new music or choral items (except for "popular repertoire"), and also when opera or ballet companies were visiting the city, or if (in some cases) there were other concerts available, or a particular concert was very highly priced.

The Hallé annual report for 1969-70 referred to the Peacock Report and the problems of regional orchestras generally, and added that "the Arts Council's compromise solution is to spread their available resources so thinly that every orchestra in the country is faced with a succession of financial crises".

---

[138]See Hallé annual reports and King-Smith, 1995: 156-7.
[139]*Report on Orchestral Resources in Great Britain* (Arts Council, 1970).
[140]Rehearsal routines at this time are described in retrospect by James Loughran as "appalling" (personal communication), but they were not untypical of the period.

The Hallé faced major financial problems in 1969 (the result, partly, of the poor financial outcome of 1967-8, referred to in chapter 6, but also of a national musicians' wage demand), and its reaction is of interest because it is the first episode in what became a series of selections from a detailed repertoire of possible measures designed to reconcile established artistic policy with limited financial resources, which extended until the end of Clive Smart's time as General Manager. It is probably this kind of detailed approach to achieving financial viability with minimal artistic deterioration – but nonetheless accepting that if finances deteriorated, some would be inevitable – which was later to be described as the "financially led" policy associated with Smart.

Initial measures listed in early 1969 were: (a) a reduction of "special concerts" in Manchester, with extra engagements elsewhere to replace them; (b) an increase in the fees charged for hiring the orchestra to other promoters; (c) increased programme booklet charges; and (d) greater use of investment income to defray operating costs. Other possible options were said by Smart to be: (a) eliminating guest orchestra and recital appearances (these were seen as inherently more risky than Hallé Orchestra performances); (b) non-replacement of orchestra members who were sick, in the rank-and-file strings; (c) lowering the standard of guest conductors and soloists; and (d) deleting works requiring extra players from the repertoire.

More radical possible changes, he added, were: (a) reducing the number of series concerts in Manchester in return for outside engagements; (b) reducing the size of the orchestra from its then establishment of 94 – this was a course of action favoured by the Arts Council, but emphatically opposed by Smart; and (c) ceasing to maintain the Hallé Choir (choral concerts then rarely achieved high attendances).

The wage award of 1969 was reflected in increased fees charged by the Hallé for hire of the orchestra, but these were already meeting with a "disturbing" reaction. Lord Goodman was involved in efforts to solve these problems, which now affected all the regional orchestras, and was trying to encourage Manchester City Council to increase its contribution to the Hallé, when it was in fact contemplating a reduction. The Hallé Committee rejected reduction of the orchestra, disbandment of the choir, and reduction of Manchester series concerts. It accepted reduction of non-profitable concerts whether in or out of Manchester, and a further increase in programme booklet prices, but no increase in ticket prices for the time being.

A meeting involving Arts Council and City Council representatives agreed there was "every justification" for the City's grant to increase to £60,000, but that there was very little hope of that happening. Smart argued that £50,000 could be acceptable, and in the summer the City grant was increased to £52,513, with conditions attached. These were nonetheless "warmly welcomed", a principal one being that the City Treasurer, Sir Harry Page, became a co-opted member of the

Hallé Committee, and Manchester City Council support for the Hallé was consistently high from this point until the formation of the Greater Manchester Council in 1975.

The effect of the Peacock Inquiry seems to have been minimal. By autumn 1969, there had been a "considerable improvement" in the Hallé's finances, and, despite the Hallé's frequent complaints about its parsimony, the Arts Council offered it supplementary funds in 1969-70 and 1970-71, and the City Council grant was increased in 1970-71. Inflation seems to have been accepted as a fact of normal life by now, and subsequent Committee discussions refer repeatedly to inflationary trends, wage escalation and ticket price increases, while references to Arts Council grant increases are usually to the effect of their inadequacy. Ticket sales, nonetheless, continued to be buoyant, although there was some resistance to increases in the higher price ranges.

The prospect of local government reorganisation gave cause for hope (well-founded, as proved to be the case) that the new Greater Manchester authority would assume "major" responsibility for the Hallé's finances (and the Hallé Committee's membership was changed in 1974 to include representatives of the new Greater Manchester Council).

The Peacock Committee had been told in 1969 that the orchestra strength of 94 was "in our opinion . . . the minimum size for an international orchestra", and it was hoped that it could be increased to 105 (the CBSO at the time had 89 members). A plan to form a second orchestra was also still alive, having been mentioned in the Hallé's annual report for 1965, after discussions on the possibility of an opera company in Manchester, in which the Hallé hoped to be involved. The Arts Council annual report for 1965 had referred to the possibility of "a great new opera house in Manchester with resident opera and ballet companies".

Smart's recommendation to the Committee was that in the long term the Society should aim for an orchestral membership of 130 musicians, and 160 if the opera project came to fruition. A summary of policy for the Arts Council in 1965 included "the establishment of a second orchestra" of about 45 members, whose purpose was to be to serve smaller towns than those accessible to the main orchestra, to provide a training ground for musicians, and to be "a suitable form of employment for players who had to be retired from the main orchestra". It could be used either instead of, or in addition to, augmentation of the orchestra for works requiring large forces. This had been accepted by the Hallé Committee "for implementation at the earliest opportunity". A meeting with the Minister for the Arts, Jennie Lee in November, raised the matter, and the Hallé resumé of the meeting records that Miss Lee welcomed the proposal, recognised that extra money would be required for it and "said that . . . we should prepare for the day when the project could be implemented...it was a proposal very much in line with her policy"

The opera project had proceeded as far as a plan for two productions at Buxton Opera House in 1967: these were to be *Savitri* by Holst and *Therese Raquin* by John McCabe, and Frederick Cox, principal of the Royal Manchester College of Music, and Maurice Handford were in the forefront of discussions. The Arts Council was to be approached for funds. But by December, 1966, there had been doubts about Buxton's suitability, and the plan was scrapped.

The 1967 annual report had mentioned in passing that the Hallé was "still unable to implement . . . plans for a second orchestra . . ." and the Arts Council's reply to a Hallé request for special funds in September, 1967, had referred to the small orchestra plan as "your project" – a distinct contrast with the Minister for the Arts' earlier view.

But the idea had not been dropped, at least not as far as Handford was concerned. In May, 1968, he was offered a three-year contract as Associate Conductor, and the decision included "the establishment on a firm basis of the work of the small orchestra, for which Mr Handford would be financially responsible." But the scheme does not appear to have been taken any further. Handford was increasingly busy, as Barbirolli conducted fewer concerts, and in late 1970 asked to be released from his contractual commitments. In early 1973, "establishing a second orchestra" was still a part of the plans for which Smart provided a costing to be submitted to Manchester's City Treasurer, in the preparation period for local government reorganisation. It does not appear to have been discussed subsequently: and later that year BBC Radio Manchester pre-empted the Hallé by founding the Manchester Camerata. (The Hallé project was reviewed for the last time in September, 1977, and though a report was ordered on the feasibility of a Hallé Chamber Orchestra, no further steps were taken).

In 1969, an awareness of the need for initiatives in publicity was apparent. The Committee authorised Smart to explore the possibilities of an arts magazine, inventing a slogan, and re-naming the Industrial Concerts. The first did not come to any significant conclusion, but the other two avenues ultimately proved fruitful. "Hear Music Live With The Hallé" was adopted as a slogan, and in 1971-2 the Industrial Concerts were re-named, and re-marketed, as the "Opus One" series. This was James Loughran's idea, and proved remarkably durable, as no better seems to have been found (at least into the beginning of the 21st century).[141]

---

[141]James Loughran recalls suggesting the idea over lunch in Sam's Chop House in Manchester – the point being that the concerts were "Opus One for the audience" (personal communication).

Money and music

The change of principal conductor in 1970 signalled a period of unprecedented financial security. For several years the Hallé received about 50% of its total income in public subvention, roughly equally split between the Arts Council and local authorities (see Table 7.1). James Loughran was able as a result to achieve a higher level of repertoire variety and challenge than any previous Hallé conductor,[142] and there is no doubt that his achievement was impressive. "Morale was good, and artistically I had a free hand with repertoire," he recalls, of the early years.[143] The transformation of the Industrial Concerts into "Opus One" produced remarkably successful results, and attendances at all the Hallé's winter season concerts from 1970-71 onwards were unprecedentedly high (see Tables 5.2, 5.4, 5.6 and chapter 12).

After 1967-8, and despite small operational losses declared in most years, the Hallé's financial reserves were re-built to a higher monetary level, by 1975, than in 1965. The fact that this was achieved must be credited to the skills of Clive Smart. But, to appreciate the effect of inflation in this period, it must also be noted that the Hallé's net total of capital and reserves, together with the balance of accumulated surplus or deficit, if measured as a percentage of annual operational costs, actually reached its absolute peak in 1965 (37.4%), and by 1975 represented only 18.2%. Hallé annual reports in 1966, 1967, 1971, 1972, 1973, 1974 and 1975 refer to inflation in various ways: conductors' and artists' fees were rising "at an alarming rate" (1966); there were increased costs of both orchestra and conductors (1967); "inflation" (1971 and 1972, and 25% in 1975); increases in ticket prices (1973); and "decline in the value of the pound" (1974).

The Arts Council's aid remained high through the late sixties and early seventies (see Table 7.3), but one qualification must be noted. Although the Hallé fairly consistently opposed the provision of support in the form of guarantee rather than grant, in this period, the Arts Council's aid was in a significant, though proportionally small, part by guarantee throughout. It is therefore not surprising that the Hallé should have budgeted for a break-even outcome each year, or a small loss. The fact that its reserves were rebuilt at all under such conditions is evidence of the skill of its financial direction.

The Hallé in the 1970s was also well-favoured through support from Manchester City Council. In 1969-70, both Hallé and CBSO received £75,000 from the Arts Council in grant, to which the CBSO could add a guarantee of £12,000 and the Hallé a guarantee of £15,000. The Birmingham city fathers gave the CBSO £50,000 – its programme of schools concerts, for which a generous grant had formerly been made, now discontinued – and other local authorities

---

[142]See the analysis in chapter 11.
[143]Personal communication.

added £9,463, while Manchester gave the Hallé £52,513, to which the "Joint Scheme" added over £20,000.

By 1974 the CBSO had built up a large accumulated deficit and claimed it received £30,000 less from local authority sources than the Hallé or Royal Liverpool Philharmonic – in fact this referred only to the aid attributable to the "Joint Scheme", not the totals of local authority support in each case.[144] These totals in 1973-4 were: Hallé, £104,836; CBSO £82,380; RLPO £92,563. The RLPO had declared itself in 1970 "more fortunate than perhaps any other symphony orchestra in the country" because of the level of its assistance from Liverpool Corporation (but after responsibility passed to the new Merseyside County Council in 1974, states Margaret Lewis, "the post-war golden age was at an end" and financial problems mounted.[145]

According to Arts Council annual reports, in 1972-3, "concerts prospered. There were no severe financial crises"; and in 1973-4, despite 17% inflation, "audiences remained good and standards high . . ."

The financial achievement over the 10 years mentioned was in fact accomplished only with the aid of higher contributions (in real terms) from both the Arts Council and Manchester City Council, than ever before. The former rose to 27% of operational costs in 1967 and never fell below 23% thereafter; and the latter rose to 15% of operational costs in 1970 and remained above 12% until the formation of the Greater Manchester Council in 1975. With the contribution of the "Joint Scheme" before 1975, and the GMC after it, the Hallé never received less than 19% of its operational costs from local authority sources, for more than a decade from 1970 onwards (see Table 7.1). Thus the apparent paradox arises that in the 1970s the Hallé was gaining higher audiences, but also a smaller proportion of income from the box office, than at any other time in its history.[146] The reason was the generosity of its public support, both national and local.

The Arts Council's annual reports of the early 1970s indicate an abrupt change in its policy in 1973-4, when the Government abandoned triennial planning and the previous target of 10% growth, in real terms, in its resources. In real terms they were cut by 2.7%. For the orchestras, it was said, "financial problems now loom large", and the following year there was comment on their "serious deficits".[147] But the Hallé took this in its stride. In 5 out of the 6 years from 1973-4, it recorded a

[144]Hallé, CBSO and RLPO annual accounts; King-Smith, 1995: 156, 157, 168, 171. The figures given by King-Smith on p146, however, do not appear to match those in the CBSO annual accounts for 1965-6.
[145]Lewis, 1998: 132, 133, 135.
[146]When Michael Kennedy says that the orchestra's earned income at this time was "spectacularly high", it should be noted that 1976-7, when it hit 57%, was actually the peak of a period (from 1966-7 to 1981-2) when it was unprecedentedly low, and was never to be so consistently low again (Kennedy, 1982: 124 – compare Table 7.1 and see chapter 12).
[147]Arts Council annual reports 1972, 1973, 1974, 1975.

surplus, and its reserves grew every year. By 1978-9, they stood at £155,177: there was no accumulated deficit.

A new Hallé Endowment Fund, proposed in the annual report in 1971, was established as the Hallé Endowment Trust Fund in 1974-5 (its accounts were published for the first time with the 1975 annual report), but at this stage its income was not used to supplement ordinary receipts.

In its Peacock Committee submission in 1969, the Hallé roundly rejected the concept that "industrial patronage" might be relied upon as a source of basic financial assistance, pointing out that it could be subject to the "whims and fancies" of company boards whose own businesses' profitability would be their chief concern, that it could disappear abruptly in the event of such companies being subject to takeover, that taxation deterred companies from such support anyway, and that the same external economic factors that would affect the Hallé's finances would simultaneously affect an industrial patron. Such patronage should, it said, be used in aid of activities additional to the orchestra's normal work, such as those supported by the Hallé Trust Fund (which was mainly devoted to helping with the costs of overseas tours).

The annual report for 1970-71 echoed this view, stating that private patronage "will never solve the economic problems of the arts satisfactorily". The arguments seem, with the benefit of hindsight, to be extremely cogent. However, from around 1973, the Hallé (and the CBSO seems to have followed the same pattern) began to record an increasing role played by sponsors in its financial affairs. The Arts Council's own view, at least in 1967 (in a "chairman's note" from Lord Goodman in the annual report of that year) was that "private bounty or investment is now totally inadequate to sustain a civilised ration of music and theatre . . ."

The Hallé's Peacock submission further suggested that in principle "public subsidy should only be provided for an orchestra devoting substantially the whole of its time to giving a public service and employing its musicians on a contractual basis" – a point, which, if admitted, would have ended public support for the London orchestras, then and now.[148]

Hard times ahead

The formation of the metropolitan county councils in the mid-1970s proved to be a landmark in the Hallé's fortunes. Continuing high inflation and what were perceived to be "hard times" economically meant that it encountered increasing financial instability in the later years of the decade. The major changes proved to be falling support from grant aid in real terms, increases in ticket prices above the rate of inflation, and declining audiences. The long-term result was that the Hallé's

---

[148]An argument put more colourfully, but no less powerfully, by Flora the feisty violist in Jilly Cooper's *Appassionata* (Cooper, 1996: 477).

financial reserves dwindled to virtual extinction. There was an element of deliberate policy in this, however, as the Arts Council had shown it would penalise the Hallé for its success in building reserves anyway. Establishing and adding to the Hallé Trust Fund and Hallé Endowment Trust Fund were ways of building capital which could not be burned away through a harsh subsidy regime, Clive Smart recalls.[149]

Manchester City Council doubled the rent it charged for the Free Trade Hall in the space of the single year to January, 1976, and froze its grant, already greatly reduced because of the establishment of the Greater Manchester Metropolitan County Council, which took on the support of the "Joint Scheme" and had primary responsibility for regional cultural funding. The City Council was now giving the Hallé only £5,000 per year more than the amount of its own rent bill. A deficit was expected on 1976-7, which "could only now be materially reduced by a change of policy and a reduction in artistic standards," Smart told the Committee in late 1975.

The Hallé did change policy in some respects, as a result. It sought further support from industrial sponsorship, and charged a "rental" fee less than normal to keep its visits going to certain towns outside Manchester. The annual report for 1975 was able to point to continuing high attendances, in particular at the Opus One concerts, and the addition of more concert sponsors.[150] The Proms of 1975 achieved 90% attendance over 20 concerts, despite a price increase of one third. The Arts Council's annual reports concentrated on "devolution" to the regions and provision for contemporary music, but made little mention of the orchestras at all, though Simon Rattle's role as Assistant Conductor of the Royal Liverpool Philharmonic (following Andrew Davis) was noted.

In late 1976 (after another good Proms series) Smart was able to forecast a break-even for 1976-7: results for 1975-6 had shown an increase in earned income of 40%, and a "very high level of attendance", including "insatiable demand" for the Opus One concerts, which resulted in their being given on Sundays as well as Wednesdays and Thursdays, the annual report stated. In November, 1976, a decision was taken to repeat certain items from Thursday programmes in the Sunday concerts, with the rider that "the differences between Thursday and Sunday concerts should still be maintained as . . . large numbers of Sunday concertgoers attended . . . more for the entertainment they provided than for any intellectual stimulus . . ."

But by the spring of 1977 there was concern about a "decline in attendances", though the resistance to ticket price increases was said to be less than expected – in itself, however, an indication of the fact that the Hallé was now beginning to

[149]Personal communication.
[150]Sponsorship was also becoming more important to the finances of the CBSO – see King-Smith, 1995: 172, 174.

put the strength of its audience support at risk by increasing prices. The City Council again limited its aid to the level of 1974, despite the high rate of inflation, and reduced its provision for Schools Concerts, for the first time, to less in cash terms than had been provided in the 1950s.

For 1977-8 the Sunday series was reduced to 15 concerts, to overcome the "temporary setback" caused by further local authority cuts in support. The 1977 Proms were also to be priced with the intention of yielding an extra 10 per cent more income than at first planned. But the books balanced in 1976-7: a small surplus was recorded, "without adversely affecting artistic standards, which had undoubtedly risen . . ." the Committee decided. The annual report said that "attendances at all concerts continued at an exceptionally high level" and predicted that recent policy changes "should . . . have substantial artistic and economic benefits . . ." (this appears to be a reference to the reduction in the Sunday series).

James Loughran had accepted an appointment as chief conductor of the Bamberg Symphony Orchestra in 1977, and his contractual minimum commitment was renegotiated to 50 concerts per year instead of 60 (although he usually conducted a larger number than the minimum – he recalls that at the beginning he conducted around 100 concerts per year for the Hallé, but the number reduced over time).[151]

The Manchester Proms of 1977 showed a 10% drop in attendance, but a 15% rise in income. In early 1978 it was decided to reduce the next Thursday series' length to 15 concerts, in line with the Sunday series, after season ticket sales for the current series had fallen, *by value*, for the first time ever, and prices were to be "stabilised". By the autumn optimism was back, with season ticket sales for the new season breaking records, the "adverse trend" of Thursday series sales "significantly reversed", and Opus One sales likely to attain new peaks. The annual report for 1977-8 (the first under Rex Hillson's chairmanship, in succession to Sir Geoffrey Haworth) recorded an increase in the size of the orchestra's woodwind section, and a new contract with James Loughran. In May, 1979, it was decided to increase the orchestra's size by nine players, phased in over the next three years.

Manchester City Council and Greater Manchester Council both increased their support in 1978-9, and ticket prices were put up again, by 10%. However, expenditure increased by 13%, the Hallé's annual report said, with earned income up by only 11% – the first time the latter increase had not exceeded the former for several years. This report is noteworthy for its avowal that "the need for private patronage has never been greater . . .", though it added that it was the Hallé Committee's "firm belief that support from the private sector must never be thought of as replacing national and local government support, but as augmenting it."

[151]Personal communication.

In the 1979-80 season, ticket prices increased by 20%, partly because of the introduction of Value Added Tax at 10%. Bradford's winter concert series was being reduced from 12 to 10, and Harrogate was replacing its week of Hallé concerts with single events for which other orchestras would compete. The Hallé Committee recorded that it considered inflation and Government policies were "seriously jeopardising concert activities". But if it expected that life would be easier under the new Conservative administration, it was soon to learn otherwise. The Arts Council's offer for 1979-80 was less than expected, and came with a demand for estimates showing how the Hallé would achieve a breakeven position: the Hallé insisted this was impossible. It resolved instead to seek greater support from local authorities, and political backing to influence the Government. Some savings were planned, but on the basis that there should be "no long-term adverse effect on the artistic standards of the orchestra or its concerts", and the search for further sponsorship was renewed.

The 1979-80 report contained a lament that "in recent years the Arts Council appear to have had far more success persuading successive Governments to provide funds to establish new ventures than in obtaining funds to sustain a realistic level of support for their existing clients." Regional orchestras in particular, it said, were getting an ever-diminishing share of the funds available, and the Hallé "an even smaller share of those". The Arts Council itself, however, did not seem overly concerned about this. Its annual report of 1980 records, without apology, that "ten years ago by far the largest part of the Council's subsidy for music went to the major orchestras and opera companies . . . [now they are] not nearly so dominant".

The General Reserve was exhausted by November, 1980, and the accounts began to include provision in case of insolvency. At the same time Smart reported to the Committee that no "special conductors" approached for the 125th season (1982-3) were able to offer any time to the Hallé in that period. Loughran was told early in the year that resources would "clearly" not be available for the orchestra augmentation planned – but renewed his contract until 1983. A plan was agreed in early 1982 to eliminate the £130,000 deficit foreseen for 1982-3 by measures including reduction in the use of the Free Trade Hall for rehearsals, reducing the Thursday and Sunday concert series each by one concert, and increasing ticket prices by 20% instead of the 10% originally planned. A £1m appeal for the Hallé Endowment Trust Fund was launched at the time of the orchestra's 125th anniversary in 1983, and, with transfers of income from the increased fund, it was hoped to write off the accumulated deficit by 1986.

Manchester City Council had once again reduced its grant to the Hallé, and again increased the rent of the Free Trade Hall, and it was felt that appeals to them now "would be of no value". The Hallé Committee was now relying firmly on "industry and commerce", which, the 1981-2 report stated, "continued to play a vital role in helping to bridge the gap between the income the Hallé can earn, the grant it receives, and the ever-increasing cost . . ." The emphasis on the role of business, which the Hallé had espoused since 1979, became a more explicit part of Arts Council philosophy, too. In 1982, Sir Roy Shaw wrote as chairman in the annual report: "The Arts Council warmly supports moves to encourage business sponsorship of the arts [which are] a very welcome supplement . . ."

Hallé season ticket sales dropped in number in 1981-2 (4% for the Thursday series and 13.3% for the Sundays): but rose in value (by 21% and 15% respectively), and the Arts Council came to the Hallé's aid with an extra grant for 1982-3 and an 8% increase for 1983-4, which were considered "a generous response to the Society's problems" by the Committee and "greatly welcomed". These decisions followed shortly after the appointment of Stanislaw Skrowaczewski as the new principal conductor.

The 1982-3 season was the Hallé Orchestra's 125th and also James Loughran's last as principal conductor. It did not break even, but with the help of the Arts Council's special grant (part of the Government's £5 million provision intended to help arts organisations clear past deficits),[152] the accumulated deficit (which had reached £130,000 in 1982) was cut by over a third. The annual report of 1983 referred to the high level of unemployment affecting ticket sales and inhibiting commercial sponsors, but said attendances at most concerts were high, "with the regrettable exception of those . . . which featured new or unfamiliar works". Industrial and commercial support, it added, was "now vital to the Society". The Government had cut the Arts Council's own grant for the following year, resulting in the Arts Council having to commit what Smart described as an "unprecedented breach of contract" in respect of its promised support for the Hallé. There was nothing in practice to be done about it.

The Hallé Committee, which had met monthly since 1951, convened only every second month from July, 1975, onwards. A "finance meeting" of the chairman, deputy chairman and two senior officers of the Hallé met frequently for some years, and from May, 1985, a Finance and Policy Committee was convened, but without formal papers.

A tour of Austria and Germany planned for 1970 with Barbirolli had gone ahead, after his death, with Jascha Horenstein and Alexander Gibson conducting, and after a few years touring momentum began again: James Loughran took the Hallé to Germany and Switzerland in 1975; Hong Kong in 1976; Switzerland in 1977; Scandinavia in 1978; Germany (including the Hallé's first appearance in Berlin) in 1979; Hong Kong and Australia in 1981; and Switzerland in 1983.

One aspect of the Hallé's work which went from being a source of pride to something of a low point was recording. Loughran had recorded Rachmaninov's *Symphony no. 2* and all the Brahms symphonies with the Hallé (and other Brahms works) for EMI's Classics For Pleasure label early in his tenure, and these were well

[152]See the Arts Council annual report of 1983.

received. A recording of Holst's *The Planets* achieved "gold disc" status for its high sales. In January, 1976, Loughran recorded works by John McCabe, including *The Chagall Windows*, for EMI's full-price label, and in March Smart reported that Loughran was to continue to record for the full-price label in 1977,[153] and that the association with the Classics For Pleasure label would also continue. But in July came the dismaying news that the contract with EMI Records Ltd "had no value", as EMI International were "blocking all worthwhile repertoire" and had cancelled the only acceptable project "at short notice for totally unacceptable reasons". Discussions began with Enigma Records Ltd – a small company selling in the top price range, whose prospects were described as a risk, but potentially far more valuable than any other's.

Six months later three Beethoven symphonies had been recorded under Loughran for Enigma, and the *Eroica*'s release had been "exceptionally well reviewed" in *The Gramophone*. The Classics For Pleasure contract was renewed in 1980, but without James Loughran as conductor, as he was contracted to Enigma. The Beethoven symphony cycle was completed (and the Beethoven piano concertos, with John Lill, were recorded under Loughran also, as were the two Elgar symphonies), but soon afterwards WEA, Enigma's owners, announced they were drastically reducing classical recording activity. All Enigma staff were dismissed, and the label was sold to ASV.

The artistic achievements of the period[154] are remarkably high when viewed objectively – particularly in terms of repertoire and attendances (see chapters 11 and 12). Loughran was respected and acclaimed, and his recordings were very successful. But after 1980 and the Enigma Records closure, he seems to have suffered in critical esteem, and the constant pressure to maintain box-office income in a period of financial instability must have had its effect. He himself recalls that after the earlier seasons "the artistic belt was tightened", and that he expressed his unease.

Perhaps over the long term Loughran also suffered from continuing comparisons with Barbirolli, on whose era Mancunians looked back with ever more rose-tinted spectacles. But his time saw better working conditions for the orchestra, an increase in its size, a reduction in the number of programmes it had to tackle each week, a variety of overseas tours, and regular appearances on TV and radio. The late 1970s were very successful for him internationally, and he turned down

---

[153]James Loughran recalls proposing Bruckner's *Symphony no 4* and Shostakovich's *Symphony no. 5*.

[154]For a survey of Loughran's programmes and other events from 1975 to 1983, see Kennedy, 1982: 123-139.

offers from elsewhere in order to be present for the Hallé's 125th season in 1982-83.

Chapter 8

Against the odds – Stanislaw Skrowaczewski

The selection of James Loughran's successor was made, it seems, with extraordinary speed and smoothness. Loughran's impending departure was announced in April, 1982, and a consultation process with the orchestra was set up, which "revealed that the views of the orchestra were almost identical to those held by the special sub-committee". There were two contenders clearly ahead of the field, in the orchestra's view, Smart recalls:[155] Bernard Haitink and Stanislaw Skrowaczewski. Haitink was not available. By November Hillson and Smart had met Skrowaczewski to discuss his appointment as Principal Conductor and Musical Advisor, and the appointment was endorsed. Skrowaczewski had to be persuaded, Smart recalls, that life as principal conductor of the Hallé would not be as exhausting as that of music director of the Minneapolis Symphony, a job he had recently relinquished with some relief.

Stanislaw Skrowaczewski, born 1923, the Polish-American composer and conductor, was chief conductor of the Katowice Philharmonic, Kracow Philharmonic and Polish National Orchestras between 1946 and 1959, and from 1960 to 1979 was music director of the Minneapolis Symphony Orchestra, later Minnesota Orchestra. He became its Laureate Emeritus in 1979, having made a large number of recordings with it and seen the opening of a new concert hall in Minneapolis. He guest conducted in Europe, the USA, Canada, Israel and South America, including the Vienna State Opera, Salzburg Festival and the Metropolitan Opera, New York. He had been a guest conductor of the Hallé since 1976, and had a reputation both for the Viennese classics and 20th century repertoire.

Skrowaczewski's first season (1983-4) was one where attendances "varied greatly", the annual report for that year said. Unfamiliar or contemporary music had poor audiences, but "popular" concerts achieved capacity. When deficits were

---

[155]Personal communication.

anticipated for 1983-4 and 1984-5, more cost-cutting (including reducing the size of the orchestra) was rejected, and the Hallé decided on measures to increase attendances (including the appointment of its first Marketing Officer) and to take more income from its trust funds.

The strategy worked, to the extent that the 1984 Proms gained extra audiences, despite increased prices, and yielded a 42% rise in income, but in 1984-85 as a whole Manchester concert income declined – which the Committee attributed predominantly to their belief "that the programmes were not sufficiently popular". This is a statement of the obvious: the wording was presumably intended to indicate that the programmes were not sufficiently conservative, in relation to the Committee's own taste. A programme of savings was instituted, including reducing spending on soloists, restricting London promotions to three per year, and cancelling a composers' competition – decisions which clearly did not meet with Skrowaczewski's whole-hearted approval.

Reference was also made to "inadequate" support from the Arts Council (its own report for 1984 stated that the real level of funding of its clients had fallen "over the past six or seven years") and local authorities, Manchester City Council in particular, and, in the annual report for 1984-5, to the need for increased self-help. However, by now the concern uppermost in every Committee member's mind was the impending dissolution of the Greater Manchester Council, on whose grant the Hallé had become fundamentally reliant. The Hallé Committee first discussed the Government's proposals for abolition in May, 1984. In relation to the arts, these included a £16m fund to be distributed by the Arts Council, designed to be used "for the first few years" in the metropolitan areas. The Hallé Committee expressed concern over long-term funding – and the fact that "there appeared to be no Council members on the Arts Council with any first-hand knowledge of the professional musical world . . . the origins and interests of members were predominantly London-based and it was unlikely they would ever be sufficiently sympathetic to regional needs." All these fears proved in time to be well-founded.

Money and music

After Luke Rittner's appointment[156] as Arts Council Secretary-General in 1984, Smart reported that it seemed apparent that the Council was not taking any immediate steps to improve the general position of the regional orchestras, and, in December, his concern that the Government had not contemplated any legislative safeguards for metropolitan-based arts organisations. The Arts Council gave its support as an outright grant (without a guarantee element) for the first time for many years in 1985-6. But it was only 2% above the previous year, while inflation was still running at 5%.

[156]Rittner had been the director of the Association for Business Sponsorship of the Arts: his appointment to the Arts Council was seen as indicative of the Thatcher government's attitude to arts funding (see Lebrecht, 1996: 209-10).

A meeting was held in May, 1985, with the Arts Council's chairman (Sir William Rees-Mogg), secretary-general (Luke Rittner), finance director, music director and music officer, at which it transpired that the Arts Council, too, felt strongly that the national total of £16m to replace "metropolitan" funding was totally inadequate, and in November it was announced that the figure was to be increased to £25m for the first year, but would decline over the following two years. The Government apparently expected the district councils in each former metropolitan county to take over the bulk of such spending. Examination of the years that followed will indicate what became of this expectation.

In mid-1985, it was reported to the Hallé Committee that the year just ended (1984-5) showed a deficit of £110,336, which was reduced by £50,000 income from the trust funds. The remaining £60,000 deficit for the year meant there was an accumulated deficit of £152,756. The Committee expressed grave concern, adding that the "failure of the Arts Council and the Manchester City Council to maintain the real value of their support in the last decade was the principal cause". But the dying GMC came to the rescue with a special additional contribution to the Hallé of £100,000, from its "closing down" balances. An annual Greater Manchester Concert was established to mark its generosity.

Estimates were sent to the Arts Council on the cost of increasing the orchestra's size and appointing an Assistant Conductor, however – such matters were admissable under the heading of "development" – and Skrowaczewski's contract was renewed for three years.

At the end of the 1975-85 decade, however, it is clear that the Hallé's long-term funding problems remained unsolved. Skrowaczewski's appointment was widely welcomed and his performances were generally held to be of superb quality, but there seems little doubt that concern about finance sapped the Hallé's will to take artistic initiatives in his first two seasons. The fact that new and unfamiliar music did not draw audiences was cited more than once as a limitation on artistic vision, and caution must have seemed to be the only viable policy against a background of hard-pressed finances. The Committee in 1985 evidently decided to blame lack of box-office success on Skrowaczewski's programming, when it should have been clear that by that year continued price increases (repeatedly above the rate of inflation) had made attending a Hallé concert more expensive, in real terms, than at any time since the Second World War (see chapter 12).

In 1984-5 the gap between the Hallé's performance income and expenditure was over £1 million for the first time, and the overall deficit on the year exceeded £110,000, even after grants and other income. This brought the accumulated deficit to over £150,000 at a time when capital and reserves together totalled £173,806, according to the annual report. The newly-established Finance and Policy Committee met in April, 1985, for the first time, charged with the duty of implementing the General Committee's policy of "not making any further cuts". In

September it recommended that members of the General Committee should be invited to secure two new sponsors for the Hallé each in the next 12 months – an indication of the prevailing assumption that the role of Committee members was not so much to monitor business or artistic affairs as to represent the Hallé to the wider world, in order to secure improved private financing.

The annual report for 1984-5 stated that Manchester concert income was up 17%, and the Summer Proms (of 1984) and Opus One concerts had had extremely high attendances. But audiences for the Thursday and Sunday series were "below average" early in the season. The General Committee expressed its apprehension about a future without the GMC, and declared that, since the funds available through the Arts Council were totally inadequate, future success would depend more than ever on self-help.

The GMC's parting gift of £100,000 in 1985-6 (in addition to an equal amount for "development" and as compensation for past underfunding, bringing its total contribution to nearly £600,000 for that year) brought the Hallé welcome relief, and the accumulated deficit was reduced to £10,000. However, in operational terms, little had changed. Attendances at the 1985 Proms and the winter season's Opus 1 concerts were as high as ever, but attendances at the more adventurous Manchester concerts continued to disappoint, the 1985-6 annual report stated. Local authorities across the region were making cuts in arts provision, and concert "rental" income from outside Manchester fell, though a 9% increase was gained in ticket income from concerts in the city.

In January, 1986, the General Committee discussed a letter from the Arts Council which told it not to be unduly concerned about the financial outlook, nor to anticipate any reduction in funding levels. And in March the District Councils Coordinating Committee, established to deal with matters formerly in the GMC's remit, agreed in principle to fund the Hallé in the future at the level provided by the GMC in 1985-6, plus inflation. But the prospect of increased aid from Manchester City Council in its own right (its contribution had been reduced to £20,000 in 1983 and subsequently frozen at that figure) was remote. A meeting with its chief executive and the chairman and deputy chairman of the Council's cultural services committee concluded that other avenues should be explored, and drew the comment from the council side that many of its members considered the Hallé "elitist". The contrast with Birmingham, where the city council took over funding for the CBSO almost entirely from the West Midlands County Council, and wrote off its accumulated deficit to the tune of almost £37,000, is very marked

The Hallé's Finance and Policy Committee was presented in April, 1986, with an analysis which showed Thursday audiences had dropped from 95% attendance in 1974-5 to 73% in 1984-5, with Sunday series attendances falling from 99% to 72% in the same 10 years, and Opus One audiences from 92% to 78%. The Thursday series drew only 68% in 1985-6, while Sundays had recovered to 75%

and Opus One was at 74%. It recommended a ticket price rise for the next season of 5% (in line with inflation), which was approved by the General Committee.

The assurances and promises given by the Arts Council and Greater Manchester District Councils in early 1986 proved to be somewhat hedged. The District Councils' grant for 1986-7 was for £103,000 only (the Arts Council was still providing a special "abolition grant" to take the place of the Greater Manchester Council's former support), but neither they nor the Arts Council included money previously given for "development", as Smart pointed out to the General Committee in May, 1986. In Birmingham, an Arts Council grant of £13,400 for "development" was received. [157]

In addition the Arts Council initiated a policy of regarding the existence of the Hallé's Endowment Trust as a reason for limiting assistance, saying it "would take into consideration the existence of the Endowment Trust when assessing the needs of the Hallé Concerts". The long-term significance of this can hardly be exaggerated, as it meant that the Hallé's self-help policy (apparently in line with the Government's principles) was likely to lead to penalties in its revenue funding, if it was successful. The warning was given at the same time as the Arts Council agreed that the old Hallé Endowment Fund's assets might be transferred to the Endowment Trust – providing the Hallé's accumulated deficit was written off first.

The implications for the future were clear. The Finance and Policy Committee considered options to eliminate annual deficits and made recommendations to the General Committee. A new series of "super-popular" winter concerts was to be tried, a Marketing and Development Officer was to be appointed, and renewed appeals to the Arts Council and local authorities were to be made, the General Committee decided in September, 1986. Options rejected included reducing the size of the orchestra, reducing the number of Manchester concerts (though there were too many concerts in Manchester for the available audience, it was the BBC Philharmonic's that were failing to attract, it was noted), and "popularising" the existing Thursday and Sunday series.

The situation meant discord with Skrowaczewski, Smart told the General Committee in November, 1986. Developments "will certainly prevent Mr Skrowaczewski from achieving and maintaining the standards that he is seeking" he reported, noting that many of the players were contemplating leaving the profession, or auditioning for other orchestras. "The morale of the orchestra is falling rapidly. They rightly feel that they are achieving high standards . . . through working very hard for Mr Skrowaczewski. Recent notices . . . endorse this belief . . .," he pointed out. "I am asked . . . if the CBSO can be offered £250,000 to keep up their standards, why can't the Hallé?"

The reference was to the CBSO's "Development Plan". It was explicitly aimed

[157]King-Smith, 1995: 208.

at recruiting "tip-top London players" to new co-principal positions in each of the five string sections, and attracting them by enhanced salaries. The Hallé chairman, Rex Hillson, made a direct approach to the Arts Council chairman, Sir William Rees-Mogg. but was rebuffed. The General Committee expressed its surprise that the Arts Council was doing so much purely to attempt to dissuade one individual – Simon Rattle – from going elsewhere.

Further correspondence having proved unsatisfactory, Smart was told by the Finance and Policy Committee to seek a meeting at the Arts Council to obtain answers to a series of questions, concluding with "What new rules are they applying and why have these not been made clear to us?" By early 1987 his report of the outcome was "noted with concern", and in May he reported that the CBSO were giving their players significant pay increases.

Hallé concerts had variable attendances again in 1986-7, despite a year of "outstanding artistic success" with "great critical and public acclaim" recorded by the annual report. Family concerts on Sunday afternoons were proving popular, and so were the summer concerts of light classics held at the large G-Mex exhibition centre, newly opened in Manchester city centre. Income from concerts outside Manchester showed a 15% increase, but expenditure was up 11%, and Manchester concert income increased by only 4%. In addition, the General Committee heard that increased charges at the G-Mex would make concerts there less attractive in future, although it endorsed the decision to present a further series of four in summer 1987.

Despite the Arts Council's "abolition grant", and the Hallé's taking almost double the amount from its trust funds compared with the previous year, the accumulated deficit for 1986-7 rose again to the same level as in 1984-5. It would have been twice as much without the trust funds' help. The annual report for 1986-7 warned of "radical changes", particularly in Manchester concerts, being forced on the Hallé if additional support was not found, and bemoaned the contrast between the combined Manchester area local authorities' grants of £130,000 and Birmingham's £500,000 to the CBSO. At the same time, Smart gave an interview in which he emphasised these points and expressed the hope that the Hallé, which was raising money from private sources, as the Government said orchestras should, rather than simply being supported by its local authority as in the case of the CBSO, might be rewarded for it. [158]

The Hallé approached the Minister for the Arts, Richard Luce, in April, 1987, with the message that "our worst fears about the post-metropolitan abolition are materialising faster than we had ever believed was possible". There was no consultation, it said, between AGMA (the Association of Greater Manchester Authorities, the successor body to the GMC in respect of arts funding) and the Hallé, or between AGMA and the local authorities; the wrong funding level had

[158]Hallé sounds out a warning. *Manchester Evening News,* October 22nd, 1987.

been established, and the Arts Council had failed to respond. In addition, the Hallé complained that the Arts Council's CBSO project was having a damaging effect, that the Arts Council was "refusing to respond to private sector funding", that Manchester City Council suffered from "left-wing elitism", and that the BBC Philharmonic (which was now giving an increasingly successful series of public concerts on Saturday nights in the Free Trade Hall, with distinguished conductors and soloists) was damaging the Hallé's position. No outcome is reported.

The Arts Council argued that the Hallé, even when it had enjoyed GMC support, had been underfunded by its local authorities for the past 12 years, and in a meeting with the AGMA Grants Committee on June 1st, 1987, a joint approach by Arts Council and Hallé representatives sought to put this point. They pressed the argument that the CBSO had gained increased funding from its local authorities in recent years along with that from the Arts Council, whereas up to 1985-6 the two orchestras' positions had been roughly comparable. Manchester City Council decided (and reported to AGMA a fortnight after the meeting just mentioned) that it and the Arts Council would make an "in depth appraisal" of the Hallé in early 1988. But it refused the Hallé's request that it should approximately double its own grant.

Appraisal and after

The appraisal team, appointed by the end of 1987, consisted of Brian Hill, the chief executive of Lancashire County Council, Fiona Grant of the Arts Council music panel, and Anthony Whitworth-Jones, director of Glyndebourne Touring Opera. The Hallé submitted a "strategic plan" to them, and also to AGMA, which had just decided that its grant for 1988-9 would be no more than an inflation-based increase on that for 1987-8.

At the same time the Arts Council introduced new arrangements of its own, requiring applications for three-year funding from its revenue clients, which meant preparation of three-year plans in support of applications, and the establishment of "Incentive Funding" to reward those "keen to take up a more enterprising stance", which (as the Secretary-General, Luke Rittner, ominously pointed out in a letter in November, 1987) "will restrict substantially the increases in the Council's basic grant-in-aid to revenue clients".

The Hallé's three-year plan was designed to follow its "strategic plan" closely, and identified four priorities: 1. Improved pay and conditions for the orchestra; 2. An increase in the size of the orchestra; 3. The need for funds to provide for early retirements; and 4. The need to develop the education programme. In addition a "survival plan" was to be drawn up, in the event of further funds not being forthcoming. The rules for Incentive Funding assessment were stated by Rittner to include review of applications by "business counsellors", for which candidates should state clearly defined targets for increasing earned income. The Hallé decided its Sponsorship Sub-Committee should deal with this.

The accounts for 1987-8, though showing a huge accumulated deficit for the first time, and a substantial deficit on all capital and reserves – i.e. technical insolvency – pinned hope on the Arts Council's appraisal of the Society's activities "as a matter of great urgency". Without that, it said, the deficit declared "clearly . . . could not have been contemplated". The background was of continued good attendances at the Proms, Opus 1 and Family concerts, disappointing support for the Thursday and Sunday series (apparently as a whole, this time), with Manchester concert income up 10%, but outside concert income down 3%. Sponsorship income was up 14%. Overall, income was up 5%, expenditure up 4%, and grants up 1.2%.

The Arts Council's response to the Hallé three-year plan came in March, 1988, and was "very depressing and disappointing", the General Committee decided. It appeared to provide a "blanket approach" to the future, which seemed to ignore local circumstances and past achievements and would force the Hallé to abandon its strategy of placing artistic quality and integrity above all other criteria, it was felt. Alan Guest, chairman of the Hallé's Finance and Policy Committee, concluded in June, 1988, that substantial increases in funding were unlikely from the local authorities in the short term, that the Arts Council would not help without them, and that therefore expenditure must be cut, with a target of break-even in two years' time.

Smart apparently did not agree. He told the committee that he was concerned that its majority view was moving away from the overall strategy that had been established, before that strategy had had an opportunity to be pursued fully. The committee, however, instructed him to prepare a detailed list of economies designed to eliminate the estimated deficit of £300,000 in 1988-9, on the grounds that, in its view, to continue trading at the present level of deficit beyond September 30th would probably be a breach of the Insolvency Act. Smart wrote to Skrowaczewski asking for reduced rehearsal hours in the next year's schedule, to make savings on overtime payments. Skrowaczewski replied with suggestions, but added: "Let us not forget that the real successful 'survival' of an orchestra depends on artistic excellence and proper preparation."

The Arts Council/AGMA appraisal report, delivered in July, 1988, was welcomed by the Finance and Policy Committee, but several of its recommendations, it was noted, depended on acceptance by the subsidising authorities of greater responsibilities. If there were no indication of an improvement in finances by September 30th, it reaffirmed, the "Retrenchment Policy" now drawn up would have to be implemented. Smart pointed out that most of the major economies contemplated would have an adverse effect on morale and artistic standards, and that almost all had been totally rejected by the appraisal team.

A meeting between representatives of the Arts Council and AGMA in

September, 1988, resulted in an undertaking by the former that if the local authorities increased support significantly in the current and subsequent years, it would respond in the next and following years. Awaiting the response, the Finance and Policy Committee extended its deadline for implementation of the Retrenchment Policy until November. The General Committee discussed the situation on September 27th, 1988, and one of the local authority representatives on it commented that AGMA wanted a greater involvement by the Hallé in local affairs and felt that the Hallé was "deliberately incurring deficits while having adequate funds to cover the deficits" – a proposition rejected by Smart.

The leading local businessman Sebastian de Ferranti, now the Hallé chairman (he took up the appointment in 1987), wrote to the leaders and chief executives of the 10 AGMA districts in October, pressing the point that the appraisal report had said that the argument for an increase in public subsidy was "unanswerable" and that a "significant" increase in local authority support was the condition of increased Arts Council funds.

At the same time a letter came on behalf of the City Council and AGMA to confirm their position regarding the Hallé. Its interpretation of the meeting with the Arts Council representatives was that the latter had said: 1. that the cumulative deficit was the Hallé's own responsibility to "sort out"; 2. that 50% of the additional £400,000 funding required should be obtained by the Hallé itself through sponsorship; and 3. that only two-thirds of the balance of £200,000 should come from the local authorities. It added that AGMA's funding for 1989-90 would not be dealt with until November and therefore no response had been given to the Hallé before its September meeting, but made no mention of funding for 1988-9. However, it said: ". . . the funding bodies have expressed determination to take positive action concerning the Hallé's base funding position in order to safeguard the standing of the Hallé in the orchestral field. You will therefore need to consider whether the Hallé should take any precipitate action at this stage . . ."

A representative of the Arts Council wrote to Smart soon afterwards, commenting on this letter, which was described as "slightly unsubtle". The Arts Council position was that AGMA and Manchester City Council were welcome to deal with the Hallé accumulated deficit if they could, but that it was the Hallé Board's responsibility to find a way forward, having chosen to incur the deficit rather than reduce its operations.

Thus the Hallé was apparently being invited by the local authorities to continue activities at a deficit-incurring level, but blamed by the Arts Council for having done so even to the extent which had already occurred. Neither was willing to give any immediate help.

Smart told the Finance and Policy Committee that he believed £500,000 per annum extra was required in base funding for the Hallé, rather than the £400,000 to which the local authorities' letter had referred, and replied the same day to the effect that the committee was "greatly encouraged" by the assurances about safeguarding the future of the Hallé, but that the cost of maintaining the Hallé as a truly international orchestra would undoubtedly require additional base funding greater than £400,000. The committee reconsidered the Retrenchment Policy at the same meeting, and decided that any major economies that might be necessary should be achieved through giving fewer concerts in Manchester. In practical terms, this meant a reduction of the Sunday series to eight concerts per season (which could be marketed alongside the Sunday Opus One concerts to offer a Sunday programme of 16 performances). This should enable the reduction of the accumulated deficit from revenue by £100,000 per annum over the next five years – and, if increased funding of £200,000 per annum were available, break-even results would be achievable.

At this meeting the decision was also taken to change the General Committee's designation to a "Board", meeting quarterly, and the Finance and Policy Committee to "Executive Committee", meeting eight times a year.

AGMA was understood to have offered the Hallé an increase of £140,000 per year from 1989-90, on condition that the Arts Council provided an extra £60,000 per annum, the Finance and Policy Committee was told on November 10th. On November 22nd the General Committee decided to offer the Hallé's musicians a 6.7% pay rise (in line with the Bournemouth Orchestras), and Smart was instructed to seek further economies to offset the cost. In December the Arts Council agreed to provide an extra £60,000 for 1989-90, but with conditions attached.

The December meeting of the Executive Committee considered the recommendations of the Arts Council appraisal report. The principal financial aspects were that the number of "uneconomic" concerts in Manchester should be reduced (which the Retrenchment Policy had already effected), that there should be no further increase in the strings strength of the orchestra (which was accepted, at least as a short term measure), and that four recently created "assistant principal" posts in the wind section would need special funding if they were to continue (which was rejected). (The CBSO, likewise, underwent appraisal in 1989, but King-Smith, 1995, its official historian, is able to dismiss the report as "disappointingly low-key"). [159]

In the event the Hallé situation was retrieved in 1988-9, mainly by large increases in performance income (12% up) and sponsorship (20% up), tight control of expenditure (7.5% up), and an unprecedentedly large contribution from the two trust funds and from the sale of investments. The annual report added that in the following year a break-even was expected, thanks to the extra grants from AGMA and the Arts Council, plus the first tranche of a £500,000 three-year

[159]King-Smith, 1995: 222.

sponsorship from Brother International Europe, the Tameside-based business machine manufacturers (a relationship which was initiated through the Hallé's Stuart Robinson).

The accumulated deficit of 1988 was not to be equalled again until 1995, but the pattern of Hallé Sunday concerts in Manchester had been irreversibly reduced.

The prediction of break-even in 1989-90 proved basically sound: a loss of £3,395 on the year was finally reported, but was clearly very small indeed. With the Brother scheme in force, sponsorship income was up 124% on the previous year, and earned income was up 25%. The AGMA grant was double the previous year, and the Arts Council grant up 7% – though, as the annual report pointed out, still the lowest of all symphony orchestra grants outside London

A report to AGMA by Manchester City Council officials, on the Hallé's new business plan (and the Arts Council's comments on it), repeated the view that the Hallé had not been underfunded since the abolition of the GMC, claiming it was a "fable" which should be "laid to rest", on the grounds that AGMA's funding was still at "base grant" originally approved by the GMC in partnership with the Arts Council, and that therefore the Hallé's accumulated deficit was a problem it had incurred because of "a risky financial strategy regarding the relationship of its costs to available funding". Smart rejected the argument, and it is noteworthy that those representing AGMA were still unwilling to accept that the support it gave had dwindled compared with the days of the GMC. Table 7.1 shows the extent to which it had.

The one-day 'assessment'

Ticket prices for the Hallé's Summer Proms were increased by 10% in 1989, and increases of the same extent for the 1989-90 season were agreed in April, 1989. The Hallé applied for Arts Council"Incentive Funding" for 1989, and the Incentive Board decided not to put the application to assessment, judging the application document to be "insufficiently clear" in certain areas, particularly in respect of the organisational strategy proposed to increase income. A revision of the plan was invited for the next year's Incentive scheme, and by October, 1989, the scheme's assessor, an accountant, had completed a one-day visit to the Hallé's offices, interviewing four senior staff and four board members, and had met the Incentive Scheme director, the Arts Council Music Director, and the Arts Council assessor for the Hallé. He decided it was not appropriate to recommend an Incentive award.

His report was remarkably wide-ranging for such a brief investigation, and claimed that although Skrowaczewski was credited with improving the technical playing standards of the orchestra and was well respected for his skills, there was little warmth in the relationship between the musicians and their principal conductor, and that he did not draw audiences "as might be expected". Its chief comment on the Hallé's financial situation was that the Board's policy of not tolerating any further deficits might lead to holding back on expenditure which could be for the long-term good of the orchestra, and that in the light of the existence of the Hallé's own trust fund, worth £1.6 million, "such a stringent policy, while apparently prudent, may not be either necessary or in the best interests of the Society". This viewpoint, it will be noted, is in line with the AGMA letter of 1988, but almost diametrically opposite to that of the Arts Council (that the Hallé should have taken steps to "reduce operations") one year before.

Indeed, the assessor concluded that the Hallé's trust funds were "a kind of back-stop security against disaster" and that more support for the Society could be provided by releasing some of their capital, if further deficits were incurred. This was not recommended, however – "it is somewhat akin to selling the family silver," the report said. Its advice was that "the Society will have to pay careful attention to the control of finances in the next period" – a point the Hallé was well aware of, without the benefit of a consultancy.

For the time being, the Hallé had no other option, it seemed to its Board, than self-help. "The financial stability of the Hallé will be more dependent than ever on the success of its own fund-raising efforts", the 1989-90 annual report declared, and announced that the Endowment Trust appeal was to be re-launched. It was the last full season both of Stanislaw Skrowaczewski as principal conductor and of Clive Smart as chief executive, the latter's last set of figures (the annual report for 1989-90) showing the Hallé was – just – solvent again. In addition to the increased income from performance, sponsorship and local authority grants, there had been a 150% increase in investment income.

At the crossroads

It was apparent well before Smart left office (in March, 1991) that the 1990-91 Hallé year would not be quite so successful financially. The Government had announced an 11% increase in support for the Arts Council for that year, and Smart had prepared a business plan and budget assuming the Hallé would benefit *pro rata*. In fact its grant increased by only 4%. Smart was instructed to prepare proposals to eliminate a deficit, and these included a 10% overall increase in ticket prices, extra performances, and a plan to gain extra sponsorship. The budget also proposed a reduction in strings strength for some concerts, to save on hiring of extras. It projected a surplus of over £100,000, but after locally concluded pay negotiations resulted in a minimum increase of 10% in all wage rates, it was clear this would need to be revised.

Audiences were good at the summer concerts of 1990: the Proms recorded an overall attendance of 70% and a 17% increase in income; and the G-Mex concerts a 17.5% increase in income. But despite initial winter ticket sales reports being similar to the previous season in volume, and 12.5% greater in value, by early 1991 the Executive heard that there was a continuing shortfall in Manchester concert income. That summer's Proms prices, it had already been decided, would rise by 13.5% (and the G-Mex concerts by almost 50%), and the next winter season's prices were to rise by a little over 10%.

In early 1991 the Hallé was at last able to secure an Incentive Funding award from the Arts Council: worth £160,000 over three years. It was, however, specifically for education, marketing and the development of the Endowment Fund appeal, and this meant bringing all the costs of the appeal into the main budget. The final result for 1990-91 was an overall loss of about £20,000, as revealed in the annual report, despite the benefit of £48,000 from the Incentive Funding Award, and with a further negative entry in the balance sheet of over £21,000 for "management re-structuring". The deficit on reserves (i.e. the extent to which the Hallé was fundamentally "in the red") was, as a result and despite some counterbalancing income, £37,000.

Artistic policy

There is more evidence in this period than in previous ones of how artistic policies were determined in the Hallé's planning and administrative machinery. Skrowaczewski's last years with the Hallé were marked by a renewed tendency on the part of the General Committee (and Finance and Policy Committee) to become involved with the details of programming – no doubt because of concerns about the financial effects of some proposals. In 1987 he questioned their unanimous view that Beethoven's *Missa Solemnis* was not a suitable work for the Opus One series, but without a change of mind on their part. When his contract was renewed in 1988, he requested a greater say in the choice of guest conductors, but Smart's refusal to concede this was endorsed by the Finance and Policy Committee. There was further disagreement shortly afterwards, as a letter from Skrowaczewski's agent complained that his availability for a concert with the Hallé in Vienna planned for September, 1989, had not been checked. Smart stated that it had. James Judd was engaged instead.

In the summer of 1989, Smart wrote to Skrowaczewski with the Board's views on some of the projected programmes for 1990-91. One Opus One programme was deemed not to be sufficiently attractive for the audience; another to be not suitable. The proposal to open the Thursday series with a symphony by Gordon Crosse was said to be not a good idea, in the Board's opinion, another suggested programme was described as very hard to sell, and a proposal to engage Luciano Berio was described as not worth the fee demanded.

The Executive discussed the possibility of a Musical Advisory Committee in September, 1989, but rejected the suggestion. Smart pointed out that inadequate funding had made it necessary for Skrowaczewski to be instructed to adopt a more conservative policy than he had wanted in each of the past four years. Skrowaczewski met the Executive Committee in October and spoke strongly in support of his programmes – but offered some changes. The committee assured him that it was only the juxtaposition of works that caused concern and not the works themselves, and decided to ask the Hallé Trust Fund to underwrite the cost of Berio's appearance. But in November, after seeing Skrowaczewski's changes, the Executive expressed continued concern. The Opus One programmes, it decided, should be significantly more "popular" and certain of the Thursday programmes lacked a major attraction of adequate significance. Skrowaczewski's suggestions for major commissions for the opening season of the projected new Manchester concert hall were also considered, but no action seems to have been taken.

After the 1989 Incentive Funding assessor's report, the Music Advisory Panel concept was accepted, and its terms of reference and composition discussed by the Executive. But in December, with the news that the Government had increased the Arts Council's funds by 11%, the Executive decided to take the financial risks inherent in the existing proposals for 1990-91. The following month, Skrowaczewski announced that he would not seek an extension to his contract beyond July, 1991. His press statement said: ". . . Although a number of my initial artistic aspirations and goals for the orchestra have still to be achieved, I do not foresee these being reached in the present financial circumstances . . ."

The Musical Advisory Committee, finally set up early in 1990, met for the first time in May. Its membership consisted of Smart, two Board members, two orchestra members, and external members, of whom the first to be appointed were Gerald Larner (then northern music critic of *The Guardian*), Trevor Green (head of music for the BBC in Manchester), Professor Ian Kemp of Manchester University, and David Patmore (Sheffield Corporation's Arts Director). It considered the 1990-91 season one of the best and most interesting for many years, but expressed a general feeling that the Summer Proms were too traditional. In January, 1991, it suggested an emphasis on Prokoviev for the 1991-2 season, but thought that guest conductor Mathias Bamert's proposal that he include a Parry symphony was not appropriate.

Whatever its disagreements with the Arts Council, the Hallé seems to have expressed no doubts about the suitability of Skrowaczewski as principal conductor until he himself decided to end the arrangement. There were doubts, however, about the wisdom of the continued arrangement with James Loughran as "Conductor Laureate", and the title was finally discontinued a year after Skrowaczewski's resignation.

The orchestra's playing standard under Skrowaczewski was widely considered to be high – as noted above, it was specifically exempted from the criticisms of artistic achievement made in the late 1980s. Its quality received exceptionally warm critical praise in spring, 1989, for a concert at the Barbican in London ("they can hold their own nowadays against any London band" – the *Financial Times*; "colourful and rhythmically incisive playing" – the *Independent*).

The orchestra went on tour to Germany, Sweden and Austria in 1986; the United States and Poland in 1987; Germany, Switzerland and Austria (Vienna) in 1989; and Germany, Austria and Switzerland in 1990.

Skrowaczewski made a number of recordings with the Hallé during his time as principal conductor, all on the Pickwick label (now IMP Classics). They included the four Brahms symphonies, Bruckner's *Symphony no. 4*, Mahler's *Symphony no. 4*, and Shostakovich's *Symphonies no. 5* and *10*.

Chapter 9

Culture change – the advent of Kent Nagano

As soon as Skrowaczewski's decision to resign was known, the Hallé Board set about seeking a successor. De Ferranti heard the orchestra's views; and the Music Advisory Panel discussed the matter in May, 1990. Lists were drawn up of possible candidates, but Kent Nagano's concerts as guest conductor in February, 1991, produced "an immediate strong feeling" on the part of the orchestra that he should be offered the position. Smart and David Richardson (who had now been appointed as the next Chief Executive) discovered in conversations with Nagano that he was positive about the idea.

Kent Nagano (born 1951), a Californian of Japanese descent, was assistant to Seiji Ozawa at the Boston Symphony Orchestra, and studied with Bernstein and Boulez, also working closely with Olivier Messiaen in preparation for the first performances of his opera, *St Francois D'Assise*, in 1983. He conducted the Berkeley Symphony Orchestra in California and in 1989 was appointed music director of the orchestra of the Opéra de Lyon, succeeding John Eliot Gardiner. He was appointed Associate Principal Guest Conductor of the London Symphony Orchestra in 1990. Several of his recordings with Opéra de Lyon and other orchestras won major awards.

Richardson was enthusiastic about the prospect of Nagano's appointment, but told the Executive at his first meeting with them that Nagano would have considerable artistic and financial requirements. He was asked to pursue negotiations, and in April, 1991, the Board empowered him "with a view to securing Kent Nagano for the Hallé". The Arts Council view was that the appointment "would change the Hallé's image overnight and position the orchestra in an entirely new way, with artistic benefits and spin-off in recording and sponsorship." In July Nagano was appointed Music Director and Principal Conductor Designate until August, 1994, and Music Director and Principal Conductor for 1994 to 1997. He immediately became involved in the Hallé's forward planning, including discussions on the acoustic requirements for the new concert hall, and by June, 1992, had planned programme outlines for the three seasons from 1993-4 through to 1995-6.

Once appointed, David Richardson did not hesitate to revise existing plans. An extensive and ambitious set of artistic aims was drafted after the appointment of Kent Nagano. These included extending the Hallé's Manchester repertoire, a programme of commissions, involvement in artistic projects in London and overseas, and a recording programme on major labels with significant repertoire. There was also to be a Principal Guest Conductor, a reduced number of concerts annually and an increase of 10 in the size of the orchestra to include 70 strings. These proposals, as Richardson made clear, would require substantial increases in the Hallé's public funding.

The rise in Manchester ticket prices for the next season was now to be 20% on average, rather than 10%, and a new ticket price structure, "rationalising and simplifying" the old one, to be introduced. Richardson expected only a 2% attrition in numbers as a result, and his belief that price was "not a major determinant of attendance at arts events" tallies with a "Pricing In The Arts Report 1990" for the Arts Council of Great Britain and the Scottish Arts Council, which appeared early in 1991 (this is discussed more fully in chapter 12). Break-even on 1991-2 was predicted.

The Arts Council told the Hallé it was "certainly the time for [it] to strengthen relationships in the North West with a view to increasing support in line with that given to the CBSO", but was unable to offer any immediately increased grant. Richardson proposed that a business plan should be prepared showing increased income from the Arts Council and local authorities, and higher earned income and sponsorship, to meet higher expenditure on the Hallé's artistic programme. This became the draft business plan for the years 1991-2 through to 1994-5, which was ready by September, 1991. It insisted the Hallé must achieve higher attendances, progressively higher ticket yields and increased public funding, all of which were "critical" to the success of its artistic development. The Arts Council would be expected to give a "substantial increase" in the Hallé's grant, AGMA and the Lancashire and Cheshire authorities should give more, and a new financial relationship with the city of Manchester was necessary.

Richardson told the Board in October, 1991, that the Nagano appointment and consequent development of artistic policy had been welcomed by the Arts Council and other bodies, and that this, allied to the opening of the new concert hall, should yield the necessary additional income. (The reference to the opening of the concert hall as a means of obtaining adequate income to balance the new plans appears to be the first time that the hope for increased prosperity from the mere existence of the new hall had been expressed).

The first signs from the city of Manchester were good. By the end of 1991, however, the news was that the Council Leader, Graham Stringer, was supportive, but that Manchester's financial situation was difficult; and also that AGMA was unlikely to increase its grant in real terms. Cheshire County Council, moreover, was changing its policy to project-based rather than revenue grants.

The Arts Council awarded the Hallé a 17.9% rise in funding for 1992-3 (most other orchestras received only 6%), but this did not give the improvements that had been sought by the Hallé, merely bringing it level with the Liverpool and Birmingham orchestras in national support – an indication of the extent to which previous Arts Council policies had worked against it.

The Executive heard in April, 1992, that ticket sales were down 4% by number on the year as a whole, but 13% up in value, and it was finally reported in July that a trading surplus had been recorded.

But Richardson's reorganisation of management was thoroughgoing and created a "considerable" cost (his own description). It was approved for implementation on a phased basis. Consequently, "management re-structuring" took a toll on the 1991-2 results, where the trading surplus (which also included increased trust fund contributions, particularly from the Hallé Trust Fund) was converted to a loss similar to the previous year's, because of the costs of restructuring and a new heading of "artistic direction", which cost £24,000. The deficit on reserves rose to over £70,000, but the annual report said this was "not an unsatisfactory result".

The budget for 1992-3 was under discussion early in 1992: its first draft showed a large deficit, partly owing to higher expenditure on "higher quality" guest conductors and soloists. Fewer concerts than in the previous year, both in Manchester and elsewhere, were planned, and a tour of South America with Stanislaw Skrowaczewski meant that the summer Proms series would be limited to eight concerts. But the tour achieved a net surplus (its proceeds, together with those of the shortened Proms, were equal to the earnings which a full series of Proms could have achieved),[160] and by October 1992, the half-year result was £35,000 ahead of budget, with a forecast outcome of near break-even, despite a serious lack of Manchester season ticket sales as against budget. The final 1992-3 results again showed "management restructuring" as a charge, this time of about £50,000 (and fees for musical direction, amounting to £48,000, were included in trading expenses), but a small surplus overall was recorded, despite an 11% drop in sponsorship income; and the annual report said a break-even was budgeted for 1993-4.

[160]David Richardson, personal communication.

Consultancy and after

Why this spectacularly failed to be achieved is one of the major questions in analysis of the Hallé's financial performance in the early 1990s, and must be related principally to the attempt to turn the summer Proms of 1993 into a festival-style event, but also to the effects of the consultancy in 1991 and 1992, embodied in the Strategic Review of 1992 and the Business Plan for 1993-4 to 1995-6, which was adopted in early 1993.

Kent Nagano took a leading part in artistic planning for the 1992-3 season and thereafter, suggesting alternative names for some of the conductors and soloists already planned, and considering the pattern for three seasons ahead. It was recognised that the Hallé would have to pay more for "higher quality" artists, in line with the artistic strategy. There were also extra costs because of changes in the leadership of the Hallé Choir. Ronald Frost, its long-standing choirmaster, retired in 1992, and Jonathan Grieves-Smith was appointed guest chorus-master, followed soon after by John Alldis. In April, 1993, John Currie was appointed guest chorusmaster for the coming season.

In April, 1992, John Owen, former head of the Britten-Pears School and a partner in Owen-White Management, was appointed to assist in the preparation of programmes and planning for the opening of the new concert hall.

Consultants were brought into the Hallé's planning process as a result of an invitation from Kent Nagano, and were asked to bring together the new artistic vision and the financial situation. They analysed the Hallé's role and market position, and their major financial proposal was that there should be standard prices for all winter season concerts, rather than the three different scales previously used for the Thursday, Sunday and Opus One series (though the differential, particularly in the case of the latter, had already decreased). Priority should be given to regaining marginal attenders lost through recent price increases, they said, at the same time maximising yield, which would mean a plan to "minimise and disguise any further ticket price increases".

They also recommended a change in Hallé "culture", from a practice based on financial criteria to one based on artistic ones, and that planning should begin with operational strategies rather than financial targets. The old approach, they said, "instigated by the last Chief Executive . . . has not led to demonstrable financial success at any level . . ." The consultancy, carried out in 1991 and 1992, was formulated in a Strategic Review presented to members of the Executive in March, 1992. One of its authors was retained as "facilitator" to implement its provisions, including the formation of a working party on communication and information, a re-structuring of the Board, and work on information technology. But its most immediate effect was on ticket pricing and marketing. It included the proposal that the Hallé should take over the management of the Free Trade Hall as a "pilot" project, with management of the new concert hall in mind; and the suggestion that fund-raising (or "development", as it was now known) should concentrate on attracting sponsorship for current activities rather than the "Hallé Appeal" for the Endowment Trust Fund.

The consultancy report made it clear that Kent Nagano was to have a leading role in artistic planning in an organisation which was now setting out be "artistically led". The subsequent appointment of Yehudi Menuhin as President and Associate Conductor of the Hallé was at Kent Nagano's request and designed to project the Hallé as an orchestra of tradition as well as of innovation, but was taken without consultation with the orchestra, because of "pressure".

Ambitions were now very high: there was a recorded aspiration of "pre-eminence in world terms within a time span of 10 years", and proposals for regular staged opera (an annual Manchester season in co-production with the Opéra de Lyon was foreseen), a summer residence for the orchestra (the Lake District the favoured place), regular performances of chamber music by Hallé orchestra members, a long-term relationship with a major record label, and overseas touring. Market research would be used to identify demand for new types of concerts, on different days of the week and in different venues, from the existing arrangements.

The approach to forthcoming seasons was to be, for 1993-4, a greater emphasis on classical repertoire, with celebrity soloists, contemporary music presented by composer-conductors, and the exclusion of "overplayed" works; then, for 1994-5, the re-introduction of large-scale romantic repertoire, along with works by living composers; and, for 1995-6, more work by living composers and British music.

A co-production with the Opéra de Lyon, of Puccini's *Turandot*, was originally planned as the Hallé's contribution to Manchester's year as European City Of Drama (1994), but was "deferred". Alternative suggestions were for a semi-staged performance of Berlioz' *Faust* with a cast from Lyon, or a staged production of John Adams' *The Death Of Klinghoffer,* but Richardson decided the latter would be too costly. The proposal did, however, surface in the Hallé members' preliminary prospectus and in a published list of forthcoming premieres for 1995 by Adams' publishers, Boosey & Hawkes, and in mid-1994, Nagano insisted in an interview, "It's going ahead" – though the Hallé line was that it would only happen if sponsorship were found,[161] and it was not included in the published season prospectus. It did not, in the event, take place.

Kees Hulsmann was appointed Leader of the orchestra in 1993 (jointly with Pan Hon Lee, who had held his post since 1980), and Thomas Ades was appointed Composer In Association, using an Arts Council grant of £10,000 per annum for two years. His duties were to spend 12 weeks of the year with the Hallé, undertaking commissions, taking part in educational work and being "fully

---

[161]Ticket To Ride, *Classical Music,* September 3rd, 1994.

involved in Manchester musical life". George Benjamin was appointed Principal Guest Artist.

The Hallé Proms were re-branded "Promfest" in 1993 and became a programme of orchestral concerts, chamber music and guest recitals. They recorded a deficit on budget of nearly £90,000. Richardson produced a plan to make savings of this amount in the rest of the financial year, and analysed the reasons for the deficit as lying in over-ambitious budgeting and pricing, a "flawed" marketing plan, and programmes which did not appeal to traditional Hallé audiences. The shortfall on income from the Proms was the first severe failure of the new plans which had been made, and, with hindsight, there seems to have been some unwillingness to face directly the implications of this failure. A first draft of 1994's Proms programmes had already been drawn up, and the programmes were now modified to try to draw a larger audience. The title was changed from "Promfest" to "Proms Festival" .

By September, 1993, the management accounts showed not only the poor results of the Promfest but also higher than budgeted overtime costs and extra players' fees, along with "special factors including the scoring requirements of the repertoire", which were blamed for a gloomier outlook. In addition, some of the new sponsorship won could not be applied in the current year but had to be carried over to 1994-5, resulting in a shortfall against budget. There was also a reduction in the Brother company's formerly very generous sponsorship.

David Richardson produced proposals for savings of £58,000 (against a projected deficit of £98,000), and listed other options, such as changing programmes, cancelling loss-making concerts, cancelling education projects and reducing strings strength for out-of-Manchester concerts, as possibilities that would "give negative signals outside the organisation". In January, 1994, the forecast loss for the year was £113,000, and, in the event, 1993-4 resulted in a net loss of nearly £140,000, the largest since 1987-8, and for the first time the Hallé balance sheet showed an accumulated deficit on reserves in excess of £250,000. AGMA's grant had been frozen, though Manchester's previously-small contribution was increased six-fold. The Arts Council had awarded a small extra amount of "Incentive Funding" – but the major factor was a decrease in performance income of over £300,000. Richardson, in an interview, admitted that without a solution to its problems, the Hallé's future as an international symphony orchestra could be at risk within two years, and re-stated the Hallé position that it would "need more than £250,000 a year [extra] in public funds". [162]

The annual report was ambivalent. Rather like a stockbroker's report in a bear market, it said the longer-term prospects for the Hallé were "reassuring", despite "short-term financial difficulties" which, it insisted, would "fall into perspective as the benefits of the new concert hall begin to flow." Three specific reasons for the

[162]Sour Note as Hallé Faces a Huge Loss, *Manchester Evening News,* March 15th, 1994.

loss were identified: 1. audiences which were "not as high as hoped" for the new-look Summer Proms of 1993 and, to a lesser extent, the winter season (nonetheless, income from Manchester performances was up by 17%); 2. a "late cancellation of sponsorship at a time when expenditure plans could not be revised" (presumably a reference to the Brother cut-back); and 3. a "loss of anticipated income from . . . hired engagements". Consequently, the increases in income were "not sufficient to meet the high income targets which had been set in order to achieve a balanced budget".

By early 1994, attention had moved to the budget for 1994-5. The dismaying fact that in future the Arts Council would not be able to carry through its long-promised three-year funding programme, and that its total grant from the Government would be reduced from 1994-5 onwards, first came in a letter in April, 1993. It was echoed in Anthony Everitt's statement in the 1993 Arts Council annual report: ". . . Now we enter a colder climate . . ." By January, 1994, Richardson had to tell the Board that, after a meeting at the Arts Council on the question of Hallé finances, there was no chance of additional money for 1994-5.

Richardson revised the budget, "at the cost of artistic policy", and told the Board he believed that the deficit was now beyond the capacity of improvements in trading to compensate for falling grants and rising costs and was a problem being experienced by all the regional orchestras. He stated that increasing the Hallé's average Manchester attendance to 75% would still reduce the deficit by only £40,000 – an indication that at this stage the Hallé's main problems lay in controlling expenditure.

Richardson drew up a new 1994-7 business plan in early 1994, which over-wrote the previous one with more modest aims. As well as the revised approach to the summer Proms, it specified that the Opus One programmes would contain more mainstream repertoire, and that the Sunday series would be somewhere in between and less adventurous than Thursdays, with, from 1995-6, repeated Thursday concerts and celebrity recitals – in most respects, a return to the artistic philosophy of pre-1991. There would also be a new winter series of four popular Saturday night concerts. Kent Nagano was clearly not the initiator of this revision of artistic strategy, as it was decided that he "should be made aware of" its effect on artistic policy, and "his agreement was required".

The presentation of the 1994-5 budget to a special Board meeting in February, 1994, showed a projected deficit of £225,000 for the year, or worse. Four lines of action were suggested, each to produce an improvement worth £100,000: 1. cutting costs; 2. funds to be raised by the Board itself from sources outside existing ones; 3. Manchester to give an increased grant; and 4. the Arts Council to give an increased grant. The Arts Council now required a balanced budget to be submitted by all its clients, but in March, 1994, Richardson told the Executive he would be submitting a deficit budget. The meeting decided it was important that Kent Nagano was fully aware of the financial position, and David Richardson and David

Wilson (deputy chairman of the Hallé) flew to New York, free of charge, to discuss the situation with him. An orchestra tour of Switzerland planned for March, 1995, was cancelled. The revised business plan showed a deficit for 1994-5 still at £225,000, but a near break-even for 1995-6 and a surplus for 1996-7.

Appraisal 1994

The Arts Council carried out an appraisal of the Hallé in May, 1994, with a team consisting of Sir James Spooner (a board member of the Royal Opera House), John Miller (a director of the Bournemouth Orchestras), and Graham Sheffield (Director of Arts at the South Bank Centre, London). A letter followed soon afterwards from Kathryn McDowell, acting music director of the Arts Council, to the Hallé chairman, Sebastian de Ferranti, expressing concern about matters which, it said "need urgent consideration". It made a number of serious criticisms, both of some of the Board's members and of some members of the Hallé management team, and of failings in relationships between them. By the Executive meeting of July 12th, 1994, Richardson had been allowed early release from his contract, although he stayed with the Hallé until September in order to manage its visit to Los Angeles that month.

The appraisal found that the Artistic Department's structure was not working well. "Gaps in communication internally [between Kent Nagano and the two senior managers in the Artistic Department, and key managers in other departments] and externally. . . appear to be making artistic planning lengthy and unsatisfactory," it said. The appraisal team suggested that the way forward was for the Chief Executive to take overall responsibility for the artistic direction of the Society, with him as the Hallé's primary point of contact with Kent Nagano. It also recommended that the Hallé should consider appointing another titled conductor in order to complement the work of Nagano, strengthen its roster of guest conductors, have clearly defined programme strands which could be aligned with target audiences, and involve Nagano integrally in the marketing as well as programme planning process.

In November, 1993, Kent Nagano had been invited to attend a special Board meeting to discuss his artistic policy and future plans. This did not take place until May, 1994. But, around the same time, he stated his own position in an interview. "Things turned sharply downwards just before I came here," he commented, referring to the economic situation for the arts in Britain generally, and compared his situation in Manchester with that at the Opéra de Lyon (where he was also music director), where, he said, he had *not* been asked "to supply a vision and change everything" but "to bring my ideas and invest them". The implication seems to have been that Manchester's expectations of him may have been unreal from the start. [163] Nagano used the meeting with the Board to make a defence of his choice of repertoire so far, and said: ". . . I have to work with a set of financial

[163]Ticket To Ride, *Classical Music*, September 3rd, 1994.

resources that I was not expecting . . . it means that I cannot do what I want in rehearsal because we cannot afford it . . ." He told them: "You have not been getting first class literature [this, in context, was a reference to the situation before he became responsible] . . . I am only choosing the best . . ." But he also admitted that "I took a risk programming Mendelssohn, Mozart and Haydn . . ." (a reference to the "classical-emphasis" seasons of 1992-3 and 1993-4). He said that, because he did not have time to rehearse enough to expose and correct problems, this was "the hardest repertoire in the world", and had been chosen "to challenge the orchestra and audience to make sure that we make progress . . ."

No precise decisions on artistic matters are recorded from this meeting, but in July, 1994, after it was known that Richardson was leaving, the Board was told that it was now necessary "to clearly define and agree the relationship with the Musical Director". Alan Dean, soon after taking office as Acting Chief Executive, met Nagano, and reported to the Board that his relationship with the Chief Executive and the Artistic Department had to be strengthened. Discussions on this subject were still continuing in early 1995.

In the interim, the 1994 summer Proms Festival had taken place. It was not a financial success, yielding £20,000 less income than budgeted, and though the Hallé's own concerts drew greater attendances than in 1993, the chamber concerts and recitals drew an average attendance of 25%. One performance in particular, including Stravinsky's *Oedipus Rex* and Schoenberg's *A Survivor From Warsaw* in semi-staged versions, given as the Hallé's contribution to Manchester's year as City of Drama 1994, added an extra £12,000 to the year's projected deficit, as hoped-for support from the Royal Exchange Theatre and the City of Drama organisation was not forthcoming. The evening was not of high quality artistically (mainly because the Hallé Choir was under-prepared) and practical arrangements were poor in that the Manchester Dancehouse Theatre was not a suitable venue.[164] Nagano said in an interview published later that year: "All the economic indicators said 'No, don't do it'. All the advisers said 'No, don't do it'. But it would have been wrong for the Hallé not to participate. I was asked to take part in the Year of Drama when I first came here."[165]

Meanwhile, the financial situation needed urgent attention. A proposal was made to make further use of the capital resources of the Hallé Trust Fund, by transferring £250,000 from it as "sponsorship" for all the 1994-5 season's unsponsored concerts – while every effort would be made to raise new money for the fund. A new fund-raising strategy would be devised, and the Board would raise the £100,000 it had committed itself to previously. By September, however, a new projection for 1994-5 showed a £308,000 deficit. The reasons given were the loss of income from the cancelled tour of Switzerland, a reduction in local authority income against the figures budgeted, over-optimism in the original budget, and an

[164]An opinion based on my own experience on the evening in question.
[165]Ticket To Ride, *Classical Music*, September 3rd, 1994.

excessive sum spent on overtime. It was also reported that a Hallé visit to Los Angeles that month with Nagano would yield less income than budgeted, and that a tour of Spain planned for November, budgeted to lose £1,000, would in fact lose £10,000, "largely due to overtime".

David Richardson formally left the Hallé in October, 1994, but from September, Alan Dean, a former Board member of some years' standing, was Acting Chief Executive, later accepting the substantive appointment. He told the Executive that he would be meeting Nagano at the earliest opportunity, as ". . . the present situation . . . could not continue." Board member John East also expressed "further concern at the adverse effect individual soloists and conductors would have on finances," and Dean told the October meeting of the Executive that when he met Nagano he "wanted to hear his views and understand his commitment to justifying the Hallé's expectations of its investment in him."

Alan Dean brought in a new management structure, under which the Executive would meet only four times a year and there would be "working groups", including both Board members and others, in the areas of business planning, fundraising, artistic matters, and marketing and customer services. He also took part in the formation of the Northern Orchestral Consortium, which was to represent the shared interests of the Hallé, Royal Liverpool Philharmonic Orchestra, BBC Philharmonic, Manchester Camerata, English Northern Philharmonia (the orchestra of Opera North, based in Leeds) and Northern Sinfonia (based in Newcastle upon Tyne). Dean's regime began with immediate attention to the financing of 1994-5's programme, and provided for a new format for marketing and sales reports to the Board. "The variance summary for future dates (comparing new forecasts with old) was meaningless without any targets for comparison," Dean told the Executive.

For the next year, 1995-6, a budget had been set for Manchester concerts, but the Business Plan was still based on the assumption of a £250,000 improvement in public funding. Dean planned a reduction in the use of extras in the orchestra, a sustainable reduction in artistic costs, the addition of revenue-earning concerts, and a review of the orchestra members' contract. His three-year plan of 1995 specified no change to the Hallé's principal concert series (or their pricing), although the new "Saturday Pops" – four winter season concerts in Manchester – were to be an ongoing feature, with a gala fund-raising concert every year. John Currie resigned as Director of the Hallé Choir, on "amicable terms", and Keith Orrell was appointed to the old post of Chorusmaster in 1995.

In the presentation of the full Arts Council appraisal report to the Hallé Board in May, 1995, the relationship of the Hallé to Nagano was still a major issue. Graham Sheffield underlined the appraisal team's conclusion, stating that "the Chief Executive is the person best able to control Kent Nagano". Dean concluded that there was a financial need to "get a return on the investment in" Nagano, and that different management resources were needed for him.

Nagano met the Board again in July, 1995. He was able to point to achievements such as the release of his first recordings with the Hallé, which he said would initiate an international enthusiasm for the orchestra, and commented that he and the orchestra had come a long way. There was still a long way to go, but maybe the future was brighter than people might think. Board members, however, referred to "a failure to convince the Manchester public of Mr Nagano's plans and take our audience with us". Kent Nagano found himself defending the fact that he was to conduct no 20th century works in 1995-6 – although Graham Sheffield had told the Hallé that the 20th century was where his greatest strengths lay. He pointed out that "What the Arts Council believed had worked in Birmingham and London may not work in Manchester . . ." and that "Lyon and the London Symphony Orchestra were selling modern music very well, but they had a very sophisticated support staff . . . The Hallé could do that when the structure was in place. . ."

The Proms of 1995 failed to raise their target in sponsorship income by £15,000, and ticket sales fell short of expectations, which was partly blamed on "hot weather". The final outcome of 1994-5 was, as expected, a further slide into debt: the deficit on reserves rose to over £340,000, despite increased performance income, an increased Manchester City Council grant and greatly increased income from the trust funds and other sources (including almost £200,000 from legacy and other sources paid to the trading account rather than the balance sheet). The Arts Council grant remained frozen, however, and costs increased dramatically. The Hallé's response to Dr Janet Ritterman's report on national orchestral provision[166] made on behalf of the Arts Council and BBC, early in 1995, contained a statement that the city of Manchester and AGMA were now "not in a position to offer increased grant support . . ." – an apparent final abandonment of the quest to restore local authority funding to the levels which had once obtained.

The 1994-5 annual report referred to "the overriding need for the Society to find strategies for balancing its budget". Manchester concerts had not shown any income growth, despite this being budgeted, it said, and overseas tours had been disappointing in financial terms. "We must examine options for re-positioning classical concert-going and developing audiences," it said – a belated acknowledgment that the Hallé was losing its way in converting its artistic aspirations into income-producing enterprise.

Kent Nagano was already under contract to the end of the first season which would take place in the new Bridgewater Hall (1996-7). The decision that had soon to be taken was whether to discuss extension of his contract beyond that point, and whether the Hallé could secure an arrangement giving the Chief Executive overall responsibility for artistic strategy, as recommended by the Arts

[166] *Joint Arts Council/BBC Review of National Orchestral Provision*, published May, 1995, Consultation Document October, 1994; Arts Council Strategy Document July, 1995.

Council appraisal.

The Nagano years

Assessment of the first five years of the Nagano regime is problematical. Nagano had promised a "wild ride" in one of his early press conferences (describing a particular season's plans), but in the event the ride was wilder than many had expected. His concerts were widely (though not universally) greeted with critical praise, and there was the undoubted achievement of his recordings with the Hallé, for Erato and Nonesuch (both part of Warner Brothers) included John Adams' *El Dorado* (released 1996), the *Violin Concertos no. 2* of Prokoviev and Shostakovich, and Britten's *The Rescue Of Penelope* and *Phaedra*. More major projects were to come. Tours included visits to Vienna in 1992, and Los Angeles (the Hollywood Bowl) and Spain in 1994.

But some policy decisions had proved controversial. The emphasis on being "artistically led", from 1992-3, raises the question of what that phrase was supposed to mean, and whether it was actually achieved. There is no doubt that Nagano and Richardson initially planned for a substantial change in the way the Hallé worked, and that it was designed to cost more. Unfortunately the expected increased grants never materialised (at least on the scale envisaged), and the projected improved business results were not forthcoming, either.[167]

It also seems that the Board no longer interfered in its principal conductor's choice of repertoire or guest artists, even when these resulted in greatly increased costs. His autonomy under the new regime was very different from that of Skrowaczewski. This was only partly changed in 1994, when Richardson attempted to secure Nagano's agreement for the amended policy then adopted. The consultants who promoted the policy of "artistic leadership", saw it as a change from a situation where, in the past, setting financial targets had resulted in "safe programming". So there was from this point an explicit move towards risk-taking without precise calculation of the financial implications.

In repertoire terms, the 1993 and 1994 Proms were no more innovative than those of 1985-6, 1986-7 and 1987-8 (see Table 6.7). The innovation was more in respect of the change to a festival-style event and the effectiveness (or lack of it) in marketing that concept. However, the 1995 series moved decisively in the direction of "pop classics" concerts, given by the whole orchestra. The Sunday concert series, however, changed in repertoire considerably in 1993-4, with

---

[167]A similar short-lived period of becoming "repertoire-led" seems to have ended, with a re-emphasis on realistic cost forecasts, at the Royal Opera House at much the same time – see Tooley, 1999: 261f, who insists that "financial control, and financial stringency for that matter, need not be the enemy of artistic endeavour and enterprise". This is one of a number of parallels discernible, from Tooley's account, between the managerial problems of the Royal Opera House and those of the Hallé at this time.

"newer" music[168] forming almost half the programme content, rather than about a quarter – but this policy was reversed almost immediately: in 1994-5 the number of Sunday concerts was reduced from eight to five, and "newer" music there diminished to about 20% (see Table 6.5).

One possible factor in the gradual decline of Hallé audiences in this period is the increased effectiveness of the BBC Philharmonic and Manchester Camerata orchestras as promoters of concerts for a mainstream audience at the Free Trade Hall during the years under scrutiny. In 1983-4, while it had given 69 concerts of its own in the Free Trade Hall, the Hallé had faced only 10 by all other bodies. [169] The BBC Philharmonic (formerly BBC Northern Symphony Orchestra) had been giving a series of "Master Concerts" at the Free Trade Hall since 1973-4, which had consistently attracted small audiences, even after being re-named BBC Philharmonic Concerts in 1983. But after 1988, when Trevor Green was appointed Head of Music for the BBC in Manchester, an energetic marketing campaign (as well as its remarkably high standards and artistic leadership) began to build its following. Manchester Camerata, which for many years had concentrated its efforts on concerts outside Manchester and at the Royal Northern College of Music, began a popular series at the Free Trade Hall also. The more competitive situation in orchestral concert-giving, including increased public activity by the BBC orchestras, was cited by the Consultation Document of the Ritterman Enquiry[170] as a reason for a downturn in orchestral incomes after 1989. The Hallé Board in the early 1990s had many concerns: selection of a new principal conductor, and the plans for the concert hall, among them. But the question of the Hallé's position in relation to the ever-more-competitive scenario of classical concert-giving in Manchester does not seem to have exercised it until 1994-5 at least. Kent Nagano was expected to give an artistic lead of international quality, and arguably did so in respect of the Thursday series, but in reality it was in the pattern of the orchestra's programmes as a whole, and its success in attracting attendances throughout its range of activity, that its financial fate lay.

It is possible that the re-introduction of the title "Music Director", which was given to Kent Nagano from 1991 (no Hallé conductor had had such a designation since Barbirolli relinquished the title of "Musical Director" to become "Musical Advisor" in 1960: Simon Rattle had been appointed "music director" by the CBSO only in 1990), was understood to carry different implications by the Hallé and by its conductor. David Richardson, with hindsight, says that it was not appreciated that "in America, the music director is king".[171] I have noted Nagano's own reference to Lyon *not* being a situation where he was expected to "supply a vision and change everything", which may reflect the way he saw the task he was being

---

[168]The term I use to denote music of living composers together with that by composers whose deaths had occurred within 50 years of the date of the performance in question.
[169]Myerscough, 1986: Table 6:3.
[170]Arts Council of England, 1994.
[171]Personal communication.

asked to perform in Manchester. It may also be that contractual arrangements had been made with him which were, at least potentially, incompatible with the position advocated by the Arts Council in its 1994 appraisal that ultimate control of artistic policy should lie with the Chief Executive.

Perhaps most significantly, it is clear that immense faith was placed in the early part of the 1990s (and to a considerable extent later, also) on the revivifying effect which it was hoped Kent Nagano's appointment and artistic contribution would have on the Hallé's commercial situation. Marketing policy concentrated strongly on the new principal conductor's name and image, to the virtual exclusion of other Hallé conductors. It does not seem to have been considered, however, that Nagano's limited availability to the Hallé necessarily restricted most of the benefits of this to a small number of "selling points", namely, the concerts he himself conducted. The same effects from Nagano's 13 to 18 appearances a year in Manchester could not be expected as those that might have been associated with Barbirolli's enormous workload (though comparisons with those days were encouraged by the Hallé's marketing efforts), or even with James Loughran's 28 or so Manchester concerts per annum. This fact was raised by a questioner as early as the 1992 annual general meeting of Hallé Concerts Society members, who referred to Nagano's "limited availability" in comparison with "all the publicity about him". He was told that this was "being dealt with partly by showing that artists and programmes were chosen by Nagano". One must question whether that was a realistic strategy or an adequate answer to the question.

It is also unfortunate that marketing policies such as the "New Beginnings" campaign of 1992-3 were based to a considerable extent on suggestions that artistic achievement had been poor in the past. The campaigns were successful to the extent that this negative "spin" was repeated by some journalists on a number of occasions subsequently, [172] but their effect may also have been to antagonise

---

[172]For example, Andrew Clark, *Financial Times* November 12th, 1994, "Eclipsed by orchestras in Birmingham and Liverpool, it needed awakening from the sleepy conservatism into which it had lapsed since the death of Sir John Barbirolli in 1970"; Hugh Canning, *Sunday Times* January 16th, 1994, "the Hallé . . . has languished somewhat since the demise of its great conductor, Sir John Barbirolli, in 1970"; Rachel Pugh, *Manchester Evening News* February 14th, 1995, "An orchestra which has been stagnating since the legendary Barbirolli days". One thing I believe this study shows is that the Hallé had not been guilty of conservatism or stagnation in the whole of the 20 years since Barbirolli's time.

those members of the concert-going public who knew better, and to create prejudice against the Hallé generally in the minds of those who did not.

Chapter 10

New hall – old problems

The search for, and planning for the prospect of, a new concert hall for Manchester form the background to much of the story of the Hallé from 1985 to 1995. The belief that the city needed to replace the Free Trade Hall with a purpose-built venue was much older than that,[173] but the matter came into particular focus in the early 1980s. By 1985 there were still three possible options. One was for the city to acquire the Theatre Royal, adjacent to the Free Trade Hall, and extend the latter on to its site. One was the "Refuge project", a plan which the Hallé had investigated in some depth, of building a new auditorium inside the Refuge Insurance building (now the Palace Hotel) on Oxford Street, Manchester, near to the Palace Theatre. The third was to build on derelict land on the Bridgewater Canal side of Lower Mosley Street alongside the G-Mex exhibition centre. Clive Smart discussed these with the Manchester City Council's Chief Executive in December, 1985.

Mr Robert Scott, known for his piloting of the refurbishment and renewal of the Palace Theatre and Opera House, Manchester, was a leading figure in the Refuge project, and won the wholehearted support of the Hallé's Finance and Policy Committee for his plan, in October, 1986. In early 1987, Smart prepared a paper on the possibilities of a new "home for the Hallé" there, predicting that an annual revenue deficit would be incurred on operating the new concert hall, on the assumption that the Hallé would want to make use of it for one-third of the total time available.

In 1988, however, Manchester Council committed itself to the Lower Mosley Street site, and in the summer of 1989 Smart and Hallé Board member Alan Dean undertook to produce the Hallé's draft specification for the hall's management, and a proposal for a contract with the hall owners. In January, 1990,

---

[173]Indeed, it was something that Charles Hallé himself had suggested before his death – Kennedy, 1960: 89.

a contractor was appointed for the building project, and discussions proceeded on the Hallé's requirements for its "occupation" of the hall. It was agreed there would not be a separate rehearsal hall, but the Hallé would use the main hall for rehearsals.

A draft agreement produced in June, 1990, stated that the Hallé would have a "life tenancy", with the time needed for its concerts safeguarded against erosion by other activities, and a "degree of control" over the artistic policy of the hall. It would pay a block rate for its use of the hall, which would be increased only in line with the Retail Price Index at the most, or in line with increases in the Hallé's public grants, and it would pay a peppercorn rent for its office accommodation. The Hallé Board of July 23rd, 1990, agreed that the Hallé should have "optimum artistic control".

After David Richardson became Hallé Chief Executive, the terms for the Hallé's relationship with the hall were clearly a high priority. Richardson was assured that the Hallé would be "the prime tenant around whose requirements the hall is scheduled".

The takeover of the management of the Free Trade Hall by a subsidiary company of the Hallé was suggested by the consultancy of 1991-1992 (it was commented that both the City of Birmingham Symphony Orchestra and Royal Scottish National Orchestra had "poor relationships" with the independent managements of their respective halls), and recommended by Richardson. Victoria Gregory, manager of the Philharmonic Hall in Liverpool, which the city council there had handed back, on lease, to the Royal Liverpool Philharmonic Society, on condition that it should be self-supporting), was engaged to prepare an outline business plan for such an arrangement, and her report was considered in July, 1992. Free Trade Hall Management Ltd was set up, with Gregory as its chief executive, to take over the Hallé's existing venue.

Discussion on arrangements for the new concert hall continued at the same time, and Warren Smith, the Hallé Board member now chiefly concerned with these, reported in September, 1993, that the business plan for it indicated that the Hallé would need to raise an additional £500,000 in revenue per annum because of the increased costs of its residency there.

The draft agreement of 1990 was adopted as the basis for negotiation of the terms of the residency, and Richardson told the Hallé Board in early 1994 that the Hallé would have a privileged position there, "built into the centre of the existence and operation of the hall", and that in musical terms the position of the Hallé would be strengthened by having control of the hall and of which other orchestras performed there. A feasibility study of the proposals was commissioned for Free Trade Hall Management Ltd.

This pointed out that it would be in the Hallé's interests if it could control artistic policy, prevent commercial exploitation and control competition in the new hall; that there would be an inevitable conflict of interest between the venue operator and the prime user; that the city of Manchester would need to underwrite the residency if the Hallé were out-of-pocket as a result of it; and that any non-profit hall operator would want to make money from the terms of the Hallé residency in order to subsidise a programme of visiting orchestras. Accordingly, it recommended that in any case the Hallé should draw up strategies to deal with competition from visiting orchestras, programmes of popular classics, and those seeking sponsorship for their own events there.

However, its principal recommendation was that the Hallé should not itself bid to run the hall, but endorse an independent "public interest" bid, acting as a major artistic partner in such a bid. This was the strategy pursued, and the Hallé formed an alliance with Ogden Entertainments Corporation, the American business already running the Manchester Arena, to bid for the operator's contract. This company was to be called Hallogen (with Gregory as its first chief executive), and its formation was on the basis that Ogden would provide £350,000 funding for the start-up costs of the new hall, but would then recover its investment by amortisation out of any profits made in subsequent years – above the first £200,000 of profit per annum, of which £100,000 would go to the Hallé, and £100,000 to Ogden. The Hallé would have no obligations in the event of trading losses or a winding up.

Meanwhile, there was doubt as to how much the city of Manchester was prepared to fund the Hallé's costs for occupying its "new home". Richardson agreed a memorandum of understanding on the subject in May, 1994, which provided for the city's grant to reflect the level of costs in the hall, and in January, 1995, Alan Dean reported that the city would "transfer its funding" to the new concert hall.

But the Hallé's role in the formation of the hall's artistic policy was now defined only as being an "input", and an artistic advisory committee including the BBC, Manchester Camerata and Royal Northern College of Music as well as the Hallé was formed for the purpose. Its outcome was a policy which, the Hallé Board was told in August, 1994, would include early music, celebrity recitals and chamber music, and visiting orchestras four or five times a year, but not as a competing series with those of the "home" orchestras. "Unlike Birmingham, it would not be possible to put on a major international series," a statement said. The major income from the hall would be from light entertainment.

Thus the Hallé was afraid from the outset that the hall itself could not be run without incurring a deficit, and this motivated its decision not to bear the risk of the hall's activities as well as those of the Hallé Orchestra and the Hallé Concerts. How much it had also forfeited the opportunity fully to control the hall's artistic policy remained to be seen. Its competitive position, with, in the event, an international orchestral series and an international recital series, as well as concerts by the Manchester Camerata and BBC Philharmonic, all marketed through the resources of the hall alongside the Hallé's concerts, and private promoters such as Raymond Gubbay offering numerous promotions of the "pop classics" kind there, too, was to be a new experience.

Making the move

In an interview in 1995, the newly-appointed Hallé chief executive, Alan Dean, drew attention to the fact that the move to the new concert hall would cost the orchestra about £300,000 per annum more in rent. Higher ticket income would cover only about £100,000 of this, he predicted. Kent Nagano, Dean said, was "a good property for our move into the new hall, despite his lack of availability" and added that the Hallé could not afford to have more of its conductor's time, anyway. [174] In July, 1995, it was reported that Manchester City Council was going to "divert" the £200,000 per annum it had formerly spent on running the Free Trade Hall to help the Hallé with the extra costs of the hall (which was now to be obliged to break even). [175]

John Whibley, the general manager of Manchester Camerata, was appointed to the post of Concerts and Artistic Planning Director of the Hallé in December, 1995, having been a contender for the post of Chief Executive which Alan Dean had won earlier in the year. [176] Whibley was to take on much of the role of Stuart Robinson, who retired as Deputy Chief Executive the following spring.

Early in 1996, Dean predicted a deficit for 1995-6 of £100,000-plus, noting that the Arts Council was giving extra funds to the Royal Liverpool Philharmonic Orchestra and City of Birmingham Symphony Orchestra (because of the RLPO's particular problems, and the level of support from the home city, respectively) which were denied to the Hallé. He had made savings on overtime and the employment of "extras", as well as freezing orchestra pay rates. He also introduced reorganisation of the Hallé Board, with a new chairman (John East) to assume office later in the year. There were outstanding vacancies in the orchestra, he said, which "I want Kent Nagano to address . . . with a firm conclusion on this fairly soon." He also expressed a desire for "one or two" conductors to be closely associated with the orchestra, instead of a wide range of visiting conductors – something which the Kent Nagano regime had not so far "afforded" – and insisted that in future, if Kent Nagano wanted to do anything, "he tells me, and we do it as a partnership". Nagano's own future relationship with the orchestra, he said, would

[174]Brass and the Band. *Manchester Evening News*, May 27th, 1995. See also All the right moves. *Classical Music*, July 29th, 1995.
[175]Hall move financial headache for Hallé. *Manchester Evening News*, July 31st, 1995.
[176]Hallé press release, December 18th, 1995. See also Hallé welcomes Camerata man. *Classical Music*, January 20th, 1996.

"not simply [be] a continuance of what it is at the moment". [177]

Shortly afterwards the Hallé announced that Kent Nagano's contract, due to expire in mid-1997, would be extended for one year only, to 1998. I wrote in the *Manchester Evening News* that the Hallé wanted to cut down on its commitment to Nagano after summer 1998 – a comment intended to reflect the ". . . not simply a continuance" comment and Dean's on-the-record view that the Hallé could not afford more of his time – but this was vigorously denied.[178] In fact his time commitment to the Hallé was slightly reduced, and he made the generous gesture of endowing the Hallé Leader's chair with a financial contribution to the orchestra of his own.

Meanwhile Whibley had created a stir of his own by bringing about secret talks between the Hallé and his former orchestra, the Manchester Camerata, on a "management merger". The suggestion was to share certain administrative functions, but the BBC Philharmonic's head, Trevor Green, expressed strong opposition to being "gazumped" shortly after having agreed a link-up of the Camerata and his orchestra for the opening season at the new Manchester concert hall.[179]

The Hallé enjoyed a highly successful tour to Japan and Hong Kong with Kent Nagano in the summer of 1996, but all attention was focussed on the new Bridgewater Hall (as it was named), which opened in September, 1996. The Hallé's first season in it included its first Manchester performance ever of Mahler's *Symphony no. 8* (the "Symphony Of A Thousand"), as well as several world premieres, including commissioned works from George Benjamin, Thomas Ades and John Adams, in the opening festival.

The Hallé's annual accounts for 1995-6, published that autumn, revealed a deficit for the year of £84,445, taking the accumulated deficit beyond £500,000 for the first time. But optimism was the order of the day. The Hallé told one columnist in January, 1997, that takings were now up by two-thirds and there should be no trouble breaking even on the new season, despite the costs of two "blockbuster" Mahler symphonies. That writer (Norman Lebrecht) was less impressed by the quality of the orchestra's playing under Nagano, which he compared unfavourably with that of the BBC Philharmonic in the same hall.[180]

The season was considered to be a memorable one, however, and there was some surprise when Alan Dean resigned as the Hallé's Chief Executive in July,

---

[177]See Hallé's debut his by cash worries. *Manchester Evening News*, January 30th, 1996, and Cold comfort in Manchester. *Classical Music*, February 17th, 1996.
[178]Just one more year for 'dear' Nagano. *Manchester Evening News*, May 2nd, 1996. Nagano threatened the *Manchester Evening News* with legal action over this article, claiming that it implied that he was "greedy and grasping", and a retraction was published.
[179]Manchester orchestras locked in merger battle. *Classical Music*, May 11th, 1996.
[180]Can the Hallé live up to its hall? *The Daily Telegraph*, January 15th, 1997.

1997. He gave "personal reasons" for his decision. The annual accounts published later in the year showed that 1996-7 had recorded, not the target of break-even, but a net deficit of £181,787, the largest single-year deficit for the Hallé since 1988-9, bringing the accumulated deficit to over £700,000. The Arts Council grant was still frozen at its 1993-4 level, with none of the extras of Incentive or Challenge Funding which had helped in two of the previous three years. The grant from the Association of Greater Manchester Authorities had finally been increased, after itself being frozen since 1992-3 (it was, however, reduced again in the following year), and Manchester City Council's "special" grant was of £140,375 (possibly an apportionment of an amount calculated to equal £200,000 per annum year-on-year).

The Hallé announced that it would be under the joint direction of John Whibley, now Deputy Chief Executive, and Finance Director Jack Whittaker, until Dean's successor was appointed. The new Hallé chairman, John East, said shortly afterwards that he was still optimistic about the future. Kent Nagano would stay with the Hallé until 2000, the Hallé would make a major impression in musical circles with the world premiere of the original version of Mahler's massive cantata, *Das Klagende Lied*, in the autumn, and the new Chief Executive, when appointed, would deal with the financial problems on the basis of established policy. He maintained that the move to the Bridgewater Hall, on balance, had not made the Hallé's financial situation any worse. [181]

One of the few beams of light in a dark situation was the appointment of Lyn Fletcher as the new Leader of the orchestra in 1997.

The crisis looms

At the Hallé annual general meeting, later in 1997, East said the Hallé was facing a stark choice. "We cannot go on as we are," he said. The prospect of an Arts Council grant increase was remote, other orchestras were making cuts, and there would have to be economies.[182] At the time, the Board was interviewing candidates for the post of Chief Executive, as Leslie Robinson later revealed, [183] but no decision was announced in 1997.

The crisis broke in February, 1998. The Hallé was reported to be facing a £500,000 loss on 1997-8, and an "investigation" by its auditors, KPMG, had said it was doomed unless a financial rescue package was assembled. They were said to be critical of a lack of financial control and urging that the entire Board should be replaced. The Hallé was far from doomed, as proved to be the case, because of its substantial trust funds, but the result of the KPMG investigation had been leaked,

[181]Hallé puts on brave face after setbacks. *Classical Music*, August 9th, 1997.
[182]Hallé 'faces stark choice'. *Manchester Evening News*, October 29th, 1997; Hallé faces 'a stark choice'. *Classical Music*, November 15th, 1997.
[183]Raising the Titanic. *Classical Music*, June 12th, 1999.

two days prior to the Hallé Board meeting which was to discuss it: the news made the front page of the *Manchester Evening News*, reported by a local government specialist, Ray King.[184]   The Hallé rushed out a press statement saying that "Manchester City Council, in particular, has offered the strongest possible support for the Hallé".

But the *Manchester Evening News* then reported that "The city council is refusing to give financial help." [185] An "Action Plan" or "Rescue Plan" was announced by the Hallé, which admitted that the accumulated deficit was likely to be "approximately £1.1 million" after 1997-8; that it was the City Council that had commissioned the KPMG report (the previous announcement had described it as part of an appraisal by the Hallé Board "in partnership with" the City Council); that Leslie Robinson had been appointed Chief Executive, on a three-month contract; that instruments belonging to the orchestra ("two pianos and a fiddle", as it was reported) would be sold to its own Endowment Fund "to capitalise £200,000 from the endowment appeal"; and that there would be a new public appeal.

Leslie Robinson was a former journalist who had risen through the BBC to become its Head of Network Radio in the North, before taking early retirement. He had had overall responsibility for the BBC Philharmonic in his previous job.

A commentary in the *Manchester Evening News* traced the history of relations between the Hallé and Manchester City Council, [186] and the newspaper's "Postbag Debate" on February 5th, 1998, asked readers whether taxpayers should "bail out" the Hallé. The vote was (perhaps surprisingly, to some) 80% for that proposition, 20% against.

Sir John Manduell, the Hallé deputy chairman with responsibility for artistic matters, insisted that a visit to the Salzburg Festival, planned for later in the year, in which the Hallé Orchestra was to play under Nagano in performances of Messiaen's opera, *St Francois D'Assise,* would go ahead. But a planned concert under Nagano at the Barbican in London, including music by Varese and Ives in the "Inventing America" series, was cancelled soon afterwards, as was a planned visit to Paris. Sir John said the "review group" which was about to look at all the Hallé's operations would have to consider its relationship with the Bridgewater Hall. "The hall . . . is expensive in rental cost . . . where it hasn't worked out is that, because we were in control at the Free Trade Hall, we were able to take a profit on it." He also forecast reductions in the size of the orchestra and "trimming" overtime.[187]

---

[184]Hallé cash crisis. *Manchester Evening News*, February 2nd, 1998.
[185]Rescue plan for Hallé but bosses face axe. *Manchester Evening News*, February 4th, 1998.
[186]Hallé prestige must be paid for. *Manchester Evening News*, February 5th, 1998.
[187]Struggling Hallé will keep Salzburg date. *Manchester Evening News*, February 7th, 1998; Hallé suspends two senior executives. *Classical Music*, March 14th, 1998.

On February 24th, 1998, the Hallé announced the suspension of John Whibley and Jack Whittaker, pending an enquiry into financial management prior to February 4th, and both later agreed terms for departure. On March 18th it was reported that the players had accepted a pay freeze and a reduction in the orchestra's size from 98 players to 80, but had passed a resolution accepting the Action Plan "on the clear understanding that the principal conductor accepts more responsibility for the costs associated with his artistic directorship and adopts a more communicative and realistic approach to the management and orchestra".[188]

Recovery

The Hallé Board announced its rescue plan on March 27th, with an aim to reach breakeven by March, 2000, shed jobs in the administration as well as the orchestra, reduce administrative budgets, increase ticket prices, launch an appeal, and begin an ongoing programme of market research. A new, "streamlined" Board structure would be put to the annual meeting in September.

In July, 1998, Leslie Robinson announced that the Hallé still needed "to raise another £250,000 by Christmas to enable it to continue to the end of the current financial year", and that its annual grant income would have to rise by £500,000 to make it financially viable, with the accumulated deficit still likely to be left at nearly £2 million after achieving break-even year-on-year.

When the accounts for 1997-8 were published in the autumn, they revealed an "operating loss" of £963,496 (much more than the £500,000 originally estimated by KPMG), and an accumulated deficit of well over £1 million. The accounts were, however, presented in a new way which consolidated the trust funds with other resources, showing an overall deterioration of slightly more than £750,000 on the year, and a net balance of £1,552,680, taking in the trust funds' combined value of £2,781,807. The interaction between operational accounts and the trust funds (whose value changed according to the fortunes of investments) was now such that results probably had to be stated in these complicated terms (in addition to the legal requirements of charity accounts), but helps to explain why precise quantification of annual "loss" was now difficult. The accounts also revealed a measure which had probably had more practical effect in the "rescue" than the "two pianos and a fiddle" arrangement – the Hallé Concerts Society could now borrow up to £1 million from the Endowment Fund, to be paid back over a 50-year period. The "family silver"[189], if not for sale, was now wrapped up and ready for the pawnbroker.[190]

---

[188]Hallé boss told: Take share of blame. *Manchester Evening News,* March 18th, 1998. See also Conductor attacked as jobs go at Hallé Orchestra. *Classical Music,* March 28th, 1998.
[189]As the Hallé's trust funds had been described by the Incentive Funding consultant's report in 1989.
[190]Both the 1998-9 and 1999-2000 Hallé accounts stated that the amount borrowed stood at £730,000.

The change in the Board, which was a condition of any further help from Manchester City Council or AGMA, meant that instead of 12 elected directors and six local authority nominees, there would be five elected members and three council nominees (plus the Chief Executive, Finance Director, Artistic Director – a post then vacant but to which Richard Wigley was appointed – and an orchestra member). There would no longer be an Honorary Treasurer, but at least two Board members would in future be qualified accountants. Reorganisation costs had already contributed £302,000 to the year's deficit.[191]

Why did the Hallé run into loss so dramatically in its first full year in its new concert hall? Some factors have been mentioned, such as the frozen Arts Council grant, and the increased rental costs which were asked by Hallogen, compared with the Free Trade Hall (Leslie Robinson said later: "The City Council's 'offsetting grant' didn't actually offset them"). Robinson [192] also cited a failure to attract as much sponsorship income as had been hoped for, a lack of control over costs, and the major artistic projects of 1997-8 – examples generally acknowledged were the world premiere and recording of *Das Klagende Lied*, a premiere recording (and performance) of the original four-act version of Britten's opera, *Billy Budd*, and a series of concert performances of Puccini's *Tosca*, in association with the European Opera Centre, a newly-established, Manchester-based "super-conservatoire" (it was suggested that the Hallé had "forgotten" to budget for the cost of the singers in this production).[193]

There was also repeated reference in Robinson's statements in 1998 to a need for better artistic planning, financial control, and monitoring of expenditure against budgets. It is of interest that one of Robinson's first actions on taking office was to bring back into the Hallé the retired Deputy Chief Executive, Stuart Robinson (no relation), and that they, as he later said, "re-budgeted everything". [194] Stuart Robinson, who for many years had been mainly responsible for detailed budgeting of all the Hallé's concerts and tours, had left the Hallé in spring, 1996, after making most of the plans for the 1996-7 season (under Dean's supervision). The 1997-8 season had gone dramatically wrong, and it appeared that one of the Hallé's problems was that of replacing his skills. Lesley Tomlinson also joined the Hallé as Finance Director.

In February, 1999, Leslie Robinson announced that he would leave the Hallé that summer, and that the Hallé would be seeking "a chief executive with considerable experience of artistic leadership in a music-based organisation" (John Summers, chief executive of the Northern Sinfonia, was later announced as his successor). Kent Nagano confirmed that he would not be renewing his contract after 2000, and before his own departure Robinson was able to announce that

[191]Hallé suspends two senior executives. *Classical Music*, March 14th, 1998.
[192]Raising the Titanic. *Classical Music*, June 12th, 1999.
[193]Is this the last blast for the concert orchestra? *The Guardian*, July 18th, 1998.
[194]Raising the Titanic. *Classical Music*, June 12th, 1999.

Mark Elder, formerly music director of English National Opera and chief guest conductor of the BBC Symphony Orchestra and CBSO, was to be the Hallé's next principal conductor.

Leslie Robinson's contribution is described by Warren Smith (who chaired the Emergency Executive for most of the critical year) as "an exceptionally good job". He comments: "With the results he achieved in one year from the appeal, and his renegotiation of the orchestra's contract and redundancies while retaining the orchestra's goodwill, the organisation owes him a great deal for bringing it back from the brink. He had to take over a large organisation in difficulty, and produce a strategy and implement it simultaneously, and he was willing to take the risk to his own reputation that it might not have worked out."[195]

Robinson was able to say, later in the year, that there was a "new climate" in relations with the Bridgewater Hall, with Howard Raynor in post as Victoria Gregory's successor at Hallogen, while the Hallé would now rehearse elsewhere wherever possible, to save money. There would be more collaboration in future, with the BBC Philharmonic, among others, and the 1998-9 accounts would state a deficit for the year of around £500,000.[196] In the event the accounts showed total accumulated debt reduced by about £400,000, after a similar figure was drawn down from the new appeal fund. The "orchestra deficit" was represented as reduced by over £1m, and the former "operating loss" as transformed to a small surplus.

The 1999-2000 results showed accumulated debt reduced by a further £200,000 approximately, after a year in which the orchestra's own activities could be presented as having achieved a small surplus. When the Arts Council had announced its revised grants for 1999-2000, the Hallé (with the other provincial symphony orchestras) was awarded a base grant of £1,500,000, an increase of £150,000 on the previous level, and promised that money would also be available to remove its accumulated debt, providing it developed "a flexible approach" to provide a "wide-ranging repertoire".[197] AGMA increased its grant by almost £100,000 (27%).

Kent Nagano's final two years with the Hallé included a tour of Germany, Switzerland, Austria and Spain in 1999, and the release of the St Francois D'Assise

---

[195]Personal communication.
[196]Raising the Titanic. *Classical Music,* June 12th, 1999.
[197]Arts Council press release, October 13, 1999. This "Stabilisation Programme" was not expected to provide funds for the Hallé, however, before April, 2001, at the earliest, according to the Hallé's accounts for 1999-2000.

recording on the Deutsche Grammophon label; with some superb concerts at the Bridgewater Hall, including visits from Alfred Brendel, Daniel Barenboim (for the Barbirolli centenary concert in December, 1999) and Mikhail Pletnev, and performances of Mahler (*Symphony no.3* and *Das Lied Von Der Erde*, and later of *Symphony no. 4*) which will long remain in the memory.

Chapter 11

Programmes, composers and performers

The emphasis in this study, as far as performed repertoire is concerned, is on statistical analysis of the Hallé's Manchester concert programmes in a series of 10-year periods spread through the 20th century. The rationale and methodology for this are outlined at the head of the Tables near the end of the book. Others have commented on the details of Hallé programming in the past – what I am seeking to do here is to draw some conclusions from what is an admittedly partial survey, and indicate points of comparison which may not be instantly obvious. For 1985 to 1995, however, I shall include more detailed accounts of the Hallé's Manchester concerts.

Richter and Balling, 1903-1913

For a commentary on variations of repertoire in the years from 1903 to 1913, see Tables 2.1 and 2.2. Although Richter's programmes[198] were very "up-to-date" by the standards of a century later, he became noticeably more conservative as time went on. His concerts of 1903-4 had a higher proportion of music by living composers and those who had died in the 50 years preceding the performance in question (I shall call this "newer" music) than in any subsequent season of his reign: 71% of items were in those two categories combined. His second-to-last season (1909-10) included 53% of "newer" music – the lowest figure in those surveyed from the early 1900s.

Variety was hardly his forté. It would seem that the financial success of his first two seasons (1902-3 and 1903-4) encouraged him to increase the range of his programmes spmewhat in 1903-4 and 1904-5, but after that it diminished. It should be borne in mind that what we now consider the "core" classical repertoire was then still in the process of formation, but it seems undeniable that it was a

---

[198]Richter's and Balling's programmes are discussed in detail, season by season, by Kennedy, 1960: 145-170 and 183-186.

time when a restricted repertoire (in comparison with later times) was played. His biographer, Christopher Fifield, points out that "Richter, having given Manchester its first hearing of works, then gave them second and third performances, providing them with firm places in the repertoire." [199] By the same token, he was restricting the variety of works heard.

There was no music played earlier than J S Bach: his name was, however, regular in programmes. Beethoven was never absent: most seasons included most of his symphonies, and the "Jubilee Season" of 1907-8 was celebrated by giving all nine in consecutive order. Mozart, Berlioz, Wagner, Tchaikovsky, Brahms (d. 1897) and Dvorak (d. 1904) were also never absent from these Edwardian Hallé seasons, and among the "moderns", neither was Richard Strauss or Elgar. Liszt's orchestral music was absent only once between 1903 and 1913.

The 23-year-old Béla Bartók appeared as a piano soloist in 1904, and Richter introduced his composition, *Kossuth*, to Manchester.[200] The 1903-4 season is accounted by Fifield to be "the apogee of Richter's decade in Manchester".[201] However, *Kossuth* was not well received and, according to Fifield, Richter's attitude to Bartók "cooled" thereafter, and he "shunned" his compositions from that point.[202] Bruckner's work also made two appearances, with the *Symphony no. 7* (1904) and the *Symphony no. 3* (1907), as did Mahler's (the English premiere of the *Symphony no. 1* under Michael Balling in 1913). Both Bruch (who died in 1913) and Cherubini were more frequently performed than in later periods. Debussy and Verdi were never played, and Rossini only once, in 1912-13.

Richter's (and Balling's) sympathies were clearly with the Germanic tradition in music, and it could no doubt hardly have been otherwise. But Richter had great admiration for Elgar: he premiered the *Enigma Variations* in London in June, 1899, and brought them to Manchester for the first time in February, 1900, followed by *The Dream Of Gerontius* in March, 1903 (it was repeated in November), and *The Apostles* in February, 1904. The premiere of Elgar's *Symphony no. 1* under him in Manchester on December 3rd, 1908, is held by some to be the high point of the Hallé's role in musical history. Richter apparently called it "the greatest symphony of modern times, written by the greatest modern composer – and not only in this country!"[203] The Hallé also premiered Elgar's *In The South* overture in March, 1904 (under Elgar, in London, as part of an Elgar festival, led by Richter and the Hallé, with 100 orchestral performers and a choir of 275),[204] and Richter introduced it to Manchester the following November. He played the *Introduction And Allegro For Strings* in 1905, repeating it there and

[199]Fifield, 1993: 410.
[200]Richter had met Bartók in Hungary the previous year and seen *Kossuth* in piano score. Bartók stayed with the Richters in Bowdon and formed an attachment to Richter's daughter, Mathilde.
[201]Fifield, 1993: 368.
[202]Fifield, 1993: 370, 378, 381.
[203]W. H. Reed: *Elgar* (London, 1946), quoted in Fifield, 1993.
[204]See Fifield, 1993.

ABOVE: The Free Trade Hall, opened in 1856 and the home of Charles Hallé's concerts from 1858 onwards. It was destroyed by bombing in December, 1940, and was re-built after the war, re-opening on November 16th, 1951. This photograph was taken in the 1970s. The hall saw its last Hallé concert on June 30, 1996.
LEFT: Hans Richter and the Hallé Orchestra, photographed on the stage of the "old" Free Trade Hall

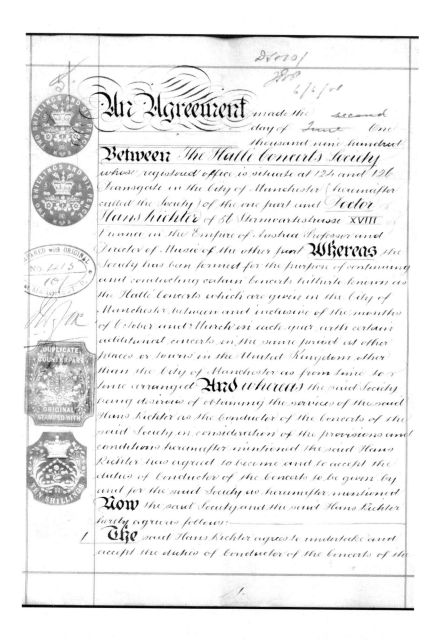

ABOVE: Hans Richter's first contract with the Hallé Concerts Society, dated June 2nd, 1900. Note that it describes his profession as "Professor and Director of Music", and states that the Hallé Society was formed "for the purpose of continuing and conducting certain concerts hitherto known as the Hallé Concerts . . ."

TOP: Sir Hamilton Harty prepares to acknowledge applause with soloists and the Hallé Orchestra in the "old" Free Trade Hall in 1930. Note that there are a number of empty seats: the Depression was beginning to hit attendances.

ABOVE: After the recording of "Nymphs and Shepherds" and "Brother Come and Dance with Me" by the Manchester Schoolchildren's Choir with the Hallé Orchestra, in the "old" Free Trade Hall, on June 4th, 1929. Sir Hamilton Harty is to be seen on the right of the rostrum: on the left are Gertrude Riall, the choirmistress, and Walter Carroll.

No.	DATE	ADVTS.	STAFF	MUSIC NOTES	HIRE OF MUSIC	ARTISTS	CONDUCTOR	ORCHESTRA	EXTRA REHEARSAL	SUNDRY EXPENSES
1	OCTOBER 19	39.18.5	6.9.0	1.1.0	—		70.0.0	125.10.6	—	39.13.8
2	OCTOBER 26	17.16.5	6.9.0	2.2.0	5.5.0	52.10.0	52.10.0	139.15.6	3.7.8	1.3.4
3	NOVEMBER 2	17.6.5	6.9.0	1.1.0	16.6.6	—	46.13.4	140.8.3	—	17.0
4	NOVEMBER 9	17.17.4	6.9.0	1.1.0	—	52.10.0	31.10.0	142.9.6	—	1.5.0
5	NOVEMBER 16	15.17.11	6.9.0	1.11.6	2.3.6	36.15.0	52.10.0	138.10.9	—	5.0.3
6	NOVEMBER 23	21.5.2	6.9.0	1.1.0	15.0.0	31.18.0	63.0.0	143.12.6	—	1.9.0
7	NOVEMBER 30	19.11.1	6.9.0	2.2.0	—	31.10.0	52.10.0	140.16.0	—	1.17.4
8	DECEMBER 7	16.11.3	6.9.0	1.1.0	—	21.0.0	70.0.0	148.7.0	64.14.8	1.12.5
9	DECEMBER 14	15.15.10	6.9.0	1.1.0	4.15.6	36.15.0	43.6.8	141.0.0	—	1.0.2
10	DECEMBER 21	23.8.8	6.9.0	10.6	—	78.15.0	32.10.0	95.18.0	—	5.5.4
11	JANUARY 11	16.18.9	6.9.0	1.11.6	—	—	31.10.0	137.3.6	—	1.2.2
12	JAN.ARY 18	16.15.11	6.9.0	2.2.0	—	15.0.0	52.10.0	144.6.0	—	17.3
13	JANUARY 25	23.3.11	6.9.0	10.6	—	52.10.0	70.0.0	145.19.6	—	2.10.9
14	FEBRUARY 1	18.17.0	6.9.0	1.11.6	—	26.5.0	51.10.0	150.4.6	70.12.3	2.7.9
15	FEBRUARY 8	17.1.0	6.9.0	1.1.0	—	84.0.0	31.10.0	125.18.0	—	3.1.1
16	FEBRUARY 15	20.11.8	6.9.0	1.11.6	—	36.15.0	31.10.0	143.9.0	—	16.4
17	FEBRUARY 22	19.12.11	6.9.0	1.1.0	18.18.0	141.15.0	inclusive fee	148.19.4	—	17.0
18	MARCH 1	20.17.2	6.9.0	2.2.0	6.6.0	52.10.0	70.0.0	158.11.6	71.2.6	3.16.4
19	MARCH 8	17.9.3	6.9.0	3.3.0	7.17.6	36.15.0	26.5.0	142.15.6	64.2.6	3.7.9
20	MARCH 15	16.11.0	6.9.0	1.1.0	—	—	70.0.0	130.2.6	—	2.17.8
	MARCH 22							274.4.7		

ABOVE: An abstract of concert receipts and expenses for the Hallé Manchester season of 1933-34. There are a several points of interest in this particular year. Conductors (see the list of names towards the right-hand side) included Sir Thomas Beecham, Pierre Monteux, Leslie Heward, Adrian Boult, Sir Henry Wood, Albert Coates, John Barbirolli, Nicolai Malko and Igor Stravinsky. Soloists also include famous names — and the Barbirolli concert with Artur Schnabel, on February 8th, 1934, drew an exceptionally high attendance (it is the only one, except for Handel's

PRINTING	RENT of HALL	CONCERT	B.B.C	EXPENSES	RECEIPTS	PROFIT	LOSS
154·19·0	37·10·0	BEECHAM	19·0·0	475·1·7	405·19·7	—	69·2·0
29·17·5	37·10·0	MONTEUX SZIGETI	—	348·6·4	282·9·7	—	65·16·9
27·15·8	37·10·0	HEGER	21·7·6	294·7·2	238·9·4	—	55·17·10
30·1·0	37·10·0	HEWARD MCISFIWITSCH	—	320·12·10	309·9·6	—	11·3·4
31·6·11	37·10·0	BOULT FISCHER	21·2·6	327·14·10	255·15·6	—	71·19·4
33·10·10	37·10·0	REQUIEM WOOD (VERDI)	—	404·15·6	224·1·6	—	180·14·0
32·4·11	37·10·0	COATES WAGNER	21·12·6	324·10·4	280·15·10½	—	43·14·5½
32·14·5	37·10·0 (5·5·0)	BEECHAM HOLST	22·10·0	405·9·9	372·12·7	—	32·17·2
29·17·5	37·10·0	HEGER CATTERALL	—	317·10·7	215·10·3	—	102·0·4
20·10·9	37·10·0 (3·0·0)	MESSIAH	—	303·17·3	461·14·2	157·16·11	—
29·7·11	37·10·0	BARBIROLLI	—	261·12·10	265·5·5½	3·12·7½	—
29·11·3	37·10·0	MONTEUX LILI KRAUSS	22·17·6	310·1·5	225·14·4	—	84·7·1
31·13·0	37·10·0	BEECHAM KIPNIS WIDDOP	22·7·6	370·5·8	353·10·1½	—	16·15·6½
35·14·5	37·10·0	WOOD MALKO	—	402·2·11	230·1·1	—	172·1·10
30·19·4	37·10·0	BARBIROLLI SCHNABEL	—	337·9·5	544·8·5	206·19·0	—
33·3·11	37·10·0	ELGAR SAMMONS	22·2·6	311·16·5	240·16·6	—	70·19·11
26·10·11	37·10·0	STRAVINSKY DUSHKIN	22·15·0	401·13·2	272·14·5½	—	128·18·8½
29·17·5	37·10·0 (5·5·0)	BEECHAM DELIUS	24·2·6	464·6·11	285·4·5	—	179·2·6
29·17·5	37·10·0 (5·5·0)	FORBES PETRI	—	380·16·11	257·2·8	—	123·14·3
30·6·11	37·10·0	BEECHAM	—	294·18·1	324·4·4½	29·6·3½	—

Messiah, to be accounted a significant profit-maker). Barbirolli, still something of an "up-and-coming" conductor at this stage, was paid only 30 guineas for it: Schnabel's fee was almost three times as much. The big conducting fees went to Beecham and Stravinsky, with Sir Henry Wood at 60 guineas, and Malko, Monteux, Coates and Boult all getting 50 guineas. The concert on February 15th was, in fact, conducted by Barbirolli in place of Elgar — which accounts for the low conductor's fee — though the programme remained all-Elgar.

LEFT: John Barbirolli, shortly after his arrival in Manchester in 1943, photographed in the ruins of the Free Trade Hall. The other figure is Manchester's city architect, L C Howitt. BELOW: The first Manchester concert of the re-formed Hallé Orchestra under John Barbirolli at King's Hall, Belle Vue, on August 15th, 1943 (Picture by permission of Manchester Libraries). Inset: A copy of the programme, signed by Barbirolli.

AN A G R E E M E N T made the   27ᵗʰ   day

October One thousand nine hundred and forty three

BETWEEN THE HALLE CONCERTS SOCIETY by *Philip Godlee*

the *Chairman* thereof of 126 Deansgate Manchester in the

County of Lancaster (hereinafter called "the Society") of

the one part and JOHN BARBIROLLI of 79 Appleby Lodge ─────

Rusholme Manchester aforesaid (hereinafter called "the

Conductor") of the other part   WHEREBY IT IS AGREED as

follows :- ───

1.   THE Society shall employ the Conductor and the Con-

ductor shall serve the Society for the period of one year

as from the Fifth day of July One thousand nine hundred and

forty three and otherwise as hereinafter provided ─────────

2.   THE Conductor's remuneration shall be the sum of TWO

THOUSAND Pounds for the said period of one year. The

Society will pay the Conductor─────────────────────────────

(a) The sum of Seven hundred and fifty pounds to recom-

pense him for his fare in respect of his journey from the

United States of America and the expenses consequent there-

upon ──────────────────────

(b) A sum not exceeding Seven hundred and fifty pounds

for the travelling expenses of himself and his Wife whilst

engaged on his duties under the terms of this Agreement to

include Hotel Expenses   and ───────────────────────────

(c) The Society will engage the services of a private

Secretary to assist in the performance of the duties of the

ABOVE: Barbirolli's first contract with the Hallé, dated October 27th, 1943. Note that "JB" did not sign anything until after the start of the main Hallé season, although the contract is back-dated to July 5th, the date of the first concert by the new Hallé Orchestra, in Bradford, Yorkshire.

WHERE HALLE GHOSTS WALK — Some present-day buildings in Manchester with great significance in the post-war history of the orchestra
Top: Inside the Albert Hall, Peter Street, where the Hallé weekday series of concerts was held from 1944 to 1951. The Methodist Mission hall held only 1,850, and for the cheapest tickets, sold at 1s, listeners had to sit literally underneath the extended platform on which the orchestra played. The ground floor of the building is now Brannigan's: this recent photograph shows the interior of the auditorium, from which the seats have been removed.
BOTTOM: The organ pipes may still be seen in the former Houldsworth Hall in Deansgate, now a restaurant (this photograph was taken during its incarnation as "Sticky Fingers"). This was the Hallé's first rehearsal room in Manchester and was used for a number of Barbirolli's classic recordings.

ABOVE: The former St Peter's Church School in Hewitt Street, behind Deansgate Station (more recently "The Boardwalk"). For many of the Barbirolli years, the upper storey here was the Hallé rehearsal room, and musicians had to climb the stairs while heavy instruments were hauled up by a hoist. It was notoriously cold, and the scene of a famous incident when Barbirolli stopped a marathon rehearsal because he heard the sound of a train whistle. When he exclaimed "What was that?", principal trumpet Sidney King replied: "The free world outside, Sir John."

BELOW: The refurbished interior of the Free Trade Hall, with Barbirolli and the Hallé Orchestra photographed in 1958, the orchestra's centenary season.

BARBIROLLI THE LEGEND:

Two studies of Sir John Barbirolli in full flight, one from early in his time with the
Hallé and one from the later years

LEFT: The lighter side of Hallé life: George Weldon and leader Martin Milner watch as the balloons cascade down on a Last Night of the Hallé Proms in the Free Trade Hall

BELOW: The finest hour. Sir John Barbarolli conducts Verdi's Otello in a concert performance to mark his own silver jubilee with the Hallé in May, 1968.

TOP: James Loughran conducts the Hallé Orchestra in the days when sideburns and hair over your ears were a must.
BOTTOM: Stanislaw Skrowaczewski pictured in action

TOP: Kent Nagano conducts the Hallé Orchestra
BOTTOM: The Bridgewater Hall, home of the Hallé from 1996

Hans Richter   Sir Thomas Beecham

Sir Hamilton Harty   Sir Malcolm Sargent

Hallé conductors in the first half of the 20th century

Sir John Barbirolli

James Loughran

Stanislaw Skrowaczewski

Kent Nagano

Hallé conductors since 1943

then when the audience response was lukewarm.[205] Elgar himself conducted the first Manchester performance of his *Symphony no. 2* on November 23rd, 1911 (but the work was not heard again in a Hallé concert until January, 1926).

The period under consideration thus included three world premieres (the Elgar symphony in 1908, the *Cello Concerto* by John Foulds, then a member of the orchestra, in 1911, and Granville Bantock's *Atalanta In Calydon* under Bantock in 1912), one English premiere,[206] and 36 first performances for Manchester (a third of them in a single season, 1911-12, when a variety of guest conductors chose programmes, in the interval between Richter's departure and Balling's permanent appointment).

It is noteworthy that Richter's introductions of new works to Manchester, though they may not have been particularly numerous, were often pieces which have since found a place in regular orchestral repertoire (as Fifield's comment, quoted above, implies). These included (in addition to the premieres mentioned above): Smetana's *From Bohemia's Wood And Fields* (January, 1905), Sibelius' *Symphony no. 2* (March, 1905), Franck's *Symphonic Variations* (October, 1905), Strauss's *Ein Heldenleben* (February, 1907), Sibelius' *Spring Song* (November, 1909), Strauss's *Don Quixote* (March, 1910) and Dukas' *The Sorcerer's Apprentice* (February, 1911).

Harty and after, 1925-1935

Analysis of the Hallé main series programmes[207] of 1925-35 (see Table 3.1) shows that repertoire overall was now more orientated to the contemporary than in Richter's time, with almost as many living composers represented as those who had died in the previous 50 years. In fact, the period 1925-35, as a whole, shows the highest proportion of music by living composers, of all five of those studied (see Table 1.1). These two groups together ("newer" music) also constitute a much larger percentage of the performed repertoire than in any other period selected.

A policy of innovation (in the sense that much of the music performed was new to Manchester ears) was carried through by Harty from 1925-6 to 1929-30 – the latter was an astonishing year, with 15 Manchester first performances and more works by living composers (42% of the total) than in any of the total of 50 seasons between 1903 and 1995 selected for this study. Philip Hammond quotes Harty as telling the *Daily Express*: "I have been accused in the past of neglecting modern works . . . Previously I have been afraid . . . However, we are going to take our

---

[205]Fifield, 1993.
[206]Fifield, 1993: 380, says that the Sibelius *Symphony no. 2* in 1905 (mentioned in the following paragraph) was also a British premiere, although the Hallé programme booklet of the time did not claim it as such.
[207]Harty's programmes are discussed in detail in Kennedy (1960): 244-263, who also includes a discussion of Harty's abilities as a musician: 214-216. There is also a discussion of Harty's programming at the Hallé in Hammond (1978).

chance."[208]   This policy of new music was maintained (courageously, against a background of economic depression) in the years that followed, until Harty's departure in 1933.

By December, 1930, when the economic tide was turning swiftly for the worse ("the present difficult times"), the Hallé Committee discussed "the poor support accorded by the audience to the modern works included . . . during the first half of the season". Harty himself suggested that programmes for the second half of the season "should be somewhat revised" and was "warmly supported" by the Musical Committee (a body which had been set up in January, 1924, at Harty's suggestion, to settle artistic arrangements in conjunction with him but whose discussions do not appear to have been minuted before December, 1933).

Audiences were considerably lower yet for each of the following three seasons. Whether matters might have been even worse without the change of policy is open to conjecture. One casualty of the new fearfulness was a planned performance of Stravinsky's *The Rite Of Spring* in February, 1932. A month beforehand, the Committee decided, "in view of the disastrous financial results of the present season", and because five extra rehearsals would be required, that the work should be "postponed".

But, despite the Committee's desire to make programmes less "modern", Harty actually made them less *varied* overall (see Table 3.2). Attendances did not recover for some time, however, although variety continued to be restricted, even after Harty left. The gradually reviving audience level by 1934-5 does, however, accompany a measureable shift away from the work of living composers: before jumping too hastily to conclusions from this fact, however, it should be recalled that Elgar, Delius and Holst died in 1934 and that they are and were among the most popular of British composers with British audiences.

Baroque music, though not the subject of "authentic" performance practice at this time, nonetheless had a firm position in the repertoire. Bach's works had a prominent place in the Hallé schedule: the programme of February 4th, 1926, proudly reported that the *Mass in B Minor* that night was the "fifth consecutive [ie, annual] performance given by the Society". Harty's own arrangements of Handel's *Water Music* and *Music For The Royal Fireworks* were widely played – not only by the Hallé – and his recordings of them with the London Symphony Orchestra sold large numbers. Vivaldi was occasionally offered to Hallé audiences, too. Beethoven, Berlioz, Brahms, Dvorak, Elgar, Haydn, Mozart, Richard Strauss, Tchaikovsky and Wagner were never absent from these Hallé seasons, and the music of Sibelius (then a living composer, as was Richard Strauss) was played every season from 1925 to 1935, except the last. Schubert was never absent, except in 1932-3, and Schumann absent only in 1927-8 and 1930-31.

[208]Hammond, 1978: 35-49.

Some whose representation suffered, in contrast, were Bruch, Cherubini, Grieg, Liszt (five performances only in 1925-35), Mendelssohn (though completely absent only in four seasons), and Weber (though absent only in three seasons). Debussy and Mahler gained more hearings than had been the case in their own lifetimes, and Rachmaninov's works began to be heard, chiefly in his personal appearances as solo pianist with the orchestra.   Other living composers introduced include Vaughan Williams, Prokoviev and Stravinsky.

Harty was an eirenic programme-maker with an eye for important new works. He gave the world premieres of Bantock's *Song Of Songs* (1926), Constant Lambert's *The Rio Grande* (Lambert conducted, and Harty played the piano, on December 12th, 1929), and Bax's *Overture To A Picaresque Comedy.* English premieres included music by Glazunov (1925), Ibert (1926), Vivaldi (1926), Respighi (1928), Mahler (the *Symphony no. 9* in 1930), Sibelius (1930), Shostakovich (the *Symphony no. 1* in 1931), and Richard Strauss (*Schlagobers* suite, 1932).

Harty's introductions of music to Manchester audiences included the following: in 1925-6 – the suite from Ravel's *Daphnis Et Chloe*, Fauré's *Ballade*, Enesco's *Rumanian Rhapsody no. 2*, Berlioz' *Requiem*, Respighi's *The Pines Of Rome*, Falla's *Nights In The Gardens Of Spain*; in 1926-7 – Sibelius' *The Swan Of Tuonela*, Chausson's *Symphony*, Vaughan Williams' *The Lark Ascending* and Bach's *First Brandenburg Concerto*; in 1927-8 – Falla's *The Three-Cornered Hat,* Mahler's *Symphony no. 4*; in 1928-9 – Kodaly's *Hary Janos* suite, Prokoviev's March from *The Love Of Three Oranges*; in 1929-30 –   Kodaly's *Psalmus Hungaricus*, Dvorak's *Te Deum*, Sibelius' *Fifth Symphony*, Walton's *Facade Suite* (conducted by the composer), Sibelius' *Violin Concerto*, Prokoviev's *Scythian Suite*, Warlock's *Capriol Suite*, Vaughan Williams' *Symphony no 3*, Sibelius' *Symphony no. 4*, Holst's *St Paul's Suite*; in 1930-31 – Sibelius' *Symphony no.3*, Ravel's *Bolero*, Prokoviev's *Piano Concerto no. 3*, Mahler's *Das Lied Von Der Erde*; in 1931-2 – Gershwin's *An American In Paris*, Sibelius' *Symphony no. 7*, Ravel's orchestration of *Pictures At An Exhibition*, Walton's *Viola Concerto*, Vaughan Williams' *Fantasia On A Theme Of Thomas Tallis*, Delius' *Mass Of Life*; in 1932-3 – Sibelius' *Symphony no. 1*, Mozart's *Symphony no. 29*, Walton's *Belshazzar's Feast,* Sibelius' *Tapiola*, Weinberger's Polka from *Schwanda The Bagpiper*, and Ravel's *Le Tombeau De Couperin.*

This remarkable list is perhaps the best evidence of Harty's gift for presenting works which have proved to be of lasting appeal. Of all Hallé conductors, he was the most successful in this respect (though it may be considered that the world of orchestral music at the time was particularly rich in new creative work). He also gave Elgar's *Symphony no. 2* its second Manchester performance (January 7th, 1926) and repeated it a fortnight later, after "many requests"; and in February, 1930, presented the *Cello Concerto*, which was only its second Manchester hearing (the first being in 1920 – it was next played in 1933).

However, some composers who have since become regularly heard were still rare in Hallé programmes. Rossini and Verdi were each played only once in the 10 years – an indication that the boundaries of Hallé repertoire at that time did not generally extend to Italian operatic overtures or excerpts (Wagner was still popular, however, usually in the form of "bleeding chunks" rather than complete works), and an item by Johann Strauss appears for the first time only in 1928.

Barbirolli 1945-1955

A look at the programmes of 1945 to 1955[209] shows that in the post-war years the Hallé's series each had its own character (see Tables 4.1 to 4.8). The mid-week series was now for the adventurous music-lover. Thus Beethoven, Schubert and Tchaikovsky took a less prominent place than before in this series (though their work was still clearly evident in the others), and Mendelssohn disappeared from it altogether. Bruckner was performed at the mid-week concerts only, as was Debussy. Grieg, on the other hand, was much more frequently found in the other, more "popular" series.

The Sunday series of concerts (held at Belle Vue from 1943, and after 1951-2 mainly at the Free Trade Hall) was a new and ambitious venture in Hallé history. It could well be that the "target audience" of the Sunday concerts was seen as the generation which had been introduced to music through the pre-war Municipal Concerts, along with an emerging audience of younger listeners who had discovered classical music through radio,[210] gramophone records and wartime concerts – and they were highly successful.

The new "Industrial" and "Proms" series, begun in 1952, show a shared concentration on works from the central part of the repertoire – that of composers who had died in the past 150 years, with a smaller representation of living composers and of those of an earlier era. Programming the Proms and Industrials in this way was undoubtedly a deliberate policy, as both series were designed to earn income principally through repertoire choice (expensive conductors and solo artists being eschewed), and the pattern reflects the most easily saleable symphony orchestra repertoire of the time.

Barbirolli's genius as a programme maker was recognised from the beginning and explicitly recalled when his achievement was assessed after his death.[211] Such was his breadth of sympathy that it is difficult to find a major composer from the Hallé repertoire of previous periods whose work was never played at this time,

---

[209]For further analysis of Barbirolli's programmes 1945-55, see Kennedy (1960: 328-330, 338-341, 347, 349-354)

[210]J M Keynes, first chairman of the Arts Council, credited the BBC with creating the new demand for orchestral music which became apparent during the war, "The Arts Council, The First Ten Years", 1955, quoted in Minihan, 1977: 227.

[211]"As musical director he had a genius for programme planning . . ." – from the Hallé Committee's formal tribute to Barbirolli recorded on September 29th, 1970.

though Cherubini was hardly ever included (I can find one example) and Turina likewise (Liszt is represented in only four of the 10 seasons studied in this period, and Bruch only once, compared with eight times in the 1903-13 seasons).

Among those whose work was introduced or assumed a more regular position were several French composers (Gounod, Bizet, Ibert, Fauré, Chabrier), along with de Falla, Verdi, Bruckner and Grieg (composers who seem to have been relatively neglected by Harty), and those who used more challenging styles, such as Bartok and Britten. Baroque music was not ignored, and the growing awareness of its being a specialist field was reflected in visits by the Boyd Neel Chamber Orchestra (the pioneers of what became the "authenticity" movement in baroque playing). However, Barbirolli included Bach, Handel, Corelli, Purcell and Vivaldi in his own programmes, using his own arrangements where symphony orchestra versions were not already available.

Barbirolli had certain favourites which alone represented their respective composers: Nicolai's *Overture to The Merry Wives Of Windsor*, Reznicek's *Overture to Donna Diana*, Wolf-Ferrari's *Overture to Susannah's Secret,* and Hindemith's *Metamorphoses On Themes By Weber,* for instance. He also introduced the "Viennese evening" to Hallé programmes, consisting mainly of a few lighter classical works (typically Mozart and Schubert), waltzes and polkas by the Strauss family, and, more often than not, the suite from Richard Strauss's *Der Rosenkavalier,* which could conveniently be set in the Viennese waltz tradition. The first such programme seems to have been on April 14th, 1946. These became immensely popular. (Johann Strauss's *Emperor Waltz* received its first Hallé performance only on November 2nd, 1947 – an indication of the new acceptability of music of that genre in the symphonic repertoire).

Themed programmes, such as selections of ballet or operatic music, began to appear. Barbirolli also championed young British composers such as Alan Rawsthorne and Lennox Berkeley. Among works which he introduced to Manchester were Barber's *Adagio For Strings* (which he had greeted enthusiastically when with the New York Philharmonic in 1939), [212] Bartok's *Violin Concerto no. 2* (then the only one extant), Moeran's *Violin* and *Cello Concertos,* Copland's *Billy The Kid Suite,* Finzi's *Dies Natalis,* Roussel's *Bacchus and Ariadne Suite,* Richard Strauss's *Oboe Concerto,* Britten's *Violin Concerto,* Mahler's *Kindertotenlieder,* Schoenberg's *Verklarte Nacht,* Hindemith's *Mathis Der Maler Symphony,* Vaughan Williams' *Symphonies nos. 4* and *6,* Richard Strauss's *Duet-Concertino* (the English premiere) and *Metamorphosen,* Bartok's *Concerto For Orchestra,* Prokoviev's *Suites* from *Cinderella* and *Lieutenant Kije,* Roussel's *Symphony no. 3,* Tippett's *Concerto For Double String Orchestra,* Ravel's *Piano Concerto,* Stravinsky's *Symphony In Three Movements,* Vaughan Williams' *Sinfonia Antartica* (its world premiere) and *Job,* Berg's *Violin Concerto,*

---

[212]Though Toscanini and the NBC Symphony gave the first performance. See Barbirolli In America 1936-1943, in: *Glorious John,* ed. Paul Brooks (The Barbirolli Society, Oxford, 1999).

Richard Strauss's *Four Last Songs*, and Donatoni's *Concerto For Timpani* (its English premiere).

Barbirolli and Loughran, 1965-1975

In the ten years from 1965 to 1975 (see Tables 5.1 to 5.8), despite the change of conductor, the level of consistency is remarkable, and the general shift of profile shown in the composer analysis (a slightly greater bias to the past than in 1945-55) is explicable as an inevitable broadening of the repertoire with the passage of time. Looking at the weekday series programmes, in 1945-55 the proportion of "newer" music had been in the range 45% to 61%, and in 1965-75 it lay in the range 46% to 60% (except for 1968-9, Barbirolli's silver jubilee year, in which it was 38% but, as the low Herfindahl Index figure shows, there was greater historical diversity than ever before).[213]

One explicit repertoire change made in the hiatus of 1970 (after Maurice Handford had accepted the post of principal conductor of the Calgary Orchestra and as negotiations were in hand for a successor to Barbirolli) was that performances of major operas should in future not exceed one per season and should be made "on merit" – this all but removed what had been a characteristic plank in Barbirolli's planning, continued by Handford. Clive Smart comments[214] that at the time this was a "partly political" decision – to impress on the Arts Council that this element in Hallé programmes would be lost if the Palace Theatre, Manchester, became (as some hoped) a second home for the Royal Opera.[215]

James Loughran's impact may be observed to the extent that in 1971-2 (the first season in which he had a hand in planning), the Composer Variety Index is higher than for any recent years, and higher yet in 1974-5. His first four seasons outdid most of the Barbirolli seasons I have analysed in composer variety. The proportion of "newer" music was also particularly high in 1972-3 (almost equalling the high point of Barbirolli's 1945-55 years) before two seasons with low figures. The explanation for what seems to have been a partial loss of nerve about "newer" music at this point (and the increase in variety in 1974-5 – possibly as a form of compensation?) may well be the unsettling effect of unprecedentedly high inflation.

The Hallé Sunday series shows a similarly wide range of composer representation, though with a slightly more pronounced bias to the past when compared with the analysis of 1945-55, though again the total proportion of "newer" music is not dissimilar from that period. The seasons of 1970-71 and 1973-

---

[213]The programmes of 1965 to 1975 are discussed in detail in Kennedy, 1982: 103-124.
[214]Personal communication.
[215] A proposal which, despite Royal Opera seasons in Manchester in 1981 and 1983, was finally vetoed by the Arts Council chairman Sir William Rees-Mogg – see Tooley, 1999: 240-1.

4 were exceptionally low in this respect – possibly a reflection of concern over the financial situation at the time – and there were five "Manchester premieres" in the 1973-4 Sunday series. A later Committee minute states that in 1973-4 the Sunday series changed "from a popular series to a more serious series", but there seems to be no contemporary evidence of a specific decision to this effect, and the evidence is not clear-cut. It is possible that memory was influenced by the fact that the second concert of the series was a Handford programme including works by Maderna and Boulez – which *was* unusual for the Sunday concerts – and the policies of James Loughran had made a difference, too.

The Industrial Concerts (renamed Opus One series from 1971-2) were, by the mid-sixties, fewer in number than in the first years from their introduction in 1952-3. They were given as pairs, with six in the series until 1967-8, four in 1968-9, five in 1969-70, six in 1970-71, and seven from 1971-2. In comparison with the early years, there is a distinct shift towards older repertoire from 1968-9 onwards (although still very little pre-classical music). Composer Variety of programmes was consistently high (except in 1966-7), and represents on average the highest degree of variety of the three winter series offered by the Hallé at the time. This was, not surprisingly, the result of a policy of providing music to appeal to the new concert-goer, within a limited series. The fact that sell-outs were recorded at every concert from 1971-2 to 1974-5 shows that this was eminently successful.

The Hallé Proms, likewise, at this stage exhibit a high degree of Composer Variety, and were increased in number from 1970-71 (when there were 11 in the series), to 12 in 1971-2, 13 in 1972-3 and 17 in 1974-5. The series of 1971-2 to 1974-5 were extremely successful in attendances, and the historical variety of their programmes increased markedly at the same time.

Consideration of individual composers' representation in the 10 years from 1965 to 1975 shows a few lost from repertoire (Bax, for instance, not played after 1967-8; Gounod, not played after 1969-70; Smetana, played only twice in the 10 years; Ibert, not played) – a few less favoured than before (Mendelssohn was not played in the weekday series at all from 1965-75, although featured in the others; Schumann appeared in only six seasons; Franck in only four) – and a few more favoured (Stravinsky and Bartok appeared in every season; Walton in every season but one; Nielsen was heard in seven). Mahler and Bruckner performances became more frequent: Barbirolli's direction of their symphonies becoming highlights of the mid-week season in the closing years of his life, and under James Loughran's principal conductorship such performances were equally highly prized.

The occurrence of "first performances in Manchester" was remarkably high compared with 1945-55 – especially in the light of the fact that Manchester had now enjoyed 20 years of Barbirolli's programming. Maurice Handford (who took an increasingly leading role after his appointment as Associate Conductor in 1966, particularly in the introduction of new music) gave the first Manchester performances of Tippett's *Concerto For Orchestra* (1966), Messiaen's *Turangalila-Symphonie* and Lutoslawski's *Concerto For Orchestra* in 1968, and Messiaen's *Et Exspecto Resurrectionem Mortuorum* in 1970.

James Loughran continued the tradition with first Manchester performances of Ligeti's *Lontano* and Goehr's *Little Symphony* in 1972, Ligeti's *Melodien* and the world premiere of Robert Simpson's *Symphony no. 4* (dedicated to Loughran) in 1973, and Havergal Brian's *Symphony no. 10* in 1975. He also explored previously unheard work (to Hallé audiences) by composers such as Berg, Schoenberg, Ives and Hindemith.

Skrowaczewski and Nagano, 1985-1995

The ten years from 1985 to 1995 are described in Tables 6.1 to 6.8. The years of Skrowaczewski's principal conductorship, dogged as they were by difficult financial circumstances, were characterised by remarkably high artistic aspirations and achievement.

The proportion of works in the main weekday series (now 15 or 16 concerts in total) by composers who were living or had died in the previous 50 years was lower than in 1965-75 or 1945-55 – an effect explicable (as in the contrast of 1965-75 with 1945-55) as due to the broadening of the repertoire with the passage of time – but nonetheless lay in the range 34%-52% (in 1965-75 it had been 38%-60%), and Composer Variety was greater than in 1965-75. The seasons from 1985-6 to 1990-1 compare, on average, to James Loughran's first years in the latter respect.

In 1986-7, Skrowaczewski's programmes produce the highest Composer Variety figure of the 1985-95 decade, but the following two seasons indicate the lowest – a sign, it may well be, of a struggle to achieve a more acceptable "box office" at that point because of financial problems. The proportion of "newer" music in 1986-7 was also the highest of the 1985-95 decade, at 52%, but this figure falls to the lowest of the decade in 1987-8 and remains low in the next two seasons. The Herfindahl Index also shows that the degree of historical concentration in the programmes was at its greatest in 1989-90.

A similar pattern is observable in the Sunday series, which between 1985 and 1990 contained 23%-37% of "newer" music, compared with a range of 26%-52% in the same series in 1965-75, and in which Composer Variety was considerably higher than 20 years before. Again, historical concentration was at its highest in 1989-90.

Taking the view that artistic decisions were likely to have been consciously influenced by financial circumstances, and bearing in mind that each season must now have been planned well before the financial results of the previous one were available, it seems likely that the effect of any one season's results would impact mainly on the second season after it. It is possible, therefore, that as a consequence of the losses of 1985-6, the programmes of 1987-8 (both Thursday and Sunday) showed a dramatic decrease in "newer" music; and that the improved results of 1986-7 resulted in the slight increase in "newer" music (in both series) in 1988-9's programmes. It has been noted that the very poor financial results of 1987-8 were seen by the Hallé Committee as acceptable only in the light of the promised Arts Council appraisal of the Hallé's situation as a whole. This may explain the relatively unchanged proportion of "newer" music in the Thursday series, and the fact that its share significantly increased in the Sunday series, in 1989-90. The Sunday series consisted of 15 or 16 concerts before 1989-90, but was reduced to 13 in that season, which may also be a factor in the increased proportion of "newer" music.

In the Thursday series in 1990-91 (Skrowaczewski's last as principal conductor) "newer" music increased to 49% (but it was reduced to 41% in 1991-2 – this was, however, a longer series, with 17 concerts in all). Works by living composers made up 26% of all items, exceeding James Loughran's highest figure in 1970-75 and any of Kent Nagano's subsequent seasons from 1992-3 to 1994-5. In the Sunday series in 1990-91, "newer" music decreased to 20%, and the series itself was reduced to eight concerts (apart from Handel's *Messiah*), while Composer Variety also decreased (and in 1991-2 "newer" music's share was 18%, in a series of nine concerts, plus *Messiah*, although Composer Variety increased). The 1991-2 season was the product of the Musical Advisory Committee and the Hallé management, in addition to Skrowcazewski.

The shortening of the Sunday series was the principal outcome of the "Retrenchment Policy" adopted late in 1988. Musical policy, though, was re-affirmed as "challenging" for the Thursday series, and "totally popular and distinct from the Thursday series" for the Opus One programmes.

Consideration of individual composers' representation in Hallé programmes from 1985 to 1995 as a whole shows no major variation from the pattern followed when James Loughran was principal conductor, except for the new living composers introduced to the Thursday (and to a lesser extent, the Sunday) series. Bax was no longer played, Bliss only once, and Verdi, Wagner and Weber were played less frequently after 1988-9. Shostakovich's music was also completely absent from three seasons between 1990-91 and 1994-5, whereas it had found a place in every one from 1965 to 1975. Saint-Saens seems to be the only composer from the past to have made a "comeback", being played in every season from 1987-88 to 1994-5, whereas his work was almost completely absent in 1965-75. Prokoviev was, unusually, played in all three series in 1991-2 – the result of a decision by the Musical Advisory Committee to feature Mozart and Prokoviev particularly in that season's concerts, although the idea of advertising it as a "Mozart-Prokoviev season" was rejected.

It is worthwhile to consider Hallé Manchester concerts after 1985 in some detail, as the Hallé's artistic standards, in particular its choice of repertoire and artists, became the subject of dispute with the Arts Council in the late 1980s, and in the 1990s of disagreement within its own management.

In January, 1986, the Hallé welcomed Witold Lutoslawski to conduct a concert of his own works – of which three were first performances in Manchester. The 1985-6 season also contained appearances in both Thursday and Sunday concerts by the violinist Anne-Sophie Mutter, in the Beethoven and Brahms *concertos*, and by Nigel Kennedy in the Walton. Guest conductors included Nicholas Cleobury, Andrew Davis, Bryden Thomson (with David Matthews' *Symphony no. 3*, commissioned by the Hallé), Lawrence Foster (with the British premiere of Mark Neikrug's *Violin Concerto*), Mark Elder, Sir Neville Marriner, Richard Hickox, Sir Charles Groves, Matthias Bamert and Neeme Jarvi. The CBSO appeared in the Thursday series as a guest orchestra. Skrowaczewski conducted a wide variety of repertoire, including Panufnik, and the first performance of Bach's *Magnificat* at the Hallé Concerts. The Proms of 1986 boasted a roster of conductors including Richard Hickox, Andrew Litton, Maurice Handford, Sian Edwards, Bryden Thomson and Vernon Handley.

The 1986-7 season included the first concerts (an Opus One set) conducted by the Hallé's new Assistant Conductor, Adrian Leaper, and guest conductors included Sir Charles Mackerras, Andrew Davis, Sir Charles Groves, Mark Elder, Bryden Thomson and Andrew Litton. Skrowaczewski gave the first Manchester performances of George Benjamin's *Ringed By The Flat Horizon,* Szymanowski's *Stabat Mater* and Penderecki's *Violin Concerto.* The 1987 Proms included Bryden Thomson, Adrian Leaper and Yan Pascal Tortelier among conductors.

Conductors for 1987-8 included Sir Michael Tippett, sharing the rostrum on January 29th, 1988, with Nicholas Cleobury and directing his own *Symphony no. 3* (part of a Tippett-Debussy Festival which involved other Manchester musical organisations besides the Hallé). Rudolf Barshai and Vernon Handley also appeared; Marc Soustrot conducted the first Manchester performance of Dutilleux' *Symphony no. 1,* and Okko Kamu the first Manchester performance of Sallinen's *Symphony no. 5,* with Igor Oistrakh the soloist in Tchaikovsky's *Violin Concerto.* The Sunday series included Tippett's *The Mask Of Time* (part of the festival) conducted by Sir Charles Groves, and Skrowaczewski gave first Manchester performances of Ravel's *Un Barque Sur L'Ocean,* Gerhard's *Violin Concerto,* Honegger's *Pastorale D'Eté,* Martinu's *Oboe Concerto,* and the first Hallé performance since 1908 of Bruckner's *Te Deum.* Murray Perahia appeared as soloist in Grieg's *Piano Concerto,* and Cho-Liang Lin in Nielsen's *Violin Concerto.* Sir Charles Groves appeared twice in the 1988 Proms, which also featured Adrian Leaper, James Judd, Yan Pascal Tortelier and Bryden Thomson.

Andrzej Panufnik appeared to conduct his own *Symphony no. 9* in the 1988-9 season, and the first Hallé performance since 1968 of Messiaen's *Turangalila-*

Symphonie was given under Serge Baudo, with Jeanne Loriod on the Ondes Martenot. Violin soloists included Kyung-Wha Chung (Bartok's *Concerto no. 2,* under Andrew Davis) and Joshua Bell (Prokoviev's *Concerto no. 1,* with Skrowaczewski). Yehudi Menuhin appeared as conductor, Radu Lupu played Mozart's *Piano Concerto no. 9,* and Sir Charles Groves conducted Berlioz' *L'Enfance Du Christ* shortly before Christmas. Skrowaczewski introduced the music of John Tavener, and John McCabe was honoured with a 50th birthday concert conducted by James Loughran. Richard Hickox, Yan Pascal Tortelier and Sian Edwards were among guest conductors, and the Proms of 1989 featured Hickox, Leaper, Judd and Jean-Bernard Pommier, among others.

The season of 1989-90 was notable for the inclusion, in the programme booklets for the opening concerts of all three series, of a statement from Skrowaczewski about his programme policy. It amounted to a defence of the inclusion of "contemporary works" although, as we have seen, there were no longer as many of these in Hallé programmes as there had been 20 years earlier. But Skrowaczewski's own concerts were dominated by major works of the established repertoire: Mahler's *Das Lied Von Der Erde* and *Symphony no. 2 ("Resurrection"),* Britten's *War Requiem* and Bruckner's *Symphony no. 3* among them. New music came from guest conductors such as George Benjamin (his own) and Jan Krenz (*Masques,* by Szymanowski arr. Krenz). Igor Oistrakh played Shostakovich's *Violin Concerto no. 1* with Adrian Leaper, and Ralph Kirshbaum Schumann's *Cello Concerto,* with Yan Pascal Tortelier. The Proms were conducted largely by James Judd, Adrian Leaper and Owain Arwel Hughes.

The 1990-91 season was Skrowaczewski's last as principal conductor and had been subject to some "critical remarks" by members of the Board, while still at the planning stage, on the grounds of the programmes' "non-saleability". It ended with Bruckner's *Symphony no. 8* and two performances (Thursday and Sunday) of Beethoven's *Missa Solemnis.* Earlier he had given the first Manchester performances of Schnittke's *Violin Concerto no. 4* (Gyorgy Pauk), Barber's *Violin Concerto,* Debussy's *Le Martyre De Saint-Sebastien,* and (for once half-breaking his self-imposed exclusion of his own compositions from Hallé programmes) Bach's *Toccata and Fugue in D minor,* arranged by Skrowaczewski. Sir Neville Marriner conducted Tippett's *A Child Of Our Time,* Hiroyuki Iwaki brought Takemitsu's *Dream Time* to Manchester, Kent Nagano (in his Hallé debut) introduced Takemitsu's *A String Around Autumn,* with Nobuko Imai, and Marc Soustrot conducted Messiaen's *L'Ascension.* Luciano Berio conducted a concert of his own and Bruno Maderna's work, all of which was new to Manchester, and James Judd gave Mahler's *Symphony no. 6,* as well as the English premiere of Herbert Willi's *Kleines Kammerkonzert.* In the Sunday series Nagano's concert included Tchaikovsky's *Piano Concerto* played by Mari Kodama – later to be his wife – and Amanda Roocroft sang in Brahms' *Requiem* under Tadaaki Otaka. Conductors in the 1991 Proms included Owain Arwel Hughes, Adrian Leaper, Yuri Simonov and James Judd.

The Musical Advisory Committee's season (1991-2) marked the 200th anniversary of Mozart's death with a complete concert performance of *Idomeneo*, under Skrowaczewski, who also conducted the first Hallé performance of Szymanowski's *Violin Concerto no. 2*, with Lydia Mordkovitch (herself a former Hallé violin section member) the soloist. George Benjamin conducted a programme including two pieces of his own new to Manchester, as well as Ligeti's *Lontano* and Berg's *Altenberglieder*. Lawrence Foster brought Enescu's *Symphony no. 1* to Manchester, and Sir Charles Groves conducted the Hallé's first performance of Mathias's *Violin Concerto* (soloist Gyorgy Pauk). Other conductors included Mark Elder, James Judd (who brought Arnold's *Symphony no. 1*, in the context of a city-wide Haydn-Arnold festival), Yehudi Menuhin, Tadaaki Otaka, Mathias Bamert and Vernon Handley, who conducted the closing all-English programme, with Tasmin Little the soloist in Elgar's *Violin Concerto* and Bryn Terfel the soloist in Walton's *Belshazzar's Feast*. Adrian Leaper, Lawrence Foster, Sir Charles Groves, Paul Daniel (with Katherine Stott the soloist in Grieg's *Piano Concerto*) and Tadaaki Otaka (with Amanda Roocroft in Richard Strauss's *Vier Letzte Lieder*) were among the Opus One series conductors. Of the seven Hallé concerts in the Summer Proms, four were conducted by James Judd and one each by Owain Arwel Hughes and Paul Daniel

Kent Nagano's musical directorship saw the proportion of "newer" music in the Thursday series stabilise around 40%, with works by living composers making up 10% to 16% of items, in a Thursday series which began with 17 concerts in 1992-3 and then reverted to 16 or 15 (in respect of "newer" music, his record is more consistent than was the case under Skrowaczewski), and includes the highest consistent degree of Composer Variety in programmes so far recorded in this analysis (an index average of 0.73) – not dissimilar to the highest figures of James Loughran's early years, but a more consistent sequence. The Herfindahl Index also shows the high level of historical differentiation of his programmes: only Barbirolli's jubilee season of 1968-9 and one James Loughran season (1974-5), from those analysed, show lower levels of concentration.

On Sundays "newer" music increased to 28% over eight concerts in 1992-3 (Composer Variety increased also), then to 46% in 1993-4 (a remarkable change in the character of the Sunday concerts), after which the series was reduced to five, with "newer" music accounting for only 20% of items played. The Herfindahl indices show higher historical differentiation in Kent Nagano's Sunday programmes, as in the case of the Thursday series.

Kent Nagano made the comment in his first press conference in 1992 that Mendelssohn and Schumann seemed to have been under-represented in Hallé programmes, a lack which he proposed to rectify. He was right to the extent that in 1990-1 Schumann was absent in all series (as was Schubert), and Mendelssohn was played only in the Opus One series, but these were aberrations in a longer-term pattern which did not show neglect of these composers compared with 1965-75, and which remained much the same (in the Hallé's Manchester programmes as a whole) in subsequent seasons under Nagano's musical directorship.

The aim of the Hallé's repertoire planning for 1993-4 was explicitly to have more Mozart, Haydn, Beethoven, Schumann and Mendelssohn, and fewer large-scale Romantic works, in the main series – and Nagano, in an interview in 1994, referred to this, with the comment "It's lamentable that one doesn't often get to hear performances geared to that repertoire in big symphonic halls".[216]

Kent Nagano had been appointed music director by the time the 1992-3 season began (though not yet officially principal conductor), and conducted the opening concerts of both the Sunday and Thursday series, plus one other Sunday concert and three Thursday ones. His own programmes were remarkable for music new to Manchester: the first Sunday one beginning with the United Kingdom premiere of Olivier Messiaen's *Un Sourire* and including *El Dorado* by John Adams, which the Hallé had premiered a few days before in Barrow-in-Furness. His second and third Thursday programmes brought to Manchester Stockhausen's *In Friendship* and two works by Boulez, and soloists in his concerts included Tatiana Nikolaeva (in Schumann's *Piano Concerto*) and Midori (in Mendelssohn's *Violin Concerto*). Other conductors in the Thursday series included Jean-Bernard Pommier, Skrowaczewski, James Judd, Mathias Bamert, Paul Daniel, Vernon Handley, Yehudi Menuhin and Gunther Herbig, and soloists included Shura Cherkassky, Steven Isserlis, Joanna McGregor and Nobuko Imai. Witold Lutoslawski conducted another concert of his own works (with Paul Crossley the soloist in his *Piano Concerto*), and the season ended with a guest appearance by the St Petersburg Philharmonic Orchestra under Mariss Jansons.

Conductors in the Sunday series included James Judd, Rudolf Barshai, Mathias Bamert, Sir Neville Marriner and Gunther Herbig, and in the Opus One series Skrowaczewski, Raymond Leppard, Vernon Handley, Sian Edwards and Yuri Simonov. Although comparisons are enormously difficult to make, it would appear that in 1992-3 the Sunday series, although made up of eight concerts only, apart from Handel's *Messiah*, became more similar than before to the Thursday series, in respect of programme contents and the distinction of artists taking part.

The Summer Proms took on a new look, designed to be a complete musical festival in themselves and including solo recitals (Amanda Roocroft, Julian Lloyd Webber, Evelyn Glennie), chamber music and a guest ensemble (the Hanover Band) as well as the Hallé's orchestral concerts. Nagano conducted the first two programmes.

The 1993-4 season may be regarded as the first on which Nagano stamped his individuality completely. His own programmes included the world premiere of *Cor D'Oeuvre* by John Casken (now Manchester University Professor of Music), and the first Hallé performances of Dutilleux' *Le Mystere De L'Instant* and George

[216]Ticket To Ride. *Classical Music,* September 3rd, 1994.

Benjamin's *At First Light* (Benjamin conducted a Sunday concert of music by himself, Berlioz, Messiaen, Ligeti and Ravel). Soloists appearing with Nagano included Viktoria Mullova in Berg's *Violin Concerto* and Franco Gulli and Nobuko Imai in Mozart's *Sinfonia Concertante for violin and viola.*

Franco Gulli also appeared as a conductor, as did Vernon Handley, Lawrence Foster, Andrew Litton, Yehudi Menuhin, Oliver Knussen (bringing Birtwistle's *The Triumph Of Time* to Manchester), Raymond Leppard, Sergiu Commissiona, Skrowaczewski and Luciano Berio (in a concert including the UK premiere of his own *Epiphanies*). Nagano conducted two of the eight Sunday concerts, and others were directed by George Malcolm, George Benjamin, Yehudi Menuhin, and John Adams (a programme including first Manchester performances of his own *The Chairman Dances* and *Fearful Symmetries*, and of John Cage's *First Construction In Metal*). Soloists in the Thursday series included Gyorgy Pauk and Ralph Kirshbaum (in the Brahms *Double Concerto*), Radu Lupu (in Mozart's *Piano Concerto no. 18*) and Shura Cherkassky (in Chopin's *Piano Concerto no. 2*), and in the Sunday series John Lill (Beethoven's *Piano Concerto no. 3*) and Midori (Prokoviev's *Violin Concerto no. 2*).

Nagano conducted a set of Opus One concerts in which the programme was Vaughan Williams' *Sinfonia Antartica* – its first Hallé performance since 1954 – and Stravinsky's *The Rite Of Spring*. Other conductors in this series were Lawrence Foster, Claire Gibault (Nagano's colleague at the Atelier Lyrique of the Opéra de Lyon), Yehudi Menuhin, Skrowaczewski, and Owain Arwel Hughes (with Evelyn Glennie the soloist in Milhaud's *Marimba Concerto* and her own arrangement of Saint-Saens' *Introduction and Rondo Capriccioso*, both new to Manchester).

The 1994 Proms were similar in concept to those of 1993, with recitals (by Simon Keenlyside, Moura Lympany and Stephen Isserlis), chamber music, and orchestral concerts including two conducted by Nagano, and the extra event mentioned in an earlier chapter, in the Dancehouse Theatre, in which the Hallé joined forces with the Royal Exchange Theatre to present Stravinsky's *Oedipus Rex*, Schoenberg's *A Survivor From Warsaw* and Mahler's *Lieder Eines Fahrenden Gesellen*, in semi-staged versions.

The Thursday series of 1994-5 included two world premieres: *The Origin Of The Harp*, by Thomas Ades, and . . .*Into The Gyre Of A Madder Dance*, by Anthony Gilbert of the Royal Northern College of Music. Nagano conducted eight programmes, which included appearances by Maxim Vengerov (Brahms' *Violin Concerto*) and Kyung Wha-Chung (Bruch's *Violin Concerto*), and by Yefim Bronfman (Bartok's *Piano Concerto no. 2*), and near the end of the season gave the first Hallé performance of *Bluebeard's Castle* by Bartok. Other conductors included Bernhard Klee, Gunther Pichler, George Benjamin (bringing his own *Sudden Time* as well as performing Ravel, Messiaen and Stravinsky), Ole Schmidt and Lukas Foss, while in the shorter-than-ever Sunday series Richard Hickox (with

Tippett's *A Child Of Our Time*) featured along with Owain Arwel Hughes, John Currie and Nagano. In the Opus One series Nagano conducted two programmes, and other conductors included Gerard Korsten (with Christian Blackshaw soloist in Mozart's *Piano Concerto no. 20*), and Raymond Leppard. Manchester Camerata appeared in this series as guest orchestra, with a baroque programme.

The Opus One series of this season, while containing relatively little new music, was characterised more clearly than before by programmes of the kind which would have been found in earlier years on Sundays or even Thursdays. Thus a process of assimilation of the characteristics of the three Hallé winter series seems to have been, by this time, all but accomplished.

The 1995 Summer Proms, however – clearly influenced by a lack of box office success with the festival concept of the two previous years – reverted almost completely to their former pattern in a wide-ranging orchestral series, with film music, Gilbert and Sullivan, Viennese waltzes, Cole Porter, Jerome Kern and Gershwin alongside the standard repertoire. Ole Schmidt conducted one programme, and Peter Donohoe gave a solo piano recital and played Rachmaninov's *Piano Concerto no. 2* with the orchestra, under Barry Wordsworth.

Analysis of the Opus One programmes throughout the 10 years from 1985 to 1995 (now firmly settled as eight programmes per season, each given three times) is notable for the almost complete disappearance of music by living composers: the average over 10 years was 2%, whereas in 1965-75 it had been 8%. The proportion of music by living composers and those who had died in the previous 50 years was in the range 15%-33% (in 1965-75 it was 25%-60%). In other words, the great majority of works played were composed before the Second World War, at the latest. Composer Variety was slightly less, on average, in these programmes than in 1965-75.

The Summer Proms programmes seem to have avoided "newer" music in proportion to the degree of anxiety, at any given time, to achieve a good "box office". Composer Variety in these programmes was similar to those in the Opus One series and slightly higher than it had been in 1965-75, but the length of the Prom series was reduced, after 1991, from a range of 11 to 13 evenings (plus two to four additional concerts in the G-Mex exhibition centre, the last of which were given in 1991), to 7 concerts in 1992, 12 in 1993, 10 in 1994 and 11 in 1995. The G-Mex concerts were an (at first) audacious method of securing large audiences for very accessible programmes in the former Central Station train hall in Manchester, where the acoustics were every bit as bad as might have been expected. But, with some effective sound reinforcement, astute marketing and a seating plan which included groups around tables, with canapés and champagne served, as well as ordinary block seats, they proved highly successful.

Chapter 12

Prices and attendances

As with the analysis of repertoire in the last chapter, the figures I draw on here are restricted to the five periods, each of 10 years, which I have selected for detailed statistical study from the century of the Hallé Concerts Society's existence.

1903-1913

Hallé attendances (see Table 2.2)[217] throughout the seasons from 1903-4 to 1912-13 showed a gradual long-term decline, except for the "Jubilee Season" of 1907-8 and the following one, which temporarily halted the process. Richter's last season (an estimated average 63% of capacity) was attended by about 17% fewer than his first (estimated average 76%): however, neither the interregnum season nor Balling's first attracted significantly greater attendances overall. Clearly the Hallé did not enjoy continuous full houses in this period (the Free Trade Hall capacity was 2,400), but box office receipts became more volatile in 1911-12 (attendance apparently ranging from 55% to 99%), the interregnum year, and 1912-13 (from 53% to 100%). The 99% and 100% attendances were for the annual Christmas-time performance of Handel's *Messiah*.

Ticket prices were stable. Subscribers paid between 2s 6d and 5s per concert, and non-subscribers from 1s, for standing room, to 7s 6d, throughout the period under consideration. Converted to 1995 values by use of the Cost Of Living and Retail Price Indices,[218] this corresponds to a price range of about £5 to £10 for subscribers and £2 to £15 for non-subscribers.[219] But applying the "leisure

---

[217]Estimated attendances based on concert receipts figures included in Hallé annual accounts.
[218]Formula adopted from Newman & Foster, 1995, and adjusted to 1995 value by reference to the Retail Price Index published by the Central Statistical Office (HMSO, London, 1995).
[219]It is important to remember that over such long periods of time the calculations produced by these indices understate the real fall in the value of money as applied to a particular item of expenditure, because the "shopping baskets" on which they are based are changed from time to time, and often novel electrical and mechanical goods are introduced when they are priced at a

spending" comparison of the cost of beer in a public bar (one of the few items of price data which were consistently recorded for the whole of the 20th century in Britain), shows that the cheapest Hallé ticket, at 1s, was equivalent in price to six pints of beer at this time, and the most expensive, at 7s 6d, to 45 pints[220] – which is the equivalent in monetary value of a range of £10 to £75 today (a consideration which may have motivated the working class of Manchester to spend their hard-earned cash on beer rather than Hallé concerts).

1925-1935

The five years beginning in 1925 were the peak of Harty's achievement with the Hallé. Knighted in that year, he attracted large audiences until the impact of the Depression from 1930-31 onwards (see Table 3.2). Manchester Hallé tickets were priced at 3s 6d to 10s in 1925, with standing room at 1s 2d – more, in nominal terms, than before the First World War. In December, 1925, the lowest seat price was reduced to 3s. This remained the price spread until November, 1931, when the top price was increased to 10s 3d, and standing room to 1s 3d.

The value of money had, however, halved between 1903 and 1925, according to the Prices and Incomes Index. The price of beer had gone up by 250%. The Hallé's prices were, in real terms, conspicuously lower than in Richter's day. Retail Price Index calculations show negative inflation from 1925 to 1933 – the value of money was rising, not falling. However, while wages may have stayed level or been cut, some costs rose. The price of beer was 5d a pint in 1925, and from 1931 was recorded as 7d. Converted to 1995 values, the Hallé price range was approximately £3 (£2.50 from 1935) to £10, and standing room was about £1.25. By the "beer standard", the cheapest Hallé ticket was worth three pints, and the most expensive 24 pints, in 1925: in 1931 the range was from two pints to 18 pints, and in 1935 from less than two pints to 15 pints.

Attendances were very variable. The annual performances of *Messiah* (there were two on succeeding evenings until 1933) were sold out in 1925, 1927, 1928, 1929 and 1930, but even they suffered thereafter. Other programmes were much less reliable: attendances were around 50% to 80% for 1925/6 (average 65%), and by the vintage season of 1929/30 they were around 55% to 85% (average 70%). But they fell drastically in the Depression years (see Table 3.2 and chapter 3).

1945-1955

Data on attendance figures in the 1945-55 period (see Tables 4.2, 4.4, 4.6 and 4.8) are difficult to assemble, as the Hallé's records are incomplete and do not facilitate comparisons. The Committee minutes state that in 1945-6, the first year of duplicated mid-week concerts in the Albert Hall, Peter Street (one of

luxury level and retained in the calculation when their prices fall with increasing mass production – see Newman & Foster,1995.
[220]Price of 1 pint of beer in a public bar taken from tables published in Newman and Foster, 1995.

Manchester's two Methodist Central Halls, with a capacity of 1,850), the Wednesdays were almost completely sold out to season ticket holders before the season began,[221] as were both series in 1946-7, when 20,000 copies of the season prospectus were sold. In 1947-8 the Wednesday series was almost completely sold by September, with the Thursday over two-thirds sold.

The annual report for 1945-6 notes "enormous audiences" at the Sunday concerts (probably in the early part of the 1946-7 season) at the King's Hall (a wooden stadium, also used for boxing, political rallies and circuses) in Belle Vue amusement park in Gorton, which "have made musical history". In his report to the 1950 annual general meeting, chairman Philip Godlee was able to record that "every concert since the orchestra came back from abroad has been sold out . . . Belle Vue was packed on a recent foggy Sunday evening with 6,000 citizens . . .." Average attendances there throughout 1945-6 to 1950-51 exceeded 5,000 per concert.

Venues and concert patterns changed from autumn, 1951, with the re-opening of the Free Trade Hall (capacity 2,450). Up to this point, the Hallé Manchester concerts consisted of a fortnightly series (from October to April) of 15 paired performances in the Albert Hall, and between 17 and 23 Sunday concerts, from October to May, at Belle Vue. The Free Trade Hall was re-opened with nine consecutive daily concerts, including the Hamburg Radio Orchestra, Concertgebouw and BBC Symphony Orchestra as well as the Hallé, followed by 20 weekly Thursday concerts, and 18 weekly Sunday ones, with four of the latter duplicated on the adjacent Saturday. But in 1952-3 the pattern of 15 paired fortnightly midweek concerts was reintroduced, with 14 Sunday concerts also at the Free Trade Hall, and eight back at Belle Vue. Subsequent years were similar, although the number of Belle Vue concerts declined, until by 1954 there were only two: a Christmas concert and the annual *Messiah*.

As far as one can gauge, attendances at the mid-week concerts were consistently high throughout the 1945-55 period (bearing in mind the duplication from 1952-3 onwards). The high popularity of classical music concerts which had begun during the war continued, and was sustained, it would seem, by pricing policies which kept tickets competitive with other mass entertainments.[222]

Halle ticket prices were stable, in nominal terms, throughout the 10-year

---

[221] The statement in Kennedy, 1960: 329, that even with 3600 seats available for each programme, every ticket was sold on the opening day of booking, thus seems to be an exaggeration, and is not borne out by the recorded income figures. It was nearly true the following year.

[222] Arts Council policy concurred: J M Hodgkinson wrote in the annual report of 1946 that there was "no possibility" of increasing admission prices for orchestral music, and in 1952 that ". . . attempts to raise admission prices have shown the public will not pay more . . .", despite the fact that "most of the permanent symphony orchestras are at present flying danger signals." The report for 1954 insisted that audiences were conditioned by the relatively cheap cost of television and the cinema, and that there was ". . . resistance to paying more than 3s 6d or 5s for a concert or play . . ."

period. In 1945 the midweek concert price range was 2s 6d to 10s (1s unreserved), and the Sunday concerts 2s 6d to 7s 6d (1s unreserved). The Free Trade Hall price range was 2s 6d to 10s in 1951-2, with top prices increased to 15s (midweek) and 12s (Sundays) from 1952-3 (and to 12s 6d on Sundays from 1953-4). Crickmore's introduction of "Industrial Concerts" in 1952-3 brought a new method of marketing: businesses were encouraged to make block bookings for their locally-based employees. Seat prices for these concerts were 2s 6d to 4s 6d, with the large majority of tickets at 3s 6d. The summer "Proms", also begun by Crickmore in 1952, were priced from 2s 6d to 7s 6d, and 1s (from 1954, 1s 6d) standing. Performed as a consecutive daily series of about 10 programmes in June (in August in 1953; eight in June and four in August in 1954; 12 in June and July in 1955), the Proms appear to have attracted high attendances – for 1955 the average audience figure is available, and is 87% of capacity.

A conversion to 1995 values, using the change in the Retail Price Index, indicates that the 2s 6d Hallé ticket would convert to just over £2 (as at 1945), declining to about £1.50 (as at 1954). The 10s top price ticket of 1945 would be equivalent to £8.25, and the 15s ticket of 1954 would be equivalent to £8.90. Standing prices of 1s (later 1s 6d) are equivalent to 80p-90p in 1995, and the Industrial Concerts' 1953 median price of 3s 6d is equivalent to £2.10. Hallé prices, in real terms, were lower than ever before. The beer price equivalents are even more striking. The standing ticket price of 1s in 1945 and 1s 6d in 1954 is very close to the price of one pint of beer; the top price ticket of 10s (in 1945) to 15s (in 1954) corresponds to 9 to 12 pints; the median price for the Industrial Concerts (3s 6d) to three pints.

It is notable that 2s 6d to 7s 6d, with 1s for standing room – the price scheme for Sunday Hallé concerts from 1945 to 1950, and for the Summer Proms of 1952 and 1953 – was exactly the same in nominal terms as that for Hallé concerts before the First World War, despite a rise in the cost of living of around 250% since that period (indeed, if measured by the price of beer, money had lost value by about 500%).[223]

1965-1975

Attendances at Manchester Hallé concerts in the mid-sixties (see Tables 5.2, 5.4, 5.6 and 5.8) were historically very high indeed, as there were still pairs of concerts in the mid-week series, filling about 70% of seats in the Free Trade Hall, and the Sunday series was long and had average attendances of 85%-90%. The

---

[223]In contrast with the Hallé's high attendance figures in this period, it is notable that the City of Birmingham Orchestra averaged less than 60% attendances at Birmingham Town Hall (capacity 1750) in 1947-8 and the following season, a pattern modified only by the introduction of Industrial Concerts in 1950 ("Saturday Pops" were also begun), which "caught on quickly" (King-Smith, 1995: 97-8). Lewis, 1998, states that Liverpool Philharmonic audiences were "in decline" by the end of the decade 1940-49, though she implies that things were not so bad after the introduction of the new, £1-a-year category of Philharmonic Society membership in 1952.

Industrial Concerts drew about 75% houses in a series of six pairs of performances, and the Proms, with about 10 performances in a fortnight, similar capacity. The change to single mid-week concerts in 1967-8 brought their average attendance figures to 90%-plus, sustained over the change of principal conductor in 1970 and for the rest of the period. The Sunday concerts also maintained their popularity.

The range of ticket prices in 1965-6 was 5s to 21s for the weekday series, 5s to 17s 6d for the Sunday series, 3s 6d to 8s for the Industrials and 3s to 10s for the Proms. The lower price for the Industrials was raised to 5s in 1967-8, and the top price of the other winter series to 25s, but, later, increases of one sort or another were applied in every season from 1970-71 onwards, taking the weekday series range to 45p-£3, the Sunday series to 45p-£2.50, the Opus One concerts to 50p-£1, and the Proms to 30p-£1.50, by 1974-5. Adjusting these prices to 1995 values by use of the Retail Price Index shows that the main series in 1965 was priced at much the same real level as 1945, though with a slighter wider spread of prices (£1.90-£10, compared with 1945's £2-£8.25). The equivalent value of beer tells the same story: 2.5 pints to 12 pints corresponds to the main series ticket price range in 1965: in 1945 it was 2.5 pints to 9 pints.

However, by 1975 the higher priced seats were more expensive in real terms, even though the cheapest were kept to a similar level to that before: £1.90-£12.70 is the range under the RPI calculation, or 2.5 pints to 15 pints in beer values. Intermediate prices were raised, too, which represents a real-value rise in the price of tickets compared with 1945-55, bringing the cost of attendance at a main series Hallé concert by 1975 close to what it had been in the unsubsidised 1930s.

The Industrial Concerts, which were originally offered (from 1952-3) with no higher-priced seats at all, kept to that pattern until 1971-2, when they were re-named the "Opus One" series: their lowest price was now slightly higher than that for weekday or Sunday concerts, although the top price was considerably lower (and group discounts meant that in most cases the real prices were lower than those quoted for single tickets). But slightly higher-than-inflation increases in succeeding years meant that in real terms the price range was higher than ever before by 1973-4 (every concert was selling out, so there was obviously no deterrent effect). The Proms, likewise begun with a low price range in 1952, had already increased in price in real terms by 1965 and were to do so slightly more over the following ten years, with a widening of the range of prices to values equivalent to £1.30 to £6.35, under the 1965 RPI comparison, by 1974 (or 1.5 pints to 8 pints in beer values).

In a time of high inflation there was a (perhaps inevitable) tendency to confuse higher income with real success, but after James Loughran's first full season (1971-72) there was evident satisfaction as the Hallé annual report recorded that attendances and income were both breaking all records; and the following year's report mentioned 93% attendances in the winter season and the Opus One series selling out. The report for 1972-3 states that attendances had been "maintained", that for 1973-4 refers to "continuing near-capacity attendances at all . . . concerts", and that for 1974-5 again claims high attendances maintained, despite 25% inflation and ticket price rises of 30%. Arts Council annual reports note the trend generally: in 1972 orchestras were seeing the "encouraging" experience of increased attendances; in 1973 "concerts prospered. There were no severe financial crises . . ." The report for 1974 said that audiences for the orchestras "remained good". The one sign of decline for the Hallé at the end of this 10-year period is a report that in December, 1974, its Sunday concerts "had not sold out this year", and there was, indeed, a slight, gradual drop in attendances after 1970-71 in this series – see Table 5.4. This was ascribed mainly to programming policy (there was a degree of programme experimentation), but also to the counter-attraction of television.

1985-1995

Data on attendance levels at Manchester Hallé concerts in 1985-95 is remarkably difficult to find, but such records as there are, together with reasonable inferences from financial data, enable the construction of the tables given (Tables 6.2, 6.4, 6.6 and 6.8). These show that in all series there had a significant decline in attendances from 1975 to 1985, which continued gradually under Skrowaczewski and was not substantially reversed after the appointment of Kent Nagano.

The most successful of the three winter series was the "Opus One" series, with attendances at the (now) eight concerts – each of which was given three times over – in the 80%-90% range before 1991-2. This represents the highest level, in the years analysed in this study, in the Hallé's audience for an entire series of programmes, as the aggregate audiences per programme were 6,000-6,500 on average. It was therefore the point of maximum "cost effectiveness" in the promotion of the orchestra in Manchester. However, average attendances subsequently fell below 80%.

Sunday concerts drew attendances between 60% and 70% for most of 1985-95, but were fewer in number from 1990-91, falling to six in 1994-5. Thursday attendances remained comfortably above 60% during Skrowaczewski's tenure as principal conductor, but fell a little (on average) under Nagano.

The Summer Proms were, as ever, highly variable, but the near-capacity levels of some years in 1965-75 were never regained (though the G-Mex concerts in 1986-7 to 1991-2 attracted very large audiences for a few days each year), and the 1993 and 1994 Proms were, as noted above, accounted considerable failures.

The effect of price rises on attendance levels at all the series must be considered. The range of ticket prices in 1985-6 was £1.50-£10 for the Thursday series, £1.20-£7 for the Sunday series, £1.50-£9 for the Opus One series, and £1-£5 for the Proms. Rises were introduced in some or all of these in every subsequent season until 1991-2, when the range was £2.75-£21 for Thursdays, the same for Sundays, £5.25-£16.50 for the Opus One series, and £2.50-£14 for the Proms. Reductions in the lowest prices were made in 1992-3 (although the highest prices were again extended for the Opus One series and Proms), but the entire range was again increased in 1993-4, with a standard price scheme ranging from £3-£22.50 for all winter season concerts, and a Proms range of £1.25-£18.50. Top prices were increased to £23.50 in 1994-5, and the Proms were sold at £2-£19.50.

Inflation was continuing throughout this period, though at a lesser rate than in 1965-75. But adjusting all the Hallé's ticket prices to 1995 values shows that they were increasing more than ever before, in real terms. The Thursday series' lowest price began, if we use the Retail Price Index adjustment, around £2.30 in 1985-6 and 1986-7, but rose to around £2.80 in 1990-91, and to over £3 in 1991-2 and 1993-4 (the year between saw a significant drop). The highest price began, by the same calculation, around £16 and climbed to more than £20 by 1990-91, and to around £24 thereafter (except for a drop back to £19 in 1992-3). These levels are well above the equivalents for 1945-55 and 1965-75 (which were fairly consistent with each other) and by the end of this period were 50% greater, in the case of the lowest price, and 150-200% greater, in the case of the highest. The pattern is very similar for the lowest price for Sunday concerts, and even more marked for the highest (which had itself increased significantly from 1967-8): this was 200% greater than 1945-55 and 1965-7, and by 1995 almost 150% greater than 1967-75.

The Opus One concerts (originally Industrial Concerts) were, as we have seen, priced well below the other series at first, but from 1967-8 had the same minimum price but a lower median price. By 1987-8 the minimum price was still level with that for the other series, but the highest price had risen to the equivalent (in 1995 values) of more than three times that of 1965-75. (Party bookings were still discounted, however, so that for most of the audience the price was not as high as single-ticket values might imply). After that the lowest prices were made higher than those for the other winter series, and the highest prices also raised, until from 1992-3 all winter concerts were priced in the same bands – with the result that by 1995 the cheapest Opus One tickets were 100% greater in real cost than in 1965-75, and the highest-priced were about 500% more expensive.

The Proms, if adjusted to 1995 values, were also more highly priced than ever before. The original pricing had been from well under £1 (equivalent) to under £5, and in 1965-75 real values (in 1995 terms) rose from about £1.20 and £4 to about £1.30 and £6.50 for the highest and lowest prices. The 1985 values were £1.60 and £8, and both rose to a peak in 1991 of over £3 and over £16, which was almost held in 1992 but fell back to £1.40 for the lowest price in the following two years, while the highest increased to around £20. In 1995 itself, the range was £2-£19.50.

In "beer values" the picture does not appear so extreme at the lower end of the price scale: the cheapest tickets for the winter concert series in 1985 cost around two pints (a little less than 1945's and substantially less than 1965's weekday and Sunday concerts, though the same as the Industrials' minimum price). But the most expensive tickets cost around 14 pints. By 1990-91 the cheapest winter season seats cost 2.5 pints of beer (4 pints for the Opus One series), but the most expensive cost 17 pints (14 for the Opus One series) – more than any 1945-55 seats, and nearly four times as much as the top price for the first few seasons of Industrial Concerts. In 1991-2 the top price rose to the equivalent of 20 pints, or nearly 16 pints for the Opus One series. Adjusted prices were lower the following season (about the same as before in the case of the Opus One concerts), but from 1993-4 the range was again at 2.5 pints to about 20 pints – and now this applied to all winter concerts including the Opus One series. In the case of the Proms, the lowest price rose from about 1.5 pints in beer values in 1986 to 2.5 in 1991 and 1992, and fell to about 1 pint from 1993. The highest rose steadily from about 7 pints in 1986 to about 16 pints from 1993 on.

The effect of these comparisons would appear to be that, whereas in 1965-75 the weekday series gradually returned in value to the levels of the 1930s (though Sunday concerts were somewhat cheaper, and the Industrial/Opus One series remained substantially cheaper in its higher rate), in 1985-95 all the winter concerts were priced at the 1930s level in real terms in respect of the cheapest seats, and in respect of the most expensive the Thursday series began at the 1930s level and then outstripped it, while the Sunday and Opus One series began at 1945-55 levels but also rose to greater than 1925-35 levels. The real price levels of pre-First World War concerts had still not been reached, but the majority of seats were sold at substantially higher real prices than at any time since 1925, and the concept of offering all seats in the hall at lower prices, pioneered in the Municipal Concerts of the 1920s and 1930s and adopted with great success for the Industrial/Opus One concerts until the end of the 1965-75 period, was first eroded and, from 1992-3, completely abandoned.

Observation (such as was available to music critics including myself) indicated that increasingly, from around 1985, the expensive blocks of seats at the Opus One concerts were selling less and less well, and this impression is confirmed by the 1991-2 consultancy comments. But it is clear that in spite of this there was a decision to assimilate all winter series prices from 1992-3 onwards. In the first year of operation, this produced the effect of a reduction in the Thursday and independent Sunday series prices, but in 1993-4 and the following season, all prices were at their highest real values of the entire 10-year period. In the case of the Proms, steady escalation of real prices continued until 1992, when an attempt was made to hold price levels in spite of inflation, and from 1993 smaller real prices were introduced at the lower end of the range, alongside greater real prices at the higher end.

Pricing policy

It is difficult to escape the conclusion that the decline in attendances the Hallé experienced in this period, and the ageing make-up of the audiences it did attract, were related to its pricing policy. The fact that cost – or perceived cost – was a major factor influencing people's decisions on whether to attend was a point which the consultants of 1991-2 made (although their recommendations seem in practice only to have exacerbated the situation). It was also alluded to by an Arts Council official in May, 1995, who said: "We would question whether your local pricing structure has sent some people away".

It is noteworthy that the Arts Council's views on this topic seem to have changed dramatically in the early 1990s – or at least there was a change in awareness of what research on the subject showed. Several Arts Council of Great Britain studies in the early 1990s had a common refrain that arts prices could (and should) be raised beyond the rate of inflation without damaging attendance levels. It was a striking and attractive proposition, and appears to have inspired the Hallé's moves in this area for a couple of critical years.

The Arts Council studies, by Millward Brown International and Research Surveys of Great Britain, were based on market research methods, including attitudinal research, by telephone and face-to-face interview, of 1298 people in four conurbations – Edinburgh, Birmingham, Manchester and Liverpool,[224] opinion and attendance sampling through interviews with 7919 adults in England, Wales and Scotland,[225] and a study of three small Welsh arts centres from 1988 to 1990 along with a second look at the first survey's results.[226] These expressed conclusions such as:

– "price is not a spontaneous barrier to attendance"[227] (only one-and-a-half per cent spontaneously mentioned price as a reason for non-attendance);
– "motivations to attend generally [were] accomplished before price entered the process";[228]
– "there was a stated intention to trade up rather than down in terms of price";[229]
– "the live arts appear to be underpriced";[230]
– "relative lack of importance of ticket price";[231]
– "once a top price payer, always a top price payer";[232]

[224]Walshe, 1991.
[225]RSGB , 1991.
[226]Walshe, Verwey and Tomlinson, 1992.
[227]Walshe, 1991.
[228]Walshe, 1991.
[229]Walshe, 1991.
[230]Walshe, 1991.
[231]Walshe, Verwey and Tomlinson, 1992.

– the second survey looked at the 39% of its sample who claimed to have been "put off" going to an arts event in the past 12 months because of price, and divided them according to the type of event they might have attended: eg. plays 10%, opera 7%, ballet 3%, orchestral music 3%. These were then split as between those who actually were regular attenders and those who were not.[233]

It is apparent that these survey reports were written to a brief, as the introduction to the third of them[234] makes clear: "The Arts Council was particularly keen to . . . find ways of increasing the earned income levels of their clients . . . Unsubstantiated claims by theatre and arts centre managers that pricing levels were a barrier to attendance had over many years gained credence."

But two responses by Chris Blamires[235] took a more objective and sophisticated approach to the issue, pointing out that there was evidence that:

– 53% of people had been put off attending an arts event by price at some time (taken from the first survey's data and comparable with the figure of 39% put off in the past 12 months);
– live arts were more price-sensitive than cinema, and price was much more relevant to arts attenders than non-attenders, facts established by re-calculating the second survey's figures as percentages of those "put-off" different art forms who were (a) attenders and (b) non-attenders in the first place: eg. 28% of attenders had been put off going to at least one opera, and 10% from going to one or more orchestral events; the equivalent figures for non-attenders were much smaller (as well they might have been – these were, presumably, people who just did not like the kind of event in question);
– 76% in the first survey's figures said ticket price was "important" or "very important" in their decision to attend (it is interesting that its author could still state his findings in the terms quoted above in view of that result).

Blamires proposed a model of the process of decision-making to attend an arts event, under which price would be a relevant issue only to those intending to go to a *specific* event, not all those interested in a particular art form. It was the effect of price increases on decisions of that kind, he wrote, which should be addressed by research. Furthermore, the experience of the Welsh centres described in the third survey actually showed that although price increases were feasible in some circumstances, they could also be "disastrous". He concluded that although price reduction could not be expected to open a mass market for any type of arts event, a price increase beyond general expectations could have a major negative impact, turning the "intenders", especially previous attenders, into the "alienated".

[232]Walshe, Verwey and Tomlinson, 1992.
[233]RSGB (1991).
[234]Walshe, Verwey and Tomlinson, 1992.
[235]Blamires, Chris (1992): What Price Entertainment? *Journal of the Market Research Society*, 34 (4) October 1992: 375-388; and Blamires, 1995.

Increasing prices by a significant margin from actual or expected levels, he wrote in 1995,[236] would not even substantially increase income. "Substantial price increases ahead of inflation appear almost universally likely to reduce audience levels and, at best, maintain income." The Hallé found that out the hard way.[237]

One of the elements in this study has been a precise consideration of the price ranges of concerts in different periods, expressed in "real" terms by taking the effects of inflation into account. Many of those who remember the prices of concerts in the fifties and sixties know that they cost more now, but assume that in real terms the prices must be worth much the same. This survey shows that (in the case of the Hallé at least, and it may well apply much more widely) this is not so. The *real* price of concert admission in the post-war years (and until the end of the 1960s) was lower than at any other time this century. This should not be forgotten when the boom in classical music attendance of those years is considered.

Attendance figures for the Hallé in the first half of the 1990s decreased in the aftermath of steep ticket price increases, and expectations of relatively small audience losses were not fulfilled (the 1991-2 increases introduced by David Richardson resulted in a 4% decrease in number of tickets sold, and extensive discounting was introduced in 1992-3 – and then the upward assimilation of the prices of the popular Opus One series to those of the "heavier" series from 1993-4 onwards coincided with a dramatic and unexpected under-performance in the Hallé's Manchester sales.

If the example of the CBSO's increased attendances in the early to mid-1990s is quoted to contradict drawing such conclusions, it should be noted that the phenomenon in Birmingham had arguably been one where attendances had increased from a low base to a level no greater than that at which the Hallé's had been for some time. The Consultation Document of the Ritterman Enquiry[238] points out that at that time attendance figures per head of population for orchestral concerts in the West Midlands region were comparatively low, compared with other regions (including the north west), despite the success of Symphony Hall, which had in itself brought increased capacity of 25% to the CBSO's concerts.

---

[236]Blamires, 1995.
[237]The previous orthodoxy is still to be found: "The notion that people do not attend classical music concerts ... principally because of the ticket price has long been discounted ..." – Phyllida Shaw, *Classical Music*, September 9th, 2000.
[238]Arts Council of England, 1994.

Chapter 13

Music's meddlesome friend – the Arts Council

Can't do with 'em – can't do without 'em. Many British arts organisations would echo the comic's misogynistic one-liner if they were honest about their feelings towards the Arts Council in the later years of the 20th century. Academic studies and others have pointed out its lack of accountability and secrecy,[239] its interventionism from the 1960s onwards,[240] its failures of critical judgment,[241] and its bureaucratic procedures.[242] An emphasis on policy declarations from its clients began in the 1960s – and John Pick comments that, by the 1980s, conformity with "arbitrary policy concepts" had become a prerequisite for Arts Council aid.[243] There seemed to be an overwhelming need to keep the Gilberts and Gwynneths[244] of this world on side, whatever the public or the professionals wanted.

The Hallé's story in the latter half of the 20th century shows how the dependent relationship established by state subsidy of the arts worked out in practice for one client organisation.

The early years

The Arts Council of Great Britain, founded in 1945, in its early years was marked by a stress on classical music, reflecting the priorities of its predecessor, the Council for the Encouragement of Music and the Arts. Indeed, Steuart Wilson, its Director of Music, stated in the annual report of 1946 that its policy was "still that

---

[239]Hutchinson, 1982.
[240]Ridley, 1987, and Tooley, 1999.
[241]Pick, 1986 and 1988, and Ridley, 1987.
[242]Tooley, 1999.
[243]Pick, 1986.
[244]The fictional Arts Council representatives in Jilly Cooper's *Appassionata*. In her story the couple were also music critics for the *Guardian* and *Independent*, respectively.

of CEMA". "Industrial music" – meaning factory concerts and visits by symphony orchestras to "industrial places" – was commended, as were "new and unusual works performed".

The Arts Council annual report of 1949 announced that the grants to the four permanent orchestras[245] "must still be regarded as an interim subsidy until more elaborate long-term arrangements can be made", and in the following year, although recommending increased help for them, enunciated the "pound for pound" policy – that their subsidy should normally be 50% Arts Council and 50% local authority – and stated that it should apply from 1951 onwards. The ensuing developments in the funding of the Hallé have been described. The CBSO faced financial crisis in 1952, too: by 1951 it had an accumulated deficit of £8,000, and in 1952 its overdraft stood at £20,000. It considered reverting to a six-months-a-year existence, but was saved in a quite different way from the Hallé – simple municipal beneficence. It was given an interest-free loan of £20,000, repayable over 10 years, by the new Labour city council in Birmingham (after an attempt at a regional scheme failed), along with an increase in total city grant from £20,000 to £31,000 per year. Its Arts Council grant was also increased to £11,000. In 1953 its city council grant went up to £36,000, and its Arts Council grant to £15,000, and a local philanthropist made generous donations which allowed it to increase its strength from 63 (at that time the smallest of the four Arts Council supported orchestras) to 71.[246] In Liverpool, the Philharmonic Society was enabled to pay off its deficit and received increased aid from the City Council in 1951 – at the price of a committee reorganisation which saw a make-up of equal numbers of Council and Society members – six of each, with three co-opted members to be approved by the Arts Council. It sustained a large loss in 1952, however, and brought in a new category of membership, for an annual subscription of £1, gaining 214 new members. These measures parallel those taken in Manchester around the same time. It benefitted equally with the Hallé from the local authorities' "Joint Scheme" from 1954-5 onwards.[247]

The Arts Council of Great Britain was now firmly wedded to the concept of sharing the burden of support for the regional orchestras between itself and local authorities – one of the earliest examples of the practice of "matching funding" (though in this case, of course, it was a second kind of public contribution, not private support, that was to be matched). Sir Kenneth Clark wrote, in his chairman's report of 1953: "Municipal patronage is taking a large and increasing share of the cost of providing the arts . . ." and the report commended Birmingham Corporation for increasing its annual grant to the CBSO.

In the early years, the Arts Council also wasted little time in expressing its

[245]At this time the London Philharmonic, Hallé, Liverpool Philharmonic and City of Birmingham Symphony.
[246]King-Smith, 1995: 106-110.
[247]Lewis, 1998: 128-30.

need for assessment of the activities of its clients. A letter in November, 1946, led to a Hallé invitation in December to J L Hodgkinson, the Regional Director, to attend the Hallé's Executive Committee meetings as "Assessor on behalf of the Arts Council". Notices of meetings and agenda papers henceforward also went to Wilson, who, it was agreed, could attend "any meeting at which matters specifically affecting the Arts Council" were to be discussed. (Wilson left to be Music Director of the BBC in 1948, and was succeeded by John Denison).

Hodgkinson attended Hallé Committee meetings from January 15th, 1947, onwards. His role seems to have been an essentially supportive one, with the initial objective of securing financial support for the Hallé from Manchester City Council which would be equal to that provided by the Arts Council. Hodgkinson was a member of the delegation which represented the Hallé in the successful first discussions with the City Council, in summer, 1947. Later, when the Hallé's financial reserves began to dwindle in 1951, and it was faced with the need to buy a new Steinway grand piano for the refurbished Free Trade Hall, it was he who suggested that the Hallé apply for two quarterly instalments of its Arts Council grant in advance, to ease the burden on its overdraft.

The Arts Council renewed its grant of £10,000 to the Hallé for the year from April 1st, 1952, on condition that it should itself review the society's financial position in August and November that year. This seems to be the first example of the Council making its aid to the orchestra subject to its own appraisal of its financial affairs. In September, 1952, after a meeting with the Arts Council's Finance Officer, it was agreed that quarterly budgetary statements would be supplied by the Hallé to the Arts Council. The Hallé Treasurer, Sir James Lythgoe, it was said, "had explained that the Society was anxious to build up, if possible, some stable reserve. He had been assured that if this object were achieved the Arts Council would not reduce its grant to the Society as a consequence." This promise was to be broken by the Arts Council as early as 1955.

There was little doubt as to the high position of the Hallé in the Arts Council's thinking at this time, however – or at least of the regard for Barbirolli's abilities. An indication can be gained from passages in its 1953 annual report, the first under the chairmanship of Sir Kenneth Clark. In the section on opera, Barbirolli's conducting "frequently" at the Royal Opera, Covent Garden, is mentioned with pride, and the introductory review of the year comments: "If Sir John Barbirolli were for any reason dissatisfied with working for the Hallé Orchestra – which he is not – he could transfer himself to Covent Garden . . ." Such invitations had, apparently, been issued, and many in the London musical establishment must have wished they had been accepted. It should be noted that it was Barbirolli's work in London, not Manchester, which elicited this public praise – an indication that the Arts Council concept of real artistic significance, even then, related to metropolitan rather than provincial enterprises.

The sixties

A factor in Hallé Committee discussions in the sixties is the beginning of overt Arts Council attempts to influence the programming policy of its client. In 1965 the Hallé Committee responded to a requirement that it should make an annual review of the representation of works by living British composers in its programmes – as a condition of receiving Arts Council support, apparently – by indignantly replying that it had "always devoted proper attention to the question of presenting British music." This was not enough, however, and the Committee reluctantly agreed to meet the requirement and send an annual list.

In October the same year the Arts Council asked for a statement of artistic policy and an indication of "likely trends" in financial and artistic policy in the future, when the estimates for 1966-7 were submitted. The Hallé responded with a detailed document in which its fundamental aims were defined (possibly for the first time in a single sentence) as: "To continue the Hallé tradition: by maintaining an orchestra of international standard in Manchester and enhancing the musical life of the city of Manchester and the North in particular, and the United Kingdom in general." On the question of contemporary music, it stated that any greater emphasis than that existing "could reduce concert income in Manchester in particular . . ."

The Arts Council then offered specific funds to enable the inclusion of more British music in the remainder of the current financial year (1965-66): notwithstanding its previous reservations, the Hallé took action to see that this could be taken up. A Manchester concerts sub-committee was set up, and when the next annual support offer was made conditional on the supply of statistics regarding "contemporary music" in the programmes, this was accepted. A wage negotiation for musicians was in progress at the time, and the Hallé Committee was far more concerned that the Arts Council might renege on what was understood to be an undertaking to provide funds to meet the entire cost of any increases.

By 1969 the Arts Council view on programmes had subtly altered. Its representative on the Hallé Committee, Eric Thompson, demanded in discussion of the programmes for 1969-70, more opportunities for works by "less established British composers". The Hallé's "Music In Our Time" series had already been launched by Handford, with specific Arts Council support, but it was not continued in 1969-70 when further special support was refused.

In 1969 the Arts Council asked that the submission made to it in respect of 1970-71 should be in two forms: one based on existing policy, and another as the requirement for "modest development". The Hallé Committee concluded that "now did not appear to be the right time" for the latter, because the Peacock

Enquiry report[248] was pending, and neither the Arts Council nor Manchester Council had in the past three years offered enough, it considered, to meet the costs of the existing policy. It drew the Arts Council's attention to its submission to the Peacock Committee – all designed to make the point that better pay for the orchestra's players was the real priority at the time, Clive Smart recalls.[249] Whatever might have been the outcome of a more compliant attitude to the Arts Council at this stage, it is clear that the requirement made of the Hallé was now to state intentions rather than report achievement.

John Cruft, the new Arts Council music director, and Eric Thompson were the Arts Council's assessors on the Hallé Committee from 1965 until 1979 – a long period during which understanding was, on the whole, effectively built. But in 1966-7 there was a serious misunderstanding involving the Arts Council and its ability to fund orchestral musicians' pay increases. A report by Lord Goodman (chairman of the Arts Council from 1965) into the London orchestras and consequent rises for their members had fuelled expectations, and in March, 1966, the Hallé confidentially informed managers of other regional orchestras that it was awarding its members an interim increase of £5 a week (worth 25% on their basic rate) pending renegotiation of the national contract, and invited the other orchestras to do the same. The explicit intention was to avoid losing any more players, as several were already planning to go. This came four days after it was reported that the Arts Council had announced its likely grant level, but said this would not preclude consideration of a further approach in the light of new salary levels that might be negotiated.

In May the Arts Council apparently told the Orchestral Employers' Association, the employers' national negotiating body, that it would make "a high contribution" to their costs in the current year, but that afterwards it would have to be a matter of "the education of local authorities" (i.e. in their duty to provide more). This was followed, however, by a more correct impression that the Arts Council was in fact prepared to offer only a half of the cost of the interim pay award. Lord Goodman assured the orchestras of his "personal view" that the Arts Council would fund the entire interim award, and the Hallé players were sent on holiday with a loan of up to £75 each, in view of the "delay in implementing" the award they had been promised.

In August the Hallé Committee heard that the Department of Education and Science had stepped in and the award was subject to a "standstill" under the Government's new White Paper on pay. The Minister for the Arts (Jennie Lee) told the orchestras that pay increases could only be made from January 1st, 1967, and could not be back-dated before October 1st, 1966. Also, the loan could not be treated as a payment on account, and so the Hallé had to tell its musicians that any who left before the end of the year would have to return it. The Arts Council

[248]See chapters 6 and 7.
[249]Personal communication.

now restated its offer as being in respect of the full award, but from October 1st only. The loan was eventually recovered, in part, by the Hallé, by being set against a "notional bonus" in December, 1967. The Arts Council's annual report of 1967 mentions the episode only by a brief comment that regional symphony orchestra players found themselves "caught by the pay freeze".

The episode no doubt reflects widely-held attitudes to pay negotiations at the time, but it seems to have left an unfortunate atmosphere of suspicion between the Arts Council and the Hallé, and there was subsequent correspondence regarding a perceived suggestion by the Council that the Hallé "did not behave responsibly in its use of public funds", a letter from the Hallé which the Arts Council accountant described as a "rebuff", and a further exchange of letters in which he denied that he had ever "interfered" with the policy or administration of the Society. When the Hallé inquired, in mid-1967, about the possibility of extra funds for 1967-8, on account of projects such as Barbirolli's special "jubilee" performances, celebration of Berlioz' centenary and the "Music In Our Time" series, it was merely told that all such ideas should simply be reflected in the budgets it submitted on which annual subsidy was based.

The 1970s and 1980s

The Arts Council's own view of the orchestral scene in the 1970s was a positive one. Its annual reports of 1971 and 1972 recorded "increased attendances" at concerts, the former describing life in provincial cities and towns where ". . . the visits of the Royal Ballet, the next Hallé concert . . . [inter alia] . . . are real events: anticipated, talked about and criticised   . . ." In 1972-3, "concerts prospered. There were no severe financial crises"; and in 1973-4, despite 17% inflation, "audiences remained good and standards high . . ."

Things were different by the beginning of the next decade. The 1981 Arts Council annual report noted that "the four great regional symphony orchestras[250] were in serious financial trouble" and said their grants were being increased as a result. The Arts Council music director met the Hallé Committee in January, 1980, and assured them that priority was being given to the funding of regional orchestras and that the Council were not prejudiced against the Hallé and were satisfied with the work they did. They would like to see more English music performed, he added, but recognised that in the present economic circumstances this was not possible.

But the Committee complained to him that the former balance between funding for the Hallé and that for the Royal Liverpool Philharmonic and City of Birmingham Symphony Orchestras had now been abandoned for an arrangement that seemed "the opposite". This was undoubtedly true: whereas in 1978-9,

[250]Now the Hallé, Royal Liverpool Philharmonic, City of Birmingham Symphony and Bournemouth Symphony.

following the pattern of the previous few years, the Arts Council gave the Hallé £251,121, the RLPO £248,253, and the CBSO £245,000 (though with an additional guarantee, newly introduced, which amounted to over £30,000 that year); in 1979-80 the RLPO received £321,747, the Hallé £315,000 and the CBSO £310,354 (in total), and in 1980-81 the CBSO gained £345,000 in total, the RLPO £338,065, and the Hallé £325,000. The Hallé was to come lowest of the three for the next few years.

The Hallé had to make programme changes in 1981-2, it decided, to reduce costs and increase returns – to offset the lack of Arts Council support. The annual report of 1981 described the Arts Council's attitude to the Hallé as "unreasonable and inequitable". The Council's representative was not able to offer any hope of amelioration of the situation, but suggested the Hallé should strengthen the musical side of its board by co-opting a representative of the Royal Northern College of Music or Manchester University. He also told the Hallé Committee that it should not be "too fearful of the effect of an adventurous programming policy on the box office" and that "the music panel would always take into account the musical policy of its clients when considering subsidy", referring to the CBSO's "very adventurous" programmes under Simon Rattle (Rattle was appointed as principal conductor of the CBSO from 1980-1 onwards) and excellent season ticket sales. However, it was felt, the Hallé minutes record, that "this was more likely to be attributable to Simon Rattle than the adventurousness of the programmes."[251]

The Arts Council's support of the regional orchestras as a whole between 1975 and 1985 did not keep pace with inflation – because of, first, an increased emphasis on contemporary music and supporting smaller ventures, and second, the Government's drastic cut-backs in the Arts Council's resources after 1983. At the same time there was a shift of balance, in 1980, which made the Hallé even less well supported than the orchestras of Liverpool and Birmingham. This was said to be based on an assessment of the respective orchestras' musical policy by the Arts Council's music panel. The Arts Council gave the Hallé £325,000 for 1980-81, whereas the CBSO received £410,000: the GMC gave the Hallé £254,000, whereas West Midlands County Council gave the CBSO £230,000, and Manchester City Council gave the Hallé £30,000, whereas Birmingham City Council gave the CBSO £38,000. So the CBSO was at this time receiving substantially more from the Arts Council, even though its supporting local authorities were less generous than the Hallé's.[252]

The CBSO was certainly enterprising: in 1980 a new weekday series had been begun in Birmingham's town hall, as well as monthly Saturday "family concerts". The town hall had a capacity of only 1750, compared with 2450 at the Free Trade Hall in Manchester, so expansion in Birmingham almost certainly had to occur

[251]Rattle had received enviable TV coverage at the outset of his appointment in Birmingham.
[252]Hallé figures from annual reports; CBSO figures from King-Smith, 1995: 272.

through scheduling new concerts.[253]

But change was on the way, as Birmingham found a new pride in its orchestra. The CBSO received over £700,000 from Arts Council and West Midlands County Council together in 1983-4 (the Hallé figure is about £800,000 in total from Arts Council and GMC), but Birmingham City Council made a special grant of £60,000 to write off its accumulated deficit, bringing the city's contribution in one year to £100,000: Manchester City Council, by contrast, gave the Hallé £20,000 in each of 1982-83 and 1983-4 – its lowest level of grant, even in cash terms, since 1962-63, and never raised its contribution above £23,450 until 1993-94.[254]

The Arts Council produced a report, *The Glory of the Garden*, in March, 1984, with a suggestion that one of the London orchestras should move to the East Midlands. The report seemed to some to indicate a new recognition of the needs of the regions (it proposed "greater investment in the regional orchestras", according to the Arts Council annual report of 1985), but the East Midlands plan came to nothing – and, says King-Smith, in the case of Birmingham the very suggestion emphasised the importance of the CBSO's Development Plan – which was already being formulated, although in "strict confidence".[255] Luke Rittner's report as Secretary-General of the Arts Council in 1985 singled out the CBSO among the "outstandingly creative regional orchestras".

After 1985

The abolition of the Metropolitan County Councils in 1985 proved a watershed for the regional symphony orchestras. Assurances that the missing portion of their income would be provided from Arts Council funds proved impossible to fulfil after 1987 – in the case of the Hallé, in the long term, the component in its income which was lost was approximately equal, in proportionate terms, to the Arts Council's own contribution throughout the ten years 1975-85.[256]

---

[253]And of course it had Simon Rattle, whose programming was undoubtedly original – but perhaps not as much as he thought: he claimed later that the CBSO, in 1980-81, was the first British symphony orchestra, apart from the BBC Symphony, to play Boulez – in fact Maurice Handford had played Boulez with the Hallé in 1973 – see King-Smith, 1995: 192, 193.
[254]Hallé figures from annual reports, CBSO figures from King-Smith, 1995: 203.
[255]King-Smith, 1995: 203-204.
[256]Sir William Rees-Mogg's statements in the 1986 Arts Council annual report that settlements with the successor authorities in the areas of the former metropolitan counties "mostly exceed previous expenditure in total", and, in the 1988 report, that "we were able to ensure that the arts took no harm", are thus particularly anomalous, and contrast with Luke Rittner's remarks (also in Arts Council annual reports of the time) that the reduction in "abolition funding" would be "a critical test" (1986), that "more and more arts organisations are staving off financial disaster . . . because the essential core funding was no longer enabling them to fulfil the demand . . ." (1987), while inflation had outstripped grant-in-aid levels by 6% (1989).

There was, it seems, a genuine hope that the emphasis on the regions in *The Glory Of The Garden* would see fruit at least in support sustained at previous real levels – the Arts Council annual report of 1986 referred to "the first year of regional development" – but it was short-lived. What actually happened was a clear divergence between the north-western cities and the Midlands. In Liverpool and Manchester the respective City Councils were reluctant to shoulder a larger burden of support than before, whereas in Birmingham the City Council resumed its old role of chief pillar of the CBSO, and its contribution from 1990 to 1995 was not far short of that of the Arts Council itself. While Manchester City Council was calling the Hallé "elitist", Birmingham City Council not only took over current support but wrote off the CBSO's accumulated deficit to the tune of almost £37,000. [257]

There was another factor. The word "development" had acquired a new and specialised meaning. The CBSO's "Development Plan" of 1986 was much more than one of widening repertoire or increasing audiences. It was aimed, as Beresford King-Smith records, specifically at recruiting "tip-top London players" to new co-principal positions in each of the orchestra's five string sections, through enhanced salaries – which would mean improved pay, and a more flexible working week, for all the orchestra members. The new Birmingham concert hall, along with plans for "adventurous" tours and projects and more contemporary music, also figured (the hall, as part of the Birmingham International Convention Centre, was already going ahead). The CBSO Development Plan had been submitted to both the Arts Council and Birmingham City Council in May, 1986, and the Arts Council music panel then invited a presentation of the case for it – "a sufficiently unusual procedure in itself," comments King-Smith, "to reinforce the feeling that everyone involved knew that they were dealing with a matter of considerable national importance." The plan was then still secret, finally being reported in October, and it received its full funding from both Arts Council and City Council the following March – "along with confirmation of Rattle's extended contract", as King-Smith delicately puts it. The Arts Council itself was not so hesitant. Its annual report for 1987 cited among the highlights of the year the fact that the City of Birmingham had "responded to the Arts Council's challenge . . .[in] . . . an adventurous development plan", and the 1988 report triumphantly hailed the fact that Rattle had extended his contract "as a result of the commitment of the City of Birmingham and the Arts Council to fund the first phase of the CBSO's development plan."

The Hallé objected to the process of focussing such generosity on one regional orchestra and not the others, but there was little, in the face of the "unusual procedure", that it could do. Liverpool City Council's policy was much more like Manchester's: it, says Lewis, saw the RLPO in the mid-eighties as "bourgeois" and "elitist", with the result that the orchestra "has clearly not had the resources to

[257]King-Smith, 1995: 208.

pursue an ambitious policy of programme planning to match, for example, the much more highly-subsidised CBSO".[258]

By 1988, CBSO attendances had climbed to 98% at Birmingham Town Hall,[259] and the admiration from the Arts Council for the Birmingham way of doing things is increasingly apparent in the annual report of 1989. Its "excitingly adventurous programming" was said to be increasing its audience (and so was that of the RLPO under Libor Pesek). Of course, no one can exceed 100% attendances in any auditorium, but it is worth noting that the CBSO's 98% house was about 1715 seats, whereas the Hallé's winter season average for all concerts in 1987-88 was about 1835 seats.

But by 1987 the Hallé knew that things had gone seriously wrong for it after the abolition of the metropolitan councils, and was unable to elicit a change of heart: instead Arts Council policy shifted in the direction of restrictions on orchestras' basic grant levels, allied with the new concept of "Incentive Funding". The reason was a belated, but nevertheless thoroughgoing, acceptance by the Arts Council of the Conservative Government's philosophy of arts finance, with an emphasis on private money and the encouragement of "enterprise". By 1989 the shift was clear. Sir William Rees-Mogg wrote, in his last annual report as Arts Council chairman (1988), that it was the Council's "objective to reduce the arts world's reliance on state subsidy . . ." and emphasised the "goal of excellence", a word which he said had fallen into desuetude while policies had had the central aim of increasing the accessibility of the arts. "The way in which the public discriminates," he wrote, "is through its willingness to pay for its pleasures". Luke Rittner added: "We must be able to show . . . that earnings and private sector income play a larger part in the turnover of arts organisations than in the past."

The Hallé's financial situation was intimately bound up with the Arts Council's attitude to it throughout the eighties, and the process which led to the decision that there should be an appraisal of the Hallé in 1988 has already been described.

But at a crucial point in negotiations with the AGMA authorities for a higher contribution, in autumn, 1988, the Hallé found itself embroiled in a dispute with the Arts Council over its artistic policy, which dragged on for the remainder of Smart's term of office. The first development was a television interview given by the Arts Council's acting music officer, in which "a very hostile and anti-Hallé attitude, particularly in relation to the Society's programme policy" was discerned by members of the orchestra and the general public, the Finance and Policy Committee was told. Programmes had not previously been criticised by the Arts Council, or by its appraisal team, it was noted [at least, not since 1980!]. But Smart wrote to the Arts Council, and received a reply that the Hallé's programmes

[258]Lewis, 1998: 135, 335.
[259]King-Smith, 1995: 217.

were not being criticised. At the same time, a new Arts Council assessor joined the Hallé General Committee.

Next an Arts Council letter to the AGMA authorities in December, 1988, stated that its extra £60,000 for the Hallé would be provisional on the Hallé Board producing a development plan with convincing evidence of "the re-invigoration of the orchestra that we all feel is now needed". The Hallé was stung by the reference to "re-invigoration", and on questioning it received a letter from Luke Rittner which said that the statement "is not intended to be all-embracing, and is likely to change . . ."

However, another Arts Council letter in February, 1989, reiterated the demand for progress in "reinvigoration" of the orchestra. The use of the phrase was again (partly) retracted, after complaints from Smart – it was now said to have referred to the Hallé Concerts Society and not the Hallé Orchestra. Waters were further muddied when discussions of the Hallé Business Plan by officers of AGMA with the Arts Council music department brought the comment from the latter that a weakness in it was the lack of mention of artistic policy: Smart pointed out that this was "completely wrong" because the Arts Council itself had said there was no need for re-statement of the artistic policy already in the Strategic Plan when submitting the Business Plan.

When the first Incentive Funding application of 1989 was rejected, Smart reported that he had been told by the scheme director (the same person who had previously been Acting Music Officer) that the Arts Council's own "inadequate resources" had been a significant factor in the Hallé's lack of success. Smart also commented that the director "appeared unaware of his predecessor's assurance that the Hallé need not restate its artistic policies in the Business Plan . . ." – implying that it seemed the Arts Council was searching for excuses for its treatment of the Hallé, even if they were illogical ones. However, the Arts Council's assessor on the Hallé Board contradicted the assertion that shortage of funds had been a factor in the decision. This implied that other factors had played a part – but the formal Arts Council decision was that the application document itself lacked clarity and therefore the application would not even be put to assessment.

A letter from the Arts Council soon afterwards detailed "the Council's criteria for subsidy", which included, under "Artistic performance and standards", "Maintenance and development of artistic standards", "Programming: range and enterprise" and "Commitment to new work"; along with two other headings ("Strategic Role" and "Organisation Effectiveness"), which included reference to education work, success in attracting and broadening audiences, local authority support, commitment to training, efficiency in management, success in generating earned income, and "success in giving overall value for money". It is clear from this list that "artistic performance and standards" were now defined by the Arts Council in a very comprehensive manner, and it seems this was the first time, as far as the Hallé was concerned, that such a statement of targets in the "artistic" field had been given to it.

The report on the second Hallé application for Incentive Funding in 1989 (also refused) reveals considerably more about the divergence of view between the Arts Council and the Hallé about artistic matters. The substantive decision was based on the grounds that "the Hallé is presently moving too fast to achieve a clear picture" (of its management's ability to implement its own plans), but offered an extensive account of the Arts Council view of the Hallé's artistic policies and standards, and acknowledged that there would "normally" be a consensus on the subject between the funding body and the applicant organisation, while observing that this was not so in the case of the Hallé.

The Arts Council view, it said, was that the Hallé had "no clear artistic policy or consensus", that there was "low morale which may affect standards" and that it was an "organisation in artistic decline". (It specifically excluded the orchestra's playing standards from this description, noting that "as in the earlier Arts Council assessment, there was complete unanimity of view that the playing standards of the orchestra were now very high and that Skrowaczewski, through his very disciplined approach, was largely responsible for this.") It noted also that "the Hallé Board members in particular were very keen to understand unambiguously the basis of any Arts Council dissatisfaction and then deal with it".

References to aspects of artistic matters are included in the report's survey of the Hallé's senior personnel, which included the view that Skrowaczewski had "a weak public persona", and that Smart "sets the style of the organisation and this style has concerned both the ACGB appraisal team and the present ACGB officers". The suggestions that an Artistic Working Group or Music Panel was needed, and the evident approval of the fact that "the Board is now deciding policy and appears genuinely open to advice from ACGB as to the best way to set artistic policy", and that "Clive Smart's dominance will inevitably diminish . . ." suggest a perception on the part of Arts Council officials that Smart had not heeded their views sufficiently in the past. (The outcome of the change to being "artistically led", which followed not long afterwards, suggests that taking greater heed of them was not to yield any obviously better results in the future).

What all this had to do with the basic concept of Incentive Funding – that of rewarding those who obtained the most from private sources – was never explained. The Hallé's Brother sponsorship of 1989-92 was actually one of the largest ever obtained by an orchestra.

The Hallé Board formed the clear impression that the assessor had been working to a brief on the Hallé which had been less than fair. The Executive expressed disquiet at "opinions . . . which were unrelated to issues discussed . . . and appeared to be unsubstantiated . . ."

The 1990s

The pattern of events in the first half of the 1990s was one of short-lived optimism (accompanying the temporary boom in the United Kingdom economy generally) followed by a standstill in the Arts Council's own budget after 1993, which had its effect on the finances of its symphony orchestra clients. The Arts Council's funding from the Government was now worth 2.75% less in real terms than two years previously, the new Secretary-General, Mary Allen, pointed out in the 1995 annual report. She made it clear that extra money was now available only for "fledgling enterprises" and "organisations facing imminent collapse", along with provision for filling gaps and helping small-scale venues. The cutbacks applied to all the regional orchestras. [260]

The Arts Council's grant to the Hallé for 1991-2 was at first set at the low level which had obtained for the preceding years. But the grant for 1992-3 was 17.9% higher and represented an adjustment of the shortfall which had existed for many years. This decision was made in the wake of David Richardson's appointment and seems to have represented Arts Council approval of the direction the Hallé was then taking. But by August, 1994, the appraisal of that year had had its effect, Richardson had decided to leave, and the Hallé was struggling to assure the Arts Council of its intention to produce a balanced budget for 1994-5. The refusal of "Challenge Funding" in early 1995 was a blow to Alan Dean's attempts to achieve this. When the Hallé Board met in May, 1995, for the formal presentation of the appraisal report, they were told that costs needed to be controlled, but also that "the Arts Council wanted to help them to recover the energy and adventure that had characterised the Hallé's work over many years". So why had there been all the previous talk about decline and a need for reinvigoration?

It was an approach which clearly puzzled others in the meeting. One Board member said: "You have been very keen to tell us what is wrong, but never . . . what you want."

---

[260]But in Birmingham the City Council gave the CBSO an extra £250,000, spread over two years, to help with cash-flow problems – King-Smith, 1995: 233.

Chapter 14

'It is axiomatic that one cannot be both great and comfortable'[261]

It is time to take the long view of the Hallé story: what kind of organisation is it, and how did it get to where it was in the late 1990s?

The Hallé Concerts Society began its life with the intention of carrying on a great man's work. It succeeded, and for many years it was very much the possession of Manchester's wealthy, who could not only afford its high admission prices but could (if they were among its guarantors) contribute to paying off its losses, too. Taking on a commitment to highly expensive artists, without large financial resources, was thus a precedent set at the very beginning, and the whole enterprise depended on the goodwill of those who loved music and had money.

But social conditions changed. Individual wealth was not what it had been, recording and broadcasting were opening up new audiences, and it is clear that by the 1920s the Hallé's top admission prices were, in real terms, substantially lower than before 1914. In addition, the support of Manchester Council enabled the Municipal Concerts to be given, with universally low admission prices, affordable by all.

In the 1930s the Hallé encountered a period of prolonged financial difficulty, but its artistic aspirations remained high. Although raising ticket prices was never considered a possibility, it took radical measures (including linking itself to the BBC) to sustain its viability without jeopardizing musical standards – in my view, that is the sense in which the "Halle tradition" may be said, at this stage, to have been born. We may also observe, however, that the business record of the 1930s gives no indication that repertoire choice alone could overcome the effect of wider economic circumstances.

[261]Rosenbaum, 1967: 167.

The period after the Second World War brought a completely new dimension to the Hallé's situation: it was a much larger and more complicated organisation, employing a full-time orchestra and also fundamentally dependent on grant income as well as box-office earnings. Public money was universally seen to have taken the place of the old philanthropy. Undoubtedly it was under severe financial pressure throughout the late 1940s and 1950s, and the fact that Sir John Barbirolli achieved so much at this time must be linked inescapably with his own artistic gifts and personality. His sacrifice of personal enrichment in order for the Hallé to prosper was unique in the orchestra's history, and his magnetism as an artist helped to build the enormous Manchester audiences which were not reflected in Birmingham or Liverpool at the time.

But there was certainly no question of his being able to work without a constant eye on the costs of everything he planned. This is the point behind the (no doubt intentional) ambiguity of the statement by Michael Kennedy[262] that "the Hallé's greatest artistic periods have also been periods of financial crisis and instability" – whereas it may have been true in Richter's time *because of* the costs which his leadership brought and which had been accepted from the start, in Barbirolli's time the artistic achievement was *despite* financial problems which were not of the Hallé's own making but were chronic and unavoidable.

Post-war admission prices were lower in real terms than ever before, and much lower than they were to become in the 1980s and 1990s. The need for "permanent" symphony orchestras (ie those providing employment full-time and round the year) to be given public subsidy was not questioned when the first four were established during the war. Previously only the BBC had been able to offer musicians such terms. But the effects of dependence on subsidy were still to be worked out – and have been ever since. The Arts Council rapidly produced the policy of requiring "pound for pound" support, which meant that local authorities were to take an equal share in supporting the orchestras and was to be applied from 1951 onwards.

The result – struggles for support from Manchester, in particular, and the other local authorities of Lancashire and Cheshire – hit the Hallé at a particularly vulnerable time, as it was preparing to enlarge its payroll of musicians and return to the re-built Free Trade Hall for its concerts. What emerged was that the removal of a part of its subsidy income – or even the threat of it – could produce radical effects in its artistic life. It abandoned attempts to reduce its number of concerts per year to the level of "the great orchestras abroad", and established new, down-market Manchester concert series which have remained part of its pattern of activity to this day.

The role of private contributions to the orchestra's finances had almost completely disappeared. It was assumed, since the advent of the Arts Council, that

[262]Kennedy, 1960.

public patronage had taken the place of private. Any appeal to guarantors or any other donors to provide funds to meet unsustainable losses was simply viewed as anachronistic.

Manchester City Council's unreliability was a major cause of the Hallé's difficult financial situation then. But the ultimate effect of the changes in 1952 was that the Hallé's public support in Manchester became more obvious than ever, and councillors were more easily able to vote financial aid to the orchestra. The identification of city and orchestra reached its high point at the orchestra's centenary in 1958.

The patient building of, first, balance sheet reserves and, later, trust funds enabled the Hallé in the sixties to adopt a measure of independence from its funding bodies. It is arguable that such independence should have enabled greater artistic freedom than was exercised in reality, but in fact the Hallé became firmly attached to its existing pattern of activity. Even in the late 1960s, Barbirolli was only permitted to plan his own projects to the extent that financial policy allowed. But his personal prestige brought prestige to the orchestra, and because he was so indefatigable a worker, it was possible for the Hallé to derive considerable artistic credit from a series of recordings which were only part of his own output.

The early years of James Loughran's conductorship (from 1970) were the Hallé's most financially comfortable period of its entire first century, in that it was receiving about 50% of its total income in the form of grants – from the Arts Council, Manchester City Council and other local authorities of Lancashire and Cheshire.[263] It was also a time of ambition and achievement artistically, but in which the effects of inflation meant that financial insecurity was ever-present.

The creation of the Greater Manchester Metropolitan Council in 1974 did not bring substantially greater resources, but fatally damaged the Hallé's links with Manchester City Council. And when the Metropolitan Counties were extinguished, the post-1985 settlement struck at the roots of the Hallé's continuing financial viability. The City Council did not, for some time, show signs of resuming responsibility for the orchestra which had once been its pride, and it was the uncertainties over the level of local authority support which, in the late 1980s, led to the abandonment of the full series of the Hallé's Sunday concerts.

In the latter part of the eighties, with one of the most distinguished musicians of his generation, Stanislaw Skrowaczewski, as principal conductor, public subsidy retreated further. Dependence on private sources (in particular, corporate

---

[263]Kennedy, 1982: 124, observes that the orchestra's earned income in 1975-76 was "spectacularly high", but it should be borne in mind that from the mid-sixties to the early 1980s it was both earning large amounts at the box office (through historically very high attendances) and receiving a high level of grant income, with the rather paradoxical result that its earned income, as a percentage of operational turnover, was at lower levels than any time before or since in the 20th century. The year 1974-5, in fact, represents the all-time low of that figure – see Table 7.3.

sponsorship) was advocated as the solution to orchestras' ills. But it proved variable in its sustainability and essentially inadequate.

When the financial situation deteriorated in the 1990s, leading to the huge crisis of 1998, who was really to blame? It is a tempting question to ask, as it implies that responsibility can be pinned to one or more individuals concerned with particular aspects of the Hallé in the last decade of the 20th century. Candidates might be chosen from the areas of artistic leadership, the orchestra's own organisation and governance, or local and national officialdom.

Artistic leadership

First, it is important to examine whether the artistic record of the Hallé prior to 1990 was a good one, as criticism of it was made, both by a succession of Arts Council officers and by Skrowaczewski's successor, Kent Nagano, after his appointment ("You have not been getting good literature . . ."). There is no doubt at all that Skrowaczewski increasingly had to work within financial limitations which he did not welcome, but also that he achieved artistic results which have seldom been bettered in the history of the Hallé.

Analysis of the Manchester programmes shows that they had remained innovative and varied to a high degree for many of the post-Barbirolli years, as far as the Thursday concert series was concerned, and the need to attract large audiences to the other series was essential to survival. The Hallé was in reality two orchestras: one playing programmes of challenge and distinction to a discerning audience, and the other churning out the "pops" to a larger group of music-lovers, whom it needed, if anything, much more. It was, in reality, one of the least elitist of symphony orchestras (whatever members of Manchester City Council may have thought).

Its music-making had actually been so successful through the 1970s and early 1980s that in audience terms there was very little room for expansion. Introducing greater challenge in repertoire – which was undoubtedly Skrowaczewski's aspiration – was thus almost bound to result in decreased attendances, by comparison with the past, and the Hallé did not have the backing, as did the CBSO, of a city council keen to attract a reputation from reflected glory.

After 1991, there is in reality no evidence that Kent Nagano's programmes were any more or less successful in attracting audiences than Skrowaczewski's. Attendances generally seem to have been lower in those seasons which Nagano designed (1993-4 onwards), but factors other than programme content could be identified as causes for poorer ticket sales, and audiences for classical music were falling as a national trend in Britain at the time. Even the pattern of the Opus One concerts did not change appreciably, although their programme content was slowly becoming assimilated with that of the other series.

But Nagano's departure was finally described as "a bathetic end" by Stephen Moss (*The Guardian*, May 28th, 1999), and Stephen Pettitt of the *Sunday Times* wrote, on June 13th: "His failure to mould a world-class orchestra has been disappointing." In my opinion, these judgments are unfair and based on limited knowledge, as those of London-based writers on Manchester musical life often are. The record of the Nagano years is one of remarkable achievement in performance, and the legacy on disc is extraordinary. To be an orchestra-in-residence at the Salzburg Festival, as it was in 1998, and to make its acclaimed CDs of the John Adams works, along with *Das Klagende Lied* and *Saint Francois D'Assise,* are peaks comparable to the greatest moments in the Hallé's past.

Pettitt's article in 1999 also reflected a judgment which has been widely made over recent years, by reporting the BBC Philharmonic's claim to be drawing 85% audiences at the Bridgewater Hall, against the Hallé's 70% – the implication being that the Hallé was failing to draw audiences, in comparison with the Philharmonic. But the 85% figure was originally given by the BBC for audience levels in the hall's opening season of 1996-97, and figures revealed since then show that the BBC Philharmonic's average paying audience for 1997-8 was about 60%, whereas the Hallé's was around 70%. In 1998-9, after ticket price increases, the average paying audience for the BBC Philharmonic was 62%, while the Hallé's average was 66% . Furthermore, the relative length of the various concerts series should be borne in mind: the BBC Philharmonic give about 15 concerts in the Bridgewater Hall each season, the Hallé about 80 in total. The Hallé Opus One series (where the eight programmes are each given three times in a week) drew 85% paying customers in 1997-8, and 76% in 1998-9. No other classical concerts at the venue draw paying audiences of 5,000 to 6,000 per programme, on a regular basis.

If judgments are to be made about Hallé attendances, the most significant point to note is that by the 1990s, Hallé admission prices were higher, in real terms, than at any time since the Second World War, in respect of the midweek and Sunday series (though the fact that the Opus One series in 1985-95 had an average attendance of 82% on a pattern of three performances of each programme means that it was achieving some of the highest aggregate audiences in Hallé history – and for most of this period it was still priced in a lower range than the other Hallé winter series). Were lower attendances than in the 1970s really so surprising in view of that?

Organisation and governance

But what of the financial record? Of course it does not look good. Was it all just a matter of management incompetence? Even a cursory look at the account of what happened in the Hallé's finances in the 1980s and 1990s must show that managing an organisation which is dependent on both the public's fickle tastes for entertainment and the fads and fancies of the grant-giving arts establishment is an exceptionally difficult skill. One might point to the enlargement of administrative staff over the years, and particularly in the 1990s (reversed, of course, to an extent in 1998). But administrative costs have never been a major cause of the Hallé's recent problems, which have stemmed far more from the risks of artistic enterprise, whether in individual events or long-term commitments. It is arguable that there should really have been more administrative back-up, to promote the artistic work effectively – as Kent Nagano pointed out in 1995, organisations such as the Opéra de Lyon and London Symphony Orchestra were able to sell 20th century music because they had the support staff to do it, but the Hallé did not.

At the most fundamental level, the success of an orchestral organisation depends on the team of people who are at its head, and the nature of the relationships between them. The Arts Council appraisal of 1994 quickly concluded that all was not well in this respect at the Hallé, and the effects of that judgment – coming at a crucial point in the preparations for the opening of the Bridgewater Hall – were critical. It is worth referring here to the research done by Erin Lehman and others in the field of orchestra management in the United States, as the Hallé's structure is in many ways similar to that of US orchestras (and unlike the self-governing London orchestras).

Adam Galinksy and Erin Lehman wrote (comparing American, East German and London orchestral organisations in 1995): "The power relations within the organization comprise a triangle with the managing director, music director and players representing the corners. The triangle rests on a base that is either a lay board of trustees, a government committee, or, in a self-governing orchestra, the players themselves . . . In the American model . . . the relationship between the managing director and music director is a balancing act . . ."[264]

Allmendinger, Hackman and Lehman studied 41 major orchestras in four countries and came to the following conclusions (among others):

"The more say the board of directors and the managing director have in orchestral decision making, the greater the orchestra's financial strength. The more say players have about orchestra decisions . . . the weaker it is financially. And, finally, orchestras in which the authority of the music director extends to organizational and operational decisions tend to be weaker financially than those in which the music director's contributions focus mainly on artistic matters . . ."[265]

Whether these verdicts "fit" the Hallé in any precise way is not the point. I think in fact they do not. But they illustrate the critical nature of the relationships between those who wield power at the top of any orchestral organisation which has a board-executive-employees governance structure (and in English contract orchestras, the crucial "triangle" is surely that of chief executive, music director and chairman). It seems clear that the Hallé had trouble clarifying the relationship

[264]Galinsky & Lehman, 1995.
[265]Allmendinger, Hackman & Lehman, 1994.

between Kent Nagano as music director and the chief executive and Board with whom he had to deal. Indeed, such relationships are not clear-cut in any orchestra – Paul Judy of the Symphony Orchestra Institute in the US writes: "Music directors typically . . . 'report' to the board of directors. It usually is unclear exactly what this means . . ."[266]

Givers of grants

What of the funding bodies? The Hallé, as we have seen, was never meant to exist, from 1943 onwards, without substantial public funding. At its most successful period in audience terms, it relied on public money for almost 50% of its entire income. And it did not encounter major problems of finance until after the abolition of the Metropolitan Counties in the mid-1980s.

The Hallé's General Committee appreciated from the start that the end of the GMC would be critical to its finances, but found itself in the middle of a buck-passing process involving the Arts Council and the local councils represented by the Association of Greater Manchester Authorities. The impression is very strong that consideration of the Hallé's position was then being simply postponed, at a time when the choice had to be made between seeking to emulate the CBSO or aiming simply to survive.

By the time of the appointment of Kent Nagano in 1991, it was apparently an Arts Council mantra that increased subsidy from itself would automatically bring greater gains from non-Arts Council sources.[267] It was tempting to suppose that the appointment of a dynamic young conductor would evoke the same enthusiasm that Simon Rattle seemed to inspire among the Birmingham city fathers – but this proved over-optimistic. Only Manchester City Council's grant for 1993-4 was significantly increased – but from such a low base that it made little difference to the Hallé's position. Nor did the Arts Council do more than bring the Hallé's grant level with comparable provincial orchestras (in 1992-3) – after which its own budget was frozen, resulting in cuts for all its clients in real terms for several years afterwards. The decision to use large amounts from the Hallé Trust Fund in an attempt to balance the accounts for 1994-5 was a measure of the desperation to which the Hallé had been brought.

But in one sense, the crisis of February, 1998, need not have been a crisis at all, because the Hallé's trust funds (the "family silver") were still there as a substantial backstop. However, the crisis enabled a thorough shake-up of the organisation, and the establishment of patterns of activity which have more relevance to the present day than before, while retaining a degree of independence for an organisation which has always guarded its autonomy.

[266]Judy, 1995.
[267] See Anthony Everitt in the annual report of 1991.

The Hallé Board believed that the existence of its trust funds had for long been a reason why the Arts Council would not assist it more generously (despite the Conservative Government's doctrine of rewarding self-help and approval of private patronage), and the most recent Hallé annual accounts have shown the funds' balances amalgamated with those of the Hallé Society itself, to show net available resources. There is clearly a charge to answer here: why should an organisation which builds up background funds be penalised, by comparison with those which do not? In the USA, the necessity for substantial endowments to support orchestras is universally assumed.

In Birmingham, things are slightly different: there is a City of Birmingham Orchestral Endowment Fund, which is not *exclusively* devoted to the work of the CBSO (although its objects name it as a particular recipient of support) which has been built up only since the mid-1980s, and in recent years has been able to make substantial donations to the orchestra. Its funds are not consolidated with those of the CBSO.

In a wider context, the relevance of the Hallé story to the debate about public subsidy for orchestras is the clear evidence it gives that the most radical effects of changes in subsidy regime arise from times of unpredictability and unreliability (as in 1952 and 1989). There is also no evidence that a provincial symphony orchestra in Britain, although it may be fully employed and draw large audiences, can be financially sustained on the proceeds of performances alone (this has been true both of the era before public subsidy and that under it, in the 20th century). Policies in the late 1980s and early 1990s which seemed calculated to encourage arts organisations to "stand on their own feet" led to near-disaster (and not only for the Hallé).

There is no doubt that over the past half-century the Arts Council has been supportive of the Hallé and relatively generous to it. But there were a number of changes of policy over the years which have meant that its aid was not as valuable as it might otherwise have been. One example was the promise made in 1952 that the Hallé would not be penalised for building up its own reserves – broken three years later. In the same way the assurances of 1986 that the Hallé's Endowment Trust Fund would not be used as a reason for restricting its grant were rapidly broken.[268]

In the sixties and seventies there was a gradual adoption of interventionist action by the Arts Council on artistic matters. It began to criticise the Hallé for the size of its orchestra and the size of its ambitions, which raises the suspicion of a view being adopted by the Arts Council of its own role as the sole arbiter of what Britain's arts bodies should do (presumably this is what the Hallé Committee meant by referring to its "blanket approach" in 1988). The procedure whereby

---

[268]Tooley, 1999, mentions the similar experience of the Royal Opera House that the achievement of surpluses brought not plaudits from the Arts Council, but reduced grants afterwards.

Stanislaw Skrowaczewski was found wanting on artistic matters by an accountant, who based his report on a one-day visit to the orchestra offices, must surely rank as an extreme of the 1980s emphasis on consultancies and the imposition of "incentive" arrangements when in reality continuity of support was needed.

The verdict

So who was to blame? Perhaps the case of the Hallé in the 1980s and 1990s could be compared to the Murder On The Orient Express. They were *all* guilty to some degree – knives went in from various quarters, for a variety of motives. To single out any one factor for blame would be to ignore the others.

The 1990s, of course, are the period during which everyone knows the problems reached crisis point. Although the verdict of "mismanagement" was easy to give at the time, it should be clear that there was very much more to it than that. The question of whether ticket price levels were raised a few times too much and too often has been discussed already. Audience loyalty can take a long time to build and a lot to destroy, but, once gone, it is very hard to bring back. Public relations campaigns can have negative as well as positive effects, and much depends, in the last resort, on the impact of individual personalities in performance. Manchester itself has long had the tendency to cry "Ichabod!"[269] when looking at the artistic achievements of the past, but it has no reason to do so as far as the Hallé is concerned.

With a core income of the level the orchestra was reduced to in the 1990s, of course there were decisions which it could not afford. But with a core function such as it has always aspired to, how could it afford anything less? And now it is in a new era, with a new holder of its purse-strings, as the Arts Council of England passes responsibility on to the regional North West Arts Board. How successful that partnership will be, in helping to sustain Charles Hallé's unique vision, remains to be seen.

[269]I Samuel 4:21.

Tables

The tables which follow are based on the belief that there is value in the empirical analysis of performed repertoire in a survey of the work of an orchestra. There are those who would divide composers into "classical", "romantic", "modern", "20th century", "contemporary", and so on, according to their own stylistic or historical definition. But it can lead to contradiction. One writer[270] for instance, defines "20th century music" as being that of composers born in 1881 or later, but bends his boundary to include Schoenberg (1874-1951) and Janacek (1854-1928). Another survey[271] attempts a definition of "20th century" music which excludes Mahler (1860-1911), Sibelius (1865-1957) and Richard Strauss (1864-1949). Another cites Mahler as an example of a "major 20th century composer".[272]

But there is little doubt that empirical assessments of performed repertoire are also used, and a variety of methods have been suggested and used[273.] Dates of composition, for instance, have been noted (or guessed) and one American survey[274] defines "20th century music" as works composed from 1900 to 1939, and "contemporary music" as those from 1940 to 1970. An Arts Council of England survey in 1994[275] found it useful to divide all repertoire into four groups

[270]Heilbrun, James (1998): The Decline in Opera Repertory Diversity in North America as Evidence of an Artistic Deficit. Revised version of paper presented at the 10th International Conference on Cultural Economics, Barcelona, 9.
[271]Heilbrun, James & Charles M Gray (1993):The Economics of Art and Culture: an American Perspective (Cambridge University Press, New York).
[272]Lewis, R M (1998): The Educational Functions of the Royal Liverpool Philharmonic Society 1840-1990. PhD thesis: University of Liverpool, Department of Education
[273]In what follows here I am greatly indebted to the findings of a thesis by E Christine Hall (1997): Survey and Analysis of the Repertory of Twenty-Six American Symphony Orchestras 1982-3 through 1993-4 (Peabody Institute of the John Hopkins University, Baltimore, Maryland).
[274]Gilmore, Samuel, 1993: Tradition and Novelty in Concert Programming (Sociological Forum 8:2) quoted in Hall, 1997.
[275]BBC/Arts Council Review of National Orchestral Provision, Consultation Document (Arts Council of England, London), 1994.

by date of composition: pre-1900, 1900-1945, 1946-1982, and post-1982. Date of composition is, of course, not always known, and can be misleading when (as in the case of Schubert's "Unfinished" Symphony) a work first became known some years after its original composition. Composers' birth dates have been used[276], and also their dates of death[277]. "Popularity" is also a concept for which empirical definitions are sought, for instance by calculation of the percentage of works by the top five or top ten most frequently performed composers in a given period.[278]
It is also clear that concepts such as "innovation", "range", "diversity", "popularity" and "accessibility" are often used by commentators, and also by the Arts Council of Great Britain, to describe aspects of programming.[279] In one form or another, the same concepts are used by critics and, not least, by ticket-buyers – perhaps in each case to draw different conclusions.

The American arts economist James Heilbrun[280] uses a mathematical measure of concentration in a study of opera repertoire: the "Herfindahl Index", borrowed from mainstream economics.[281]   This can indicate comparative concentration (a higher figure) or diversity (a lower figure) in a set of percentage divisions of a group of data.

This survey has been based on a selection of five periods in Hallé history, each of 10 years. It would have been an enormous task to survey the whole century: as it is, half has been covered. These periods were selected to make up a fairly even spread, avoid wartime, include at least a half-decade of the incumbency of each major Hallé conductor of the 20th century, and relate to those periods where the archive evidence is at its best (thus allowing for estimates of average attendance to be included alongside repertoire analysis).

The tables for each period of ten years are made up of two kinds of

---

[276]eg the definition of "20th century" just cited.
[277]Percentages of works by composers who were living, or not, at the time of performance are quite often calculated.
[278]Gilmore, 1993; Lewis, 1998.
[279]For instance, the Arts Council of Great Britain's "Criteria for Subsidy" announced in 1989 included "Programming: range and enterprise"; and "Commitment to new work", and "Success in attracting and broadening audiences". A telephone enquiry to the Arts Council of England in October 1997 produced the response that (inter alia): "We look at the percentage of new work put on, and whether little-done pieces are included" . The Orchestras Officer, Olivia Lowson, replied that priorities included seeking evidence of "adventurous and innovative" programming, and "moving away from the broad mainstream" of orchestral works.
[280]Heilbrun, 1998.
[281]Used by the U.S. Justice Department since 1982 to evaluate company mergers, this assesses the extent to which a few companies or products dominate a market. It is based on a previously calculated set of "market share" figures: each percentage is squared and the totals added together – thus an absolute monopoly scores 10,000 (100 X 100), and 100 companies with 1% each would produce an index of 100 (1 X 1 added 100 times). The squaring gives higher values to sets which have a small number of components possessing a high "market share" in each case. Thus a high number means greater concentration, and a lower one greater diversity.   In this particular application where there are six percentage figures the minimum Herfindahl Index is 1634.

empirical analysis: one relating to the historical pattern of all the works performed in each Hallé concert series in Manchester, season by season, designed to measure, and to facilitate comparison of, factors such as novelty, modernity, and degree of historical diversity or concentration in repertoire; the other illustrating the variety of composers whose work was performed – set alongside the average attendance level (as a percentage of hall capacity).

The first table (in respect of each series) contains nine columns: the first three are the numerical totals of world premieres, English premieres and "first performances in Manchester" of each season. This is an indication of the novelty of the music played, by simple and consistently recorded criteria. The next five columns show a percentage division of the total works performed, according to the dates of the deaths of their composers, grouped in 50-year segments (retrospectively from the date of the concert concerned). This provides a form of historical analysis of the works performed, and identifies the percentage of works by living composers given in each season, and also that of works by those who were near-contemporary and those who were figures from the past, divided by specific periods of time. This analysis of the music avoids division by style, school, "period", etc., but demonstrates the historical range of repertoire at different times. The Herfindahl Index, given in the last column, shows the degree of historical concentration indicated by the five percentage divisions.

The second table's three columns represent two different assessments of the make-up of all programmes in a series. The Composer Variety Index measures overall variety, by the ratio of the number of composers represented to the total of works performed (so 20 works representing 10 composers give an index of 0.5; 20 works by 20 different composers give an index of 1). The "Enterprise rating" multiplies this figure by the actual number of concerts in the series, to give a weighting to the variety figures according to the length of the series (clearly, variety measured in the way just described is more easily achievable in a short concert series than a long one). These are set alongside the estimated average paid-for attendance level (based on recorded data) for the series.[282] For the purpose of this survey, repeated concerts such as the weekday series in the 1950's and early 1960's, and the Opus One series in all periods) are considered as single instances. But most comparisons are within series, rather than across them, so the point makes little difference to my conclusions.

---

[282] For a fuller account of the methodology used in this repertoire survey and tables, readers are referred to the Appendix of the author's research thesis for City University ("The Halle Concerts Society 1899-1999: Financial constraints and artistic outcomes").

TABLE 1.1

Composer analysis averages in 10-year periods in Hallé history
(a = living; b = died in past 50 years; c = died in past 100-51 years; d = died in past 150-101 years; e = died in past 200-151 years; f = died in past 201 years or more)

Period	World Prems	English Prems (per series)	Mcr Prems	a %	b %	c %	d %	e %	f %	Herfindahl Index
1903-13	0.3	0	3	23	40	25	7	5	0	2828
1925-35	0.5	1	7	31	34	11	18	6	0	2598
1945-55 midweek	0.4	0.8	8	27	27	18	15	11	1	2129
1945-55 weekend (Sat & Sun)	0.2	0.2	4	14	28	30	21	6	0	2357
1952-55 Industrial	0	0	0	10	38	34	14	2	2	2904
1952-55 Proms	0	0	0	17	37	31	12	3	0	2772
1965-75 midweek	0.6	0.6	9	20	33	22	14	9	3	2259
1965-75 Sunday	0	0.1	3	13	26	28	21	9	3	2160
1965-75 industrial (renamed Opus One)	0	0	0	8	31	34	18	8	1	2570
1965-75 Proms	0.1	0	0	13	34	36	11	4	1	2759
1985-95 midweek	0.3	0.4	7	14	27	29	9	17	3	2145
1985-95 Sunday	0	0.1	2	5	23	33	13	18	8	2200
1985-95 Opus One	0	0	1	2	21	33	19	18	6	2340
1985-95 Proms	0.1	0	0.5	5	29	39	13	9	5	2662

Commentary:

The general trend is towards a wider and more even historical spread in the repertoire over time, as concentration on the music of living and recent composers decreases (see the Herfindahl Index in all comparable instances), but the high rates of diversity established in the midweek series in 1945-55, and in the Sunday series in 1965-75, have not been subsequently exceeded.

In 1925-35 the proportion of work by living composers in the midweek series was higher than at any other time, and the combined total of music by living composers and those who had died in the preceding 50 years ("newer" music) was 65%. In the midweek series of 1945-55 the proportion of music by living composers was the second highest of the periods studied – 27% – and that of "newer" music 54%, and the degree of historical diversity (see the Herfindahl Index) was at its highest of all the periods analyzed. The pattern of concerts in 1965-75 shows a midweek series with 20% of music by living composers and 53% of "newer" music, and a Sunday series with the highest degree of historical diversity (see the Herfindahl Index) of all periods for this series. From 1985-95, in the midweek series, works by living composers made up 14% of the total, and "newer" music 41%. The degree of historical variety was high, exceeded only, in the periods studied, by that of 1945-55 – see the Herfindahl Index, the second lowest of all for midweek concerts (and the Composer Variety Index – see Table 1.2 – is the highest for the midweek series in all periods). But the proportion of works by living composers in the Sunday concerts fell to 5% (though Composer Variety – see Table 1.2 – here was still at its highest for the Sunday series of all periods), and in the Opus One series to 2%.

The Industrial concerts (later Opus One) and Proms, introduced in the early 1950s, have been characterised by a more historically concentrated repertoire than the other series since that time, but whereas the Industrial/Opus One repertoire became significantly more diverse in 1965-75 and again in 1985-95 (by that decade it attained characteristics, in this respect, similar to the series of 1945-55), the Proms repertoire has not changed so markedly.

TABLE 1.2

Variety, "enterprise" and attendance averages in 10-year periods in Halle history

Period	Variety Index	Average No of concerts per series	"Enterprise Rating"	Attendance
1903-13	0.43	21	9.0	69%
1925-35	0.49	21	10.3	62%
1945-55 midweek	0.65	15	9.9	86%
1945-55 weekend (Sat & Sun)	0.58	18	10.7	89%
1952-55 Industrial	0.59	9	5.3	93%
1952-55 Proms	0.77	11	8.3	87%
1965-75 midweek	0.66	18	11.7	89%
1965-75 Sunday	0.58	20	11.4	90%
1965-75 Industrial (renamed Opus One)	0.84	6	5.1	86%
1965-75 Proms	0.81	12	9.4	68%
1985-95 midweek	0.71	16	11.1	64%
1985-95 Sunday	0.76	11	8.7	66%
1985-95 Opus One	0.82	8	6.6	82%
1985-95 Proms	0.82	12	9.6	69%

Commentary:

In 1903-13 and 1925-35 the Hallé series was all midweek and consisted of 20 or 21 concerts; in 1945-55 and 1965-75 the weekday series was usually 15 concerts, the Sunday 20. By 1985-95 the weekday series varied between 15 and 17 concerts; the Sunday series was 15 or 16 until 1988-9, reducing thereafter to a range of 6-13 concerts in different years.

Audiences in 1945-55 were very high indeed, especially when the size of Belle Vue as the venue for the Sunday series for part of that period is considered – admission prices were also as low as they have ever been, in real terms, during this period.

The Composer Variety Indices for the weekday and Sunday series are higher in 1985-95 than ever before, and attendances lower than for any except 1925-35.

The Enterprise Rating for the main (ie, midweek) and Sunday series are at their highest in 1965-75: attendances for those series were also at their highest ever in that period.

The Composer Variety Index of the Industrial/Opus One concerts was significantly higher in 1965-75 and 1985-95 than in 1952-55, when these concerts were first introduced, though a lower Enterprise Rating reflects the reduction in number of separate programmes in the series in 1965-75. In 1985-95 that number stabilised at 8, a longer series than 1965-75.

The Proms series have varied greatly in number, but the Composer Variety of their programmes has always been high.

By the 1990s, attendances were lower (and real admission prices higher) than at any time since the Second World War, in respect of the midweek and Sunday series, though the fact that the Opus One series, 1985-95, had an average attendance of 82% on a pattern of three performances of each programme means that it was achieving some of the highest aggregate attendances in Hallé history (and for most of this period it was still priced in a lower range than the other Hallé winter series).

Unless otherwise stated, data has been sourced from Hallé programme booklets and other records.

TABLE 2.1

Hallé Manchester concerts: Composer analysis main series 1903-13
(a = living; b = died in past 50 years; c = died in past 100-51 years; d = died in past 150-101 years; e = died in past 200-151 years; f = died in past 201 years or more)

Season	World prems	English prems	Mcr prems	a %	b %	c %	d %	e %	f %	Herfindahl Index
1903-4	0	0	3	28	43	23	3	3	0	3180
1904-5	0	0	3	25	40	24	8	3	0	2874
1905-6	0	0	1	16	41	22	13	5	3	2624
1906-7	0	0	2	18	49	22	8	3	0	3282
1907-8	0	0	0	20	36	34	7	3	0	2910
1908-9	1	0	1	17	48	20	1	5	0	3019
1909-10	0	0	4	22	31	34	5	8	0	2690
1910-11	1	0	5	27	32	31	3	7	0	2772
1911-12	1	0	12	30	38	21	7	4	0	2850
1912-13	0	0	5	25	39	32	10	4	0	3286

Commentary:

In almost every season, the largest segment of works played was of those by composers who had died in the preceding 50 years. In Richter's time (until 1912), considered overall, this category accounted for 40% of items, with those by living composers, and those by composers who died between 51 and 100 years previously, each amounting to about a quarter of works played. Richter's programmes of 1903-4 had a higher proportion (71%) of music by living composers or those who had died in the preceding 50 years than in any subsequent season of his reign. His second-to-last season (1909-10) included 53% of this category – the lowest figure in this survey decade: pointing to an increasing emphasis on the music of the past.

The rate of occurrence of premieres and first performances in Manchester was lower than in the main weekday series in any of the subsequent periods studied, but the interregnum year (1911-12) included a larger number of items new to Manchester audiences than any other year in this survey decade and a higher proportion of music by living composers than before (30%) – an indication of the individual tastes of the visiting conductors that season, and of the relative conservatism of Richter's choices compared with those of a number of his contemporaries. Balling's first programmes (1912-13) were slightly more concentrated in historical spread than any of the previous decade – see the Herfindahl Index.

TABLE 2.2

Hallé Manchester concerts: Variety and popularity 1903-13 (see beginning of Tables for methods of calculation)

Season	Variety Index	"Enterprise rating"	Est. attendance
1903-4	0.46	9.6	76%
1904-5	0.49	10.3	73%
1905-6	0.36	7.6	72%
1906-7	0.37	7.8	71%
1907-8	0.36	7.6	75%
1908-9	0.36	7.6	73%
1909-10	0.42	8.9	67%
1910-11	0.39	8.3	63%
1911-12	0.43	9.1	64%
1912-13	0.62	13.0	61%

Number of concerts in series: 21
Concerts held in the Free Trade Hall (capacity 2450)

Commentary:

In this period as a whole, the variety of composers heard was less than in those of later times (see Table 1.1). 1903-4 and 1904-5 show greater Variety than any subsequent season under Richter (the figure was exceeded only in Balling's first season, 1912-13). After the financial loss of 1904-5, however, variety reduces and remains approximately level from 1905-6 to 1908-9. Two years which were profitable (1907-8 and 1908-9) are followed by somewhat higher figures for 1909-10 and 1910-11 (Richter's last). The interregnum year index is similar to that for 1909-10.

Attendances show a gradual decline, except for the "Jubilee Season" of 1907-8 and the following one. Richter's last season was attended by about 17% fewer than his first: however, neither the interregnum season nor Balling's first attracted significantly greater attendances overall.

TABLE 3.1

Hallé Manchester concerts: Composer analysis main series 1925-35
(a = living; b = died in past 50 years; c = died in past 100-51 years; d = died in past 150-101 years; e = died in past 200-151 years; f = died in past 201 years or more)

Season	World prems	English prems	Mcr prems	a %	b %	c %	d %	e %	f %	Herfindahl Index
1925-26	2	1	10	32	34	15	13	7	0	2594
1926-27	1	1	6	22	32	21	16	9	0	2286
1927-28	1	3	5	23	34	14	20	7	2	2234
1928-29	0	1	4	30	35	6	18	9	2	2570
1929-30	1	1	15	42	37	8	11	2	0	3223
1930-31	0	1	7	31	36	8	18	7	0	2694
1931-32	1	1	8	39	30	8	16	7	0	2790
1932-33	0	1	7	39	31	9	17	3	1	2862
1933-34	0	0	2	31	32	8	24	5	0	2650
1934-35	0	1	2	17	38	12	29	4	0	2734

Commentary:

Programming is more orientated to the contemporary than in Richter's time, with (on average) almost as many living composers represented as those who had died in the previous 50 years. However, the work of composers who had died between 101 and 150 years previously is (overall) more frequently represented than that of those who had died 51 to 100 years before: a sign, perhaps, of reaction against the predominant taste of the previous generation.

The Herfindahl Index shows that the degree of repertoire differentiation in an historical sense was higher than in 1903-13, with 1926-7 the season with the highest figure in this respect, and generally more concentration from 1929-30 onwards.

A policy of innovation was carried through from 1925-6 to 1929-30 (note the high numbers of "Manchester premieres" in the two seasons mentioned, and the percentages of works by living composers) and maintained in the years that followed until Harty's departure in 1933, but the emphasis on living composers was abandoned in 1934-5.

TABLE 3.2

Hallé Manchester concerts: Variety and popularity 1925-35 (see beginning of Tables for methods of calculations)

Season	Variety Index	"Enterprise rating"	Est. attendance
1925-26	0.59	12.4	65%
1926-27	0.53	11.1	65%
1927-28	0.48	10.2	70/5
1928-29	0.57	12.0	67%
1929-30	0.51	10.7	70%
1930-31	0.42	8.8	60%
1931-32	0.47	9.9	*51%
1932-33	0.46	9.6	53%
1933-34	0.44	9.2	56%
1934-35	0.45	9.5	59%

Number of concerts in series: 21
(* Data incomplete: this is an average of 16 concerts, not 20)
Concerts held in the Free Trade Hall (capacity 2450)

Commentary:
The degree of Composer Variety of Hallé programmes clearly fell from 1930 onwards. Comparison with the analysis in Table 3.1 shows that although Harty said then that he would make the programmes less "modern", he actually maintained relatively high levels of innovation and of music by living composers, but made the programmes somewhat less varied. Attendances fell, however, and did not recover for some time, both before and after Harty's departure in 1933, while Composer Variety remained at the new, lower level.
The impact of one of the Hallé's most enterprising principal conductors of the 20th century contrasts clearly with his predecessor and with subsequent programming styles (see also Table 3.1).

TABLE 3.3

Hallé Municipal Concerts: Composer analysis 1926-35
(a = living; b = died in past 50 years; c = died in past 100-51 years; d = died in past 150-101 years; e = died in past 200-151 years; f = died in past 201 years or more)

Season	World prems	English prems	Mcr prems	a %	b %	c %	d %	e %	f %	Herfindahl Index
1926-27	0	0	0	4	45	41	10	0	0	3822
1927-28	1	0	0	17	50	21	8	0	4	3310
1928-29	0	0	1	10	43	14	14	14	5	2562
1929-30	0	0	0	7	45	14	21	10	3	2820
1930-31	0	0	0	20	51	9	11	6	3	3248
1931-32	0	0	0	22	45	11	22	0	0	3114
1932-33	0	0	0	25	50	17	8	0	0	3478
1933-34	0	0	0	8	50	8	34	0	0	3784
1934-35	0	0	0	17	49	17	17	0	0	3268

TABLE 3.4

Hallé Municipal Concerts: variety 1926-35 (attendance and receipts data not available)

Season	Variety Index	"Enterprise rating"
1926-27	0.77	6.1
1927-28	0.79	4.7
1928-29	1.00	5.0
1929-30	1.00	7.0
1930-31	0.80	6.4
1931-32	0.83	4.2
1932-33	0.58	2.9
1933-34	0.83	3.3
1934-35	1.00	2.0

Number of concerts in series: variable (data incomplete)
Concerts held in the Free Trade Hall (capacity 2450)

Commentary on Tables 3.3 and 3.4:

Records have not survived of all the concerts in these series – figures are based on those that have. It is clear that the proportion of music by living composers and those of the recent past is lower than in the case of the main series, and that the programme contents were more historically concentrated – as one would expect of a series designed to be "popular". The series contained fewer concerts than the main series (varying between five and ten) and not all the programme details have survived: consequently the high Composer Variety figures have to be seen in the light of the Enterprise Rating in each case.

TABLE 4.1

Hallé Manchester concerts: Composer analysis main series 1945-55
(a = living; b = died in past 50 years; c = died in past 100-51 years; d = died in past 150-101 years; e = died in past 200-151 years; f = died in past 201 years or more)

Season	World prems	English prems	Mcr prems	a %	b %	c %	d %	e %	f %	Herfindahl Index
1945-46	0	1	10	33	28	16	12	10	1	2374
1946-47	0	0	4	30	27	12	12	17	2	2210
1947-48	0	0	9	24	31	20	13	12	0	2250
1949-50	0	1	16	38	17	8	17	20	0	2486
1950-51	0	0	11	17	30	23	19	9	2	2164
1951-52	0	0	12	21	24	21	24	8	2	2102
1952-53	2	0	5	24	27	25	10	12	2	2178
1953-54	1	0	+	23	34	15	15	11	2	2260
1954-55	0	5	6	27	26	17	20	10	0	2194

Commentary:

The series shows a considerable broadening of repertoire, compared with Tables 2.1. and 3.1, in terms of the historical range of music included – the Herfindahl Index figures are clearly lower than those for 1925-35, and much lower than for 1903-13. More works by composers whose death was more than 200 years prior to the date of performance are included than in the earlier tables, while the proportion of work by living composers and those who died in the previous 50 years remains comparably high.

The number of first performances in Manchester and the proportion of work by living composers both decline in the financially troubled years after 1950. However, the end of the ten-year period to 1955 shows signs of a return to the more adventurous pattern of its outset.

TABLE 4.2

Hallé Manchester concerts: Variety and popularity main series1945-55 (see beginning of Tables for methods of calculations)

Season	Variety Index	"Enterprise rating"	Est. attendance
1945-46	0.72	10.9	68%
1946-47	0.68	10.2	92%
1947-48	0.73	10.9	98%
1948-49	0.62	9.2	99%
1949-50	0.62	9.2	99%
1950-51	0.62	9.3	98%
1951-52	0.58	11.6	82%
1952-53	0.61	9.2	75%
1953-54	0.62	8.7	74%
1954-55	0.66	9.9	72%

Before 1951/2, this series was given as 15 concerts each on two consecutive nights at the Albert Hall Methodist Mission, Peter Street (capacity 1850). In 1951/2 it became a weekly series of 20 concerts at the rebuilt Free Trade Hall (capacity 2450), but thereafter reverted to 15 pairs of concerts on consecutive nights, with occasional extras such as special performances of The Dream Of Gerontius and the Pension Fund concert.

Commentary:

The variety of composers represented is higher than in 1903-13 or 1925-35 – but the series was usually shorter: 15 paired concerts, rather than 20 individual ones. The one season which offered 20 different midweek programmes, on the old Hallé pattern, was 1951-2, and the Composer Variety Index and "Enterprise Rating" here are very similar to those of Harty's heyday.

Attendances were quite consistently high, bearing in mind the demanding nature of the programmes, and their duplication from 1952-3 onwards in the Free Trade Hall.

TABLE 4.3

Composer analysis Sunday (1951-2: Sat & Sun) series 1945-55
(a = living; b = died in past 50 years; c = died in past 100-51 years; d = died in past
150-101 years; e = died in past 200-151 years; f = died in past 201 years or more)

Season	World prems	English prems	Mcr prems	a %	b %	c %	d %	e %	f %	Herfindahl Index
1945-46	0	0	3	8	28	35	21	8	0	2578
1946-47	0	0	3	16	20	32	24	8	0	2320
1947-48	0	0	5	15	32	33	13	7	0	2556
1949-50	0	0	5	16	29	29	17	9	0	2308
1950-51	0	0	5	16	26	30	20	7	1	2282
1951-52	0	1	8	11	28	29	21	11	0	2308
1952-53	1	0	4	13	28	23	30	4	2	2402
1953-54	0	0	3	11	29	35	24	1	0	2764
1954-55	1	1	4	18	33	25	19	5	0	2424

TABLE 4.4

Variety and popularity Sunday (1951-2: Sat & Sun) series 1945-55
(see beginning of Tables for methods of calculation)

Season	Variety Index	"Enterprise rating"	Est. attendanc
1945-6	0.53	12.4	50%
1946-7	0.58	9.9	97%
1947-8	0.62	10.5	97%
1948-9	0.56	11.8	98%
1949-50	0.63	12.6	93%
1950-1	0.56	11.8	89%
1951-2	0.55	12.0	97%
1952-3	0.57	7.9	91%
1953-4	0.67	10.0	89%
1954-5	0.56	8.4	86%

Before 1951-2, this series was given as 23 (in 1945-6), then 17 (1946-7 to 1947-8), then 20 or 21 (1949-50 to 1950-51) weekly concerts at the King's Hall, Belle Vue (capacity 6,000). From 1951-2, it was given at the Free Trade Hall (capacity 2450), with a few exceptions. The first of these seasons consisted of 22 Sunday concerts. four of them duplicated on Saturday, plus four Belle Vue Sunday concerts. In 1952-3 there were 14 Free Trade Hall Sunday concerts and seven at Belle Vue. In 1953-4 there were 15 at the Free Trade Hall and four at Belle Vue; in 1954-5 there were 15 at the Free Trade Hall and two at Belle Vue; thereafter the Christmas *Messiah* was the only regular Hallé event at Belle Vue. The shortening of the Sunday series after 1951-2 no doubt relates, among other factors, to the introduction of the Industrial series – a form of competition by the Hallé itself for the "popular" audience.

* Data incomplete

Commentary on Tables 4.3 and 4.4:

The pattern bears some resemblance to that of the Municipal Concerts of 1925-35, with a large predominance of "central" repertoire in historical terms (ie, that of the b,c, and d segments). Composer Variety is consistently lower than in the main series. The Sunday programmes were highly successful, with average audiences at Belle Vue from 1945-6 to 1950-51 of well over 5,000.

TABLE 4.5

Composer analysis Industrial series 1952-55
(a = living; b = died in past 50 years; c = died in past 100-51 years; d = died in past 150-101 years; e = died in past 200-151 years; f = died in past 201 years or more)

Season	World prems	English prems	Mcr prems	a %	b %	c %	d %	e %	f %	Herfindahl Index
1952-53	0	0	0	14	33	29	20	0	0	2534
1953-54	0	0	0	8	40	36	14	2	0	3160
1954-55	0	0	0	8	42	36	8	3	3	3206

TABLE 4.6

Variety and popularity Industrial series 1952-55
(see beginning of Tables for methods of calculation)

Season	Variety Index	"Enterprise rating"	Est. attendance
1952-53	0.43	3.8	?%
1953-54	0.66	6.7	?%
1954-55	0.69	5.5	93%

This series began in 1952-3, at the Free Trade Hall (capacity 2450), as nine programmes, seven of which were given as pairs. In 1953-4 there were 10 programmes: two given three times over, the remainder as pairs. In 1954-5 there were eight programmes: four given three times, three as pairs, one only once.

TABLE 4.7

Composer analysis Hallé Proms 1952-55
(a = living; b = died in past 50 years; c = died in past 100-51 years; d = died in past 150-101 years; e = died in past 200-151 years; f = died in past 201 years or more)

Season	World prems	English prems	Mcr prems	a %	b %	c %	d %	e %	f %	Herfindahl Index
1952-53	0	0	0	23	33	27	11	4	2	2488
1953-54	0	0	0	15	33	37	9	6	0	2800
1954-55	0	0	0	14	40	35	11	0	0	3142

TABLE 4.8

Variety and popularity Hallé Proms 1952-55
(See beginning of Tables methods of calculation)

Season	Variety Index	"Enterprise rating"	Est. attendance
1952-53	0.75	7.5	?%
1953-54	0.67	8.1	?%
1954-55	0.86	10.4	87%

The "Coronation" Proms of 1953 consisted of 10 concerts on consecutive nights in August. In 1954 eight concerts were given on consecutive nights in June, and four in August, followed by a gala concert in September. In 1955 12 concerts were given on consecutive nights in June and early July. All were in the Free Trade Hall (capacity 2450)

Commentary on the Industrial Concerts and Proms:
The new "Industrial" series, begun in 1952, showss a concentration on works from the "central" part of the repertoire – that of composers who had died in the past 150 years, with a smaller representation of living composers and of those of an earlier era. The Proms' programmes were more orientated to the present, but still with a high concentration level.

Composer variety, particularly after the first "Industrial" series, was higher than in the Sunday series, for both "Industrials" and "Proms".

Despite the limited data available, it appears that both these series were very successful in audience terms, with the frequency of the Industrial series rapidly increasing, and the number of Proms also gaining.

TABLE 5.1

Hallé Manchester concerts: Composer analysis main series 1965-75
(a = living; b = died in past 50 years; c = died in past 100-51 years; d = died in past 150-101 years; e = died in past 200-151 years; f = died in past 201 years or more)

Season	World prems	English prems	Mcr prems	a %	b %	c %	d %	e %	f %	Herfindahl Index
1965-66	1	1	4	19	40	19	12	10	1	2567
1966-67	0	0	5	16	30	32	10	8	4	2360
1967-68	0	1	11	19	34	23	11	10	3	2276
1968-69	1	0	9	17	21	32	15	9	6	2096
1969-70	1	0	11	22	36	20	16	4	2	2456
1970-71	1	5	8	19	33	21	19	5	3	2286
1971-72	0	0	8	23	33	19	10	13	2	2252
1972-73	1	0	9	23	37	10	16	12	2	2402
1973-74	1	0	9	16	31	23	18	10	2	2174
1974-75	0	2	16	21	31	21	13	10	4	2128

Commentary:

The high level of consistency in the programmes offered in this period (until 1973-4 and 1974-5) is remarkable in view of the change of principal conductor in 1970. The general shift of profile shown (a slightly greater bias to the past than in 1945-55) is explicable as an inevitable broadening of the repertoire with the passage of time, but the proportion of music by composers who were living or had died in the previous 50 years (or "newer" music) is in the range 46%-60% (except for 1968-9) – very similar to the range for 1945-55 (1968-9 was Barbirolli's silver jubilee year and the figure was 38%). The low Herfindahl Index figures show a greater historical diversity in the programmes than ever before.

TABLE 5.2

Variety and popularity main series 1965-75
(see beginning of Tables for methods of calculations)

Season	Variety Index	"Enterprise rating"	Est. attendance
1965-66	0.67	10.1	70%
1966-67	0.54	8.6	70%
1967-68	0.69	15.1	95%
1968-69	0.60	11.5	90%
1969-70	0.58	11.6	90%
1970-71	0.67	12.1	95%
1971-72	0.71	12.0	93%
1972-73	0.67	11.4	92%
1973-74	0.67	11.4	97%
1974-75	0.75	12.8	95%

The midweek series still consisted of 15 concerts, each given twice, in 1965. In 1966-7, 16 pairs were given, but from 1967-8 onwards the concerts became single programmes – at first a series of 22, in 1968-9 a series of 19, in 1969-70 a series of 20, in 1970-71 a series of 18, and from 1971-2 on, a series of 17.
Sources: Hallé programme booklets and records. Attendance figures are difficult to infer in this period, as precise records do not appear to be available, and the effect of inflation makes calculation from income problematical.
Hall capacity: approx. 2450.

Commentary:
The average Composer Variety Index for 1965-75 is 0.66 (for 1945-55 the average is 0.65) – with 1966-7 exceptional, having the lowest index of the period (0.54). The link with the falling attendances at the "pairs" of concerts seems clear, and the programmes of 1966-7 seem to have been a last attempt to change matters by a less adventurous policy. Once the decision to move to single Thursday concerts was taken, the previous pattern reasserted itself. It is interesting to compare the seasons from 1967-8 to 1969-70 with 1951-2 (see Table 4.2), the only previous post-war season to offer 20 non-repeated concerts – Composer Variety is extremely high in 1967-8, and this season shows a record "Enterprise rating" for all Hallé seasons; but the figures for the next two seasons are similar to 1951-2 (in the case of 1969-70, identical, although attendances were much higher than two decades earlier).

James Loughran's impact may be observed to the extent that in 1971-2 (the first season in which he had a hand in planning), the Composer Variety Index is higher than for any of the previous few years, and higher yet in 1974-5. His first four seasons outdid most of the Barbirolli seasons analysed, in Composer Variety.
Attendances at Manchester Hallé concerts in the mid-sixties were historically very high indeed, bearing in mind the pairing until 1966-7. The change to single mid-week concerts in 1967-8 brought attendance figures to 90%-plus, sustained over the change of conductor and for the rest of the period here under scrutiny.

TABLE 5.3

Composer analysis Sunday series 1965-75

(a = living; b = died in past 50 years; c = died in past 100-51 years; d = died in past 150-101 years; e = died in past 200-151 years; f = died in past 201 years or more)

Season	World prems	English prems	Mcr prems	a %	b %	c %	d %	e %	f %	Herfindahl Index
1965-66	0	1	2	12	25	33	16	12	2	2262
1966-67	0	0	7	19	33	26	16	4	2	2402
1967-68	0	0	2	16	27	30	19	7	1	2296
1968-69	0	0	3	12	30	31	17	7	3	2352
1969-70	0	0	3	14	26	33	17	5	5	2300
1970-71	0	0	2	9	17	29	34	9	2	2452
1971-72	0	0	4	18	22	35	17	5	3	2356
1972-73	0	0	3	7	26	24	20	17	6	2026
1973-74	0	0	5	10	18	22	28	16	6	1984
1974-75	0	0	2	10	36	19	23	10	2	2390

Commentary:

This series shows a similarly wide range of composer representation to that of the main series, though with a slightly more pronounced bias to the past when compared with the analysis of 1945-55, though the total proportion of "newer" music is not dissimilar from that period (the seasons of 1970-71 and 1973-4 were exceptionally low in this respect, but the range is otherwise 33% to 52%, compared with 36% to 51% for 1945-55 – and there were five "Manchester premieres" in the 1973-4 Sunday series).

TABLE 5.4

Variety and popularity Sunday series 1965-75
(see beginning of Tables for methods of calculations)

Season	Variety Index	"Enterprise rating"	Est. attendance
1965-66	0.60	10.7	85%
1966-67	0.56	10.7	87%
1967-68	0.60	13.2	90%
1968-69	0.58	13.4	87%
1969-70	0.52	12.5	90%
1970-71	0.60	10.1	95%
1971-72	0.63	12.0	93%
1972-73	0.50	9.5	92%
1973-74	0.56	10.6	90%
1974-75	0.63	11.3	87%

The number of concerts in the Sunday series rose from 18 (1965-6) to 19 (1966-7), 22 (1967-8), 23 (1968-9) and 24 (1969-70). But in 1970-71, only 17 were given; in 1971-2, 1972-3 and 1973-4 there were 19, and in 1974-5 there were 18. All concerts were in the Free Trade Hall – capacity 2450.

Sources: Hallé programme booklets and records. Attendance figures are difficult to infer in this period, as precise records do not appear to be available, and the effect of inflation makes calculation from income problematical.

Commentary:
The degree of Composer Variety remained high until 1969-70, rose again in 1970-71, and remained relatively high except for 1972-3.
The Sunday concerts maintained and increased their popularity after James Loughran's appointment in 1970.

TABLE 5.5

Composer analysis Industrial (from 1971-2, Opus One) series 1965-75
(a = living; b = died in past 50 years; c = died in past 100-51 years; d = died in past 150-101 years; e = died in past 200-151 years; f = died in past 201 years or more)

Season	World prems	English prems	Mcr prems	a %	b %	c %	d %	e %	f %	Herfindahl Index
1965-66	0	0	0	23	34	31	9	0	0	2940
1966-67	0	0	0	4	43	31	9	13	0	3076
1967-68	0	0	0	14	41	32	14	0	0	3097
1968-69	0	0	0	0	25	56	0	13	6	3966
1969-70	0	0	0	5	26	32	26	11	0	2522
1970-71	0	0	0	11	16	42	31	0	0	3102
1971-72	0	0	0	9	31	31	19	11	0	2468
1972-73	0	0	0	0	44	32	20	4	0	3376
1973-74	0	0	0	9	17	30	35	9	0	2576
1974-75	0	0	0	7	33	26	19	15	0	2400

Commentary:
In comparison with the early years of this series, there is a distinct shift towards older repertoire from 1968-9 onwards (although still very little music of any great antiquity – but its repertoire becomes less concentrated in 1973-4 and 1974-5).

TABLE 5.6

Variety and popularity 1965-75 Industrial (from 1971-2 Opus One) series.
(see beginning of Tables for methods of calculation)

Season	Variety Index	"Enterprise rating"	Est. attendance
1965-66	0.91	5.5	75%
1966-67	0.65	3.9	75%
1967-68	0.91	5.5	70%
1968-69	0.88	3.5	80%
1969-70	0.89	4.5	70%
1970-71	0.84	5.1	90%
1971-72	0.77	5.4	100%
1972-73	0.84	5.9	100%
1973-74	0.91	6.4	100%
1974-75	0.78	5.4	100%

This series consisted of 6 repeated concerts in 1965-6, 1966-7, and 1967-8; 4 in 1968-9; 5 in 1969-70; 6 in 1970-71, and 7 (renamed "Opus One") from 1971-2. All were held in the Free Trade Hall (capacity 2450).

Sources: Hallé programme booklets and records. Attendance figures are difficult to infer in this period, as precise records do not appear to be available, and the effect of inflation makes calculation from income problematical. The "sell-outs" of the last four years are specifically noted, however.

Commentary:
The Composer Variety of these programmes is consistently high (except in 1966-7), and represents on average the highest degree of variety of the three winter series offered by the Hallé at the time – the result of a policy of providing music to appeal to the new concert-goer, within a limited series. The fact that sell-outs were recorded at every concert from 1971-2 to 1974-5 shows it was eminently successful.

TABLE 5.7

Composer analysis Proms 1965-75 (no Proms were held in 1968)
(a = living; b = died in past 50 years; c = died in past 100-51 years; d = died in past 150-101 years; e = died in past 200-151 years; f = died in past 201 years or more)

Season	World prems	English prems	Mcr prems	a %	b %	c %	d %	e %	f %	Herfindahl Index
1965-66	0	0	0	28	26	37	7	2	0	2882
1966-67	0	0	0	22	39	30	3	3	3	2932
1968-69	0	0	0	11	33	47	9	0	0	3500
1969-70	0	0	0	9	37	37	14	3	0	3024
1970-71	0	0	0	5	38	43	11	2	0	3443
1971-72	0	0	0	9	31	42	9	9	0	2968
1972-73	0	0	0	6	33	31	19	4	7	2512
1973-74	1	0	0	13	40	25	11	11	0	2636
1974-75	0	0	1	12	35	32	16	3	2	2662

Commentary: (see next page)

TABLE 5.8

Variety and popularity 1965-75 Proms series
(see beginning of Tables for methods of calculations)

Season	Variety Index	"Enterprise rating"	Est. attendance
1965-66	0.72	7.2	75%
1966-67	0.97	9.7	80%
1968-69	0.86	8.6	60%
1969-70	0.86	7.7	70%
1970-71	.075	8.3	75%
1971-72	0.80	9.6	80%
1972-73	0.79	10.3	75%
1973-74	0.81	10.5	80%
1974-75	0.75	12.8	90%

There were 10 Hallé Proms concerts in each of 1965-6 and 1966-7; none in 1967-8; 10 in 1968-9; 9 in 1969-70; 11 in 1970-71; 12 in 1971-2; 13 in 1972-3 and 1973-4; and 17 in 1974-5. All were held in the Free Trade Hall (capacity 2450).

Sources: Hallé programme booklets and records. Attendance figures are difficult to infer in this period, as precise records do not appear to be available, and the effect of inflation makes calculation from income problematical. Several of the above averages, however, are specifically minuted.

Commentary:
There is a high degree of Composer Variety. The series of 1971-2 to 1974-5 were extremely successful in attendances, and the overall historical variety of their programmes increased markedly at the same time (see the Herfindahl Indices).

TABLE 6.1

Hallé Manchester concerts: Composer analysis main series 1985-95
(a = living; b = died in past 50 years; c = died in past 100-51 years; d = died in past 150-101 years; e = died in past 200-151 years; f = died in past 201 years or more)

Season	World prems	English prems	Mcr prems	a %	b %	c %	d %	e %	f %	Herfindahl Index
1985-86	0	1	6	14	24	31	2	27	2	2470
1986-87	0	0	8	16	36	24	12	12	0	2416
1987-88	0	0	6	10	24	37	12	17	0	2478
1988-89	0	0	5	14	26	28	9	23	0	2266
1989-90	0	0	5	6	33	30	6	22	3	2554
1990-91	0	0	11	26	23	28	6	17	0	2314
1991-92	0	0	11	13	28	32	6	13	8	2246
1992-93	0	0	8	15	26	28	11	18	2	2134
1993-94	1	1	6	16	22	25	11	13	13	1824
1994-95	2	1	4	10	30	27	15	13	5	2148

Commentary:

The combined proportion of works by composers who were living or had died in the previous 50 years is lower than in 1965-75 or 1945-55 – an effect explicable (as in the contrast of 1965-75 with 1945-55) as due to the broadening of the repertoire with the passage of time – but nonetheless lies in the range 34%-52% (in 1965-75 it had been 38%-60%). The figure is at its highest in 1986-7, but falls to the lowest of the decade in 1987-8 and remains low in the next two seasons. The Herfindahl Index also shows that the degree of historical concentration in those programmes was at its greatest in 1989-90.

Possible linked effects are that after the losses of 1985-6, the programmes of 1987-8 show a dramatic decrease in "newer" music; and the improved results of 1986-7 are followed by a slight increase in "newer" music in 1988-9's programmes. The poor financial results of 1987-8 were seen by the Hallé Committee as acceptable only in the light of the promised Arts Council appraisal of the Hallé's situation as a whole. This may explain the relatively unchanged proportion of "newer" music in 1989-90.

In 1990-91 (Skrowaczewski's last as principal conductor) "newer" music increases to 49%, but reduces to 41% in 1991-2 (this was, however, a longer series, with 17 concerts in all). In 1990-91, works by living composers make up 26% of all items, which exceeds James Loughran's highest figure in 1970-75 and any of Kent Nagano's subsequent seasons from 1992-3 to 1994-5.

Kent Nagano's musical directorship sees the proportion of "newer" music stabilise around 40%, with works by living composers making up 10% to 16% of items. The Herfindahl Index shows the high level of historical differentiation of his programmes: only Barbirolli's jubilee season of 1968-9 and one James Loughran season (1974-5), from those analysed, show lower indices of concentration.

TABLE 6.2

Variety and popularity main series 1985-95
(see beginning of Tables for methods of calculation)

Season	Variety Index	"Enterprise rating"	Est. attendance
1985-86	0.65	10.4	68%
1986-87	0.81	12.1	?%
1987-88	0.61	9.1	*69%
1988-89	0.63	9.4	65%
1989-90	0.72	10.8	65%
1990-91	0.74	11.9	65%
1991-92	0.72	12.3	57%
1992-93	0.74	12.6	?%
1993-94	0.71	11.4	*60%
1994-95	0.73	10.9	?%

The midweek series consisted of 16 concerts in 1985-6, 15 from 1986-7 to 1989-90, 16 in 1990-91, 17 in 1991-2 and 1992-3, 16 in 1993-4, and 15 in 1994-5.

Sources: Hallé programme booklets and records
* Estimates from income figures. Data for some years appears not to be recorded for individual series.

Hall capacity: approx. 2450.

Commentary:

Composer Variety was generally greater than in 1965-75: and the seasons from 1985-6 to 1990-1 compare, on average, to those of James Loughran's first years. In 1986-7, Skrowaczewski's programmes produce the highest Composer Variety figure of the 1985-95 decade, but the following two seasons produce the two lowest – a sign, it may well be, of a struggle to achieve a more acceptable "box office" at that point because of financial problems.

Kent Nagano's period includes the highest overall degree of Composer Variety in programmes so far recorded in this analysis (an index average of 0.73) – which is not dissimilar to the highest figures of James Loughran's early years, but represents a more consistent sequence of high figures.

Attendances remain comfortably above 60% during Skrowaczewski's tenure as principal conductor, but fall a little (on average) under Nagano.

TABLE 6.3

Composer analysis Sunday series 1985-95
(a = living; b = died in past 50 years; c = died in past 100-51 years; d = died in past 150-101 years; e = died in past 200-151 years; f = died in past 201 years or more)

Season	World prems	English prems	Mcr prems	a %	b %	c %	d %	e %	f %	Herfindahl Index
1985-86	0	0	2	0	32	27	14	27	0	2678
1986-87	0	0	0	0	28	35	19	16	2	2630
1987-88	0	0	4	4	19	42	14	19	2	2702
1988-89	0	0	0	3	23	40	17	14	3	2632
1989-90	0	0	1	0	37	43	7	10	3	3376
1990-91	0	0	3	6	26	36	20	40	5	2600
1991-92	0	0	3	0	18	45	9	14	14	2822
1992-93	0	1	3	4	24	32	16	12	12	2160
1993-94	0	0	6	23	23	9	14	18	13	1828
1994-95	0	0	2	10	10	30	10	10	30	2200

Commentary:

In 1990-91 "newer music" decreased to 20%, and the series itself was reduced to eight concerts (apart from Handel's *Messiah*); and in 1991-2 "newer" music's share was 18%, in a series of nine concerts (plus *Messiah*), although Composer Variety increased.

"Newer" music increased to 28% over eight concerts in 1992-3 , then to 46% in 1993-4 , after which the series was reduced to five concerts, with "newer" music accounting for only 20% of items played. The Herfindahl indices show higher historical differentiation in Kent Nagano's Sunday programmes, as in the case of the Thursday series.

TABLE 6.4

Variety and popularity Sunday series 1985-95
(see beginning of Tables for methods of calculation)

Season	Variety Index	"Enterprise rating"	Est. attendance
1985-86	0.71	10.6	75%
1986-87	0.65	9.8	?%
1987-88	0.72	10.8	*65%
1988-89	0.74	11.9	68%
1989-90	0.77	9.9	64%
1990-91	0.65	5.8	60%
1991-92	0.73	7.3	66%
1992-93	0.92	8.3	?%
1993-94	0.82	7.4	*62%
1994-95	0.90	5.4	?%

The series consisted of 15 concerts from 1985-6 to 1987-8; 16 in 1988-9; 13 in 1989-90; 9 in 1990-91; 10 in 1991-2; 9 in 1992-3; 10 in 1993-4, and 6 in 1994-5. They were held in the Free Trade Hall (capacity 2450).

* Estimates from income figures. Data for some years appears not to be recorded for individual series.

Hall capacity: approx. 2450.

Commentary:
Between 1985 and 1990 Composer Variety is considerably higher than 20 years previously. In 1990-91 it increases, though reducing the following season. In 1992-3, under Kent Nagano, it increases again. The series was reduced in length in 1994-5, so the "Enterprise rating" falls, although the CVI increases.
These concerts drew attendances between 60% and 70% for most of the period, but were of course fewer in number from 1990-91.

TABLE 6.5

Composer analysis Opus One series 1985-95
(a = living; b = died in past 50 years; c = died in past 100-51 years; d = died in past 150-101 years; e = died in past 200-151 years; f = died in past 201 years or more)

Season	World prems	English prems	Mcr prems	a %	b %	c %	d %	e %	f %	Herfindahl Index
1985-86	0	0	2	4	12	24	24	24	12	2032
1986-87	0	0	0	4	11	31	4	38	11	2679
1987-88	0	0	0	0	21	29	29	21	0	2564
1988-89	0	0	0	4	29	32	14	21	0	2518
1989-90	0	0	0	0	19	39	15	27	0	2836
1990-91	0	0	2	0	23	31	35	11	0	2836
1991-92	0	0	4	4	28	28	11	25	4	2346
1992-93	0	0	1	0	26	50	14	5	5	3422
1993-94	0	0	2	0	31	38	23	4	4	2966
1994-95	0	0	1	4	13.	25	25	4	29	2292

Commentary:
This is notable for the almost complete disappearance of music by living composers: the average over 10 years is 2%, whereas in 1965-75 it is 8%. The proportion of music by living composers and those who had died in the previous 50 years is in the range 15%-33% (in 1965-75 it was 25%-60%). Historical concentration increased after the arrival of Kent Nagano (though Composer Variety also increased).

TABLE 6.6

Variety and popularity 1985-95 Opus One series
(see beginning of Tables for methods of calculations)

Season	Variety Index	"Enterprise rating"	Est. attendance
1985-86	0.8	6.4	74%
1986-87	0.73	5.8	??%
1987-88	0.79	6.3	86%
1988-89	0.86	6.9	82%
1989-90	0.77	6.1	88%
1990-91	0.85	6.8	89%
1991-92	0.78	6.3	77%
1992-93	0.82	6.5	??%
1993-94	0.88	7.1	76%
1994-95	0.96	7.7	??%

There were eight concerts in each series, each given three times over, all in the Free Trade Hall (capacity 2450).

Sources: Hallé programme booklets and records
Data for some years is not recorded for individual series.

Commentary:
Composer Variety is slightly less, on average, in these programmes than in 1965-75 (it increased in the Kent Nagano seasons, however). This is the most successful of the three winter series before 1991-2, with average attendances for four years being in the range 82%-89%. However, average attendances subsequently fell below 80%.

TABLE 6.7

Composer analysis Proms 1985-95
(a = living; b = died in past 50 years; c = died in past 100-51 years; d = died in past 150-101 years; e = died in past 200-151 years; f = died in past 201 years or more)

Season	World prems	English prems	Mcr prems	a %	b %	c %	d %	e %	f %	Herfindahl Index
1985-86	0	0	0	9	35	30	14	12	0	2546
1986-87	0	0	0	7	28	43	13	8	1	2916
1987-88	0	0	0	9	33	38	11	9	0	2816
1988-89	0	0	0	3	18	40	12	18	9	2482
1989-90	0	0	0	2	27	37	12	17	5	2560
1990-91	0	0	0	2	24	48	13	9	4	3150
1991-92	0	0	0	7	30	44	11	4	4	3038
1992-93	0	0	3	4	34	21	10	7	24	2338
1993-94	1	0	1	3	38	44	6	6	3	3470
1994-95	0	0	1	0	26	43	24	5	2	3130

Commentary:
These programmes seem to have avoided "newer" music in proportion to the degree of anxiety, at any given time, to achieve a good "box office": in 1986-8 it is in the range 35%-44%; in 1988-9 it is 21%, but by 1991-2 and 1992-3 it is up again to 37% and 38%, and in the Proms of 1993-4 it rises to 41% – though in the same two seasons the historical concentration of the programmes changes from its lowest of the decade (1992-3) to its highest (1993-4).

After the poor financial results of 1993-4 (and, although those related to the Proms of 1993, the poor sales of 1994's Proms were also known by the time plans for 1995 were made) the proortion of "newer music" falls again, to 26%, in 1994-5.

In 1965-75 as a whole, the equivalent range is 39%-61%.

TABLE 6.8

Variety and popularity 1985-95 Proms series
(see beginning of Tables for methods of calculation)

Season	Variety Index	"Enterprise rating"	Est. attendance
1985-86	0.70	11.2	??%
1986-87	0.80	12.9	??%
1987-88	0.95	10.5	??%
1988-89	0.74	8.1	??%
1989-90	0.78	9.4	66%
1990-91	0.8	9.6	70%
1991-92	0.93	6.5	71%
1992-93	0.83	9.9	??%
1993-94	0.91	9.1	??%
1994-95	0.81	8.9	??%

All concerts given in the Free Trade Hall (capacity 2450).

Data for some years is not recorded for individual series.

Commentary:
Composer Variety is similar to the Opus One series and slightly higher than in 1965-75, but the length of the series varies: until 1991, it was between 11 and 13 evenings; there were seven concerts in 1992, 12 in 1993, 10 in 1994 and 11 in 1995.
Attendances (though not recorded precisely) seem to have been variable, and the near-capacity levels of some years in 1965-75 were never regained. The 1993 and 1994 Proms were taken to be considerable failures in attendances and income.

TABLE 7.1

Earned income and subventions as percentages of Halle operational turnover
1946-1999

Year	Earned Income	Arts Council	Manchester Council	Cit Joint Scheme/GMC/ AGMA
1946-47	93	6	-	-
1947-48	85	6	7	-
1948-49	81	8	8	-
1949-50	79	8	7	-
1950-51	80	8	5	-
1951-52	76	7	7	-
1952-53	85	8	6	-
1953-54	90	9	7	-
1954-55	87	8	-	2
1955-56	87	5	-	3
1956-57	82	6	-	6
1957-58	78	7	3	6
1958-59	78	8	3	7
1959-60	79	9	3	6
1960-61	72	14	5	6
1961-62	70	14	4	7
1962-63	66	13	7	6
1963-64	63	20	9	7
1964-65	61	21	9	7
1965-66	62	21	8	6
1966-67	55	27	8	6
1967-68	51	26	7	5
1968-69	50	38	14	8*
1969-70	52	26	15	6
1970-71	52	24	15	6
1971-72	53	25	14	6
1972-73	56	23	12	7
1973-74	53	26	13	7
1974-75	48	24	5	18
1975-76	52	23	4	18
1976-77	57	22	3	17
1977-78	56	21	3	16
1978-79	55	20	3	17
1979-80	51	23	3	18
1980-81	56	19	2	15
1981-82	53	22	2	17
1982-83	60	21	1	16
1983-84	59	21	1	16
1984-85	55	22	1	16
1985-86	58	21	1	20
1986-87	58	30	1	4
1987-88	56	29	1	4
1988-89	68	28	1	4
1989-90	65	26	1	7
1990-91	64	27	1	7
1991-92	66	28	1	7
1992-93	67	27	0.5	7
1993-94	59	26	3	6
1994-95	63	23	4	6
1995-96	58	29	5	7
1996-97	62	23	3	8
1997-98	49	19	3	5
1998-99	58	21	4	5**

1968-9 was an 8-month year, because of a change in the Halle financial year-end
** In 1998-9, 12% of income was from the proceeds of the Hallé Appeal
From 1982-3, earned income includes contributions from the Halle's trust funds as well as
performance income

TABLE 7.2

Earned income and subventions as percentages of CBSO total income 1946-1995

Year	Earned income	Arts Council	Birmingham City Council	Others/W Mids CC
1946-47	56	4.5	39	-
1947-48	54	9	36	-
1948-49	46	16	38	-
1949-50	52	18	30	-
1950-51	60	18	22	-
1951-52	53	20	24	1
1952-53	49	25	25	
1953-54	56	13.5	28	2
1954-55	57	13	27	2
1955-56	58	13	27	2
1956-57	58	13	27	2
1957-58	54	15	28	-
1958-59	53	16	29	-
1959-60				*
1960-61				*
1961-62	52	21	26	-
1962-63	55	21	22	-
1963-64	50	26	22	
1964-65	50	26	22	-
1965-66	52	26	26	-
1966-67	50	28	20	
1967-68	48	29	21	2
1968-69	44	26	19	4
1969-70	41	33	19	4
1970-71	43	31	18	3
1971-72	45	32	19	4
1972-73	42	36	18	4
1973-74	42	35	18	3
1974-75				*
1975-76				*
1976-77	45	30	5	20
1977-78	47	29	4	20
1978-79	46	32	3	19
1979-80	47	30	3	18
1980-81	51	28	3	6
1981-82	49	30	3	17
1982-83	50	31	2.5	16
1983-84	52	26	6	15
1984-85	54	23	8	14
1985-86	54	23	10	13
1986-87	56	32	12	-
1987-88	58	27	15	-
1988-89	58	26	16	-
1989-90	57	23	19	-
1990-91	59	21	19	-
1991-92	61	21	18	-
1992-93	61	22	17	-
1993-94	58	21	18	-
1994-95	59	21	20	-

*   Data incomplete

The West Midlands County Council contributed from 1974-5 to 1985-6
Source: CBSO annual reports and accounts

TABLE 7.3

Earned income and subventions as percentages of RLPO total income 1946-1995

Year	Earned income	Arts Council	Liverpool City Council	Joint Scheme/ Merseyside/ others
1946-47	85	11	5	-
1947-48	87	3	9	-
1948-49	81	10	9	-
1949-50	77	12	11	-
1950-51	77	12	11	-
1951-52	75	12	13	-
1952-53	74	13	13	-
1953-54	65	13	22	-
1954-55	52	12	4.5	11
1955-56	56	10	25	9
1956-57	64	11	17	8
1957-58	63	13	16	9
1958-59	61	16.5	12	10
1959-60	58	17	15	10
1960-61	55	20	17	8.5
1961-62	49	20	21	9
1962-63	52	20	18	9
1963-64	50	24.5	16	9
1964-65	53	25	13	9
1965-66	53	25	13	8
1966-67	52	30	10	7.5
1967-68	44	31	18	7
1968-69	46	29	18	7
1969-70	43	30	19	7
1970-71	45	29	18	7
1971-72	44	29	18	9
1972-73	46	30	16	8
1973-74	42.5	33	16	8
1974-75	40	33	5	23
1975-76	42	30	4	24
1976-77	40	31	3	27
1977-78				*
1978-79	41	29	3	27
1979-80	40	32	2	26
1980-81	44	29	2	25
1981-82				*
1982-83	47	30	1	22
1983-84	51	26	1	22
1984-85	51	25	1	23
1985-86	54	25	1	20
1986-87	50	45	1	4
1987-88	54	29	1	7
1988-89	57	26	1	6
1989-90	63	31	1	5
1990-91	65	29	1	5
1991-92	67	29	0.5	3.5
1992-93	61	35	1	3.5
1993-94	56	37.5	1	5
1994-95	57	40	1	2

*   Data incomplete

The "Joint Scheme" of Lancashire and Cheshire local authorities operated from 1954-5 to 1973-4; Merseyside County Council contributed from 1974-5 to 1985-6; the Merseyside District Councils after that Source: RLPO annual reports and accounts

TABLE 7.4

Net balances of Hallé capital, reserves and accumulated surplus or deficit, as a percentage of operational turnover, 1946–1998

Year		Year	
1946-47	20.3	1978-79	14.4
1947-48	10.6	1979-80	11.8
1948-49	7.8	1980-81	4.7
1949-50	7.3	1981-82	2.6
1950-51	11.1	1982-83	4.4
1951-52	15.9	1983-84	3.7
1952-53	25	1984-85	0.9
1953-54	37.2	1985-86	6.5
1954-55	35.7	1986-87	0.8
1955-56	36.2	1987-88	-8.1
1956-57	35.5	1988-89	0.03
1957-58	34.5	1989-90	0.04
1958-59	36.1	1990-91	-1
1959-60	34.2	1991-92	-1.8
1960-61	36	1992-93	-1.5
1961-62	35	1993-94	-5.3
1962-63	34.7	1994-95	-6.3
1963-64	36.9	1995-96	-9.1
1964-65	37.4	1996-97	-11.3
1965-66	37.3	1997-98	-24.5
1966-67	33.5		
1967-68	21		
1968-69	21.7		
1969-70	21.8		
1970-71	20		
1971-72	19.7		
1972-73	16.7		
1973-74	17		
1974-75	18.2		
1975-76	15.4		
1976-77	18.9		
1977-78	17.4		

Calculated from published figures in Halle annual reports. The four largest falls in a single year were in 1998 (16 percentage points), 1968 (9.5 percentage points) 1948 and 1988 (9 percentage points in each case).

*Calculated by adding the declared "operating loss" to the previous year's "deficit on reserves". The accounts show consolidated balances including the Halle Endowment Fund.

Bibliography

Allmendinger, Jutta, J Richard Hackman and Erin V Lehman (1994). Life and Work in Symphony Orchestras: An Interim Report of Research Findings, report no. 7, Cross-national Study of Symphony Orchestras (Harvard University, Cambridge, Mass.)

Arian, Edward (1971). Bach, Beethoven and Bureaucracy: The case of the Philadelphia Orchestra (University of Alabama Press, University, Alabama)

Atkins, Harold and Peter Cotes (1983). The Barbirollis: A Musical Marriage (Robson Books, London)

Blamires, Chris (1995). Pricing Research Manual (Arts Council of England, London)

Cooper, Jilly (1996). Appassionata (Bantam Press, London)

Fifield, Christopher (1993). True Artist and True Friend: A biography of Hans Richter (Clarendon Press, Oxford)

Galinsky, Adam D and Erin V Lehman (1995). Emergence, Divergence, Convergence: Three Models of Symphony Orchestras at the Crossroads. *European Journal of Cultural Policy* 2 (1): 117-139)

Greer, David, ed. (1978). Hamilton Harty: His life and music (Blackstaff Press Ltd., Belfast)

Hammond, Philip (1978). Dublin and London; and The Hallé Years and After. In: Hamilton Harty: His life and music, ed. David Greer (Blackstaff Press Ltd., Belfast)

Hart, Philip (1973). Orpheus In The New World: The Symphony As An American Cultural Institution (W W Norton & Co, New York)

Hewison, Robert (1995). Culture and Consensus: England, art and politics since 1940 (Methuen, London)

Hirsch, Leonard (1978). Memories of Sir Hamilton. In: Hamilton Harty: His life and music, ed. David Greer (Blackstaff Press Ltd., Belfast)

Hutchinson, Robert (1982). The Politics of the Arts Council (Sinclair Browne, London)

Judy, Paul R (1995). The Uniqueness and Commonality of American Symphony Orchestra Organizations. *Harmony* 1: 11-21.

Kennedy, Michael (1960). The Hallé Tradition (Manchester University Press, Manchester)

Kennedy, Michael (1971). Barbirolli: Conductor Laureate (MacGibbon & Kee, London)

Kennedy, Michael (1982). The Hallé 1858-1983: A History of the Orchestra (Manchester University Press, Manchester)

King-Smith, Beresford (1995). Crescendo! 75 years of the City of Birmingham Symphony Orchestra (Methuen, London)

Lebrecht, Norman (1991). The Maestro Myth – Great Conductors. In: Pursuit of Power (Simon & Schuster Ltd., Sydney)

Lebrecht, Norman (1996). When the Music Stops ... : Managers, Maestros, and the Corporate Murder of Classical Music (Simon & Schuster, London)

Lewis, R M (1998). The Educational Functions of the Royal Liverpool Philharmonic Society 1840-1990. PhD thesis: University of Liverpool, Department of Education

McCaldin, Denis (1987). Hallé Orchestra. In: Symphony Orchestras of the World, ed. Robert R Craven (Greenwood Press, New York)

Minihan, Janet (1977). The Nationalization of Culture (Hamish Hamilton, London)

Myerscough, John (1986). Facts About the Arts 2 (Policy Studies Institute, London)

Newman, Oksana & Allan Foster (1995). The Value of a Pound: Prices and Incomes in Britain 1900-1993 (Gale Research International Ltd., Andover, Hants.)

Peterson, Richard A (1986). From Impresario To Arts Administrator. In: Nonprofit Enterprise in the Arts, ed. Paul J DiMaggio (Oxford University Press, New York)

Pick, John (1986). Managing the Arts? The British Experience (Rhinegold Publications, London)

Pick, John (1988). The Arts in a State (Bristol Classical Press, Bristol)

Pick, John and Malcolm Anderton (1999). Building Jerusalem: Art, Industry and the British Millennium (Harwood Academic Publishers, Amsterdam)

Procter-Gregg, Humphrey (1976). Beecham Remembered (Duckworth, London)

Reid, Charles (1962). Thomas Beecham: An independent biography (Gollancz, London)

Reid, Charles (1971). John Barbirolli: A biography (Hamish Hamilton, London)

RSGB (Research Surveys of Great Britain) (1991). Omnibus Survey: Report on a Survey of Arts and Cultural Activities in Great Britain (Arts Council of England)

Ridley, F F (1987). Tradition, Change and Crisis in Great Britain. In: The Patron State, ed Cummings, Milton C Jr & Richard S Katz (Oxford University Press, Oxford)

Rosenbaum, Samuel R (1967). Financial Evolution of the Orchestra. In: The American Symphony Orchestra, ed. Henry Swoboda (Basic Books, Inc., New York)

Shanet, Howard (1975). Philharmonic: A History of New York's Orchestra (Doubleday & Co., New York)

Street, Sean & Ray Carpenter (1993). The Bournemouth Symphony Orchestra: A Centenary Celebration (The Dovecote Press, Wimborne, Dorset)

Tooley, John (1999). In House: Covent Garden, 50 Years of Opera and Ballet (Faber & Faber, London)

Walshe, Peter (1991). Pricing in the Arts Report 1990 (Arts Council of Great Britain, London)

Walshe, Peter, Peter Verwey and Roger Tomlinson (1992). What Price the Live Arts? (Arts Council of Great Britain, London)

Wyatt, Margaret (1994). BBC Philharmonic: A celebration 1934-1994 (BBC Philharmonic, Manchester)

Index